ITI: THE MODEL

INTEGRATED THEMATIC INSTRUCTION

Third Edition

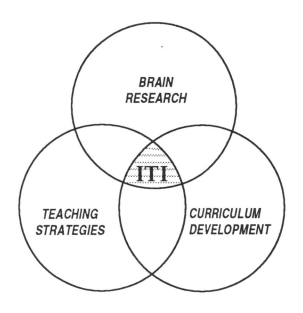

SUSAN KOVALIK

with

Karen Olsen

INTEGRATED THEMATIC INSTRUCTION: THE MODEL

1997 Updated Third Edition

Published by Susan Kovalik & Associates

Graphics by Linae Frei
Drawings by Cynthi Black

©1994 by Susan Kovalik

Distributed by Books for Educators, Inc.
Covington Square
17051 S.E. 272nd Street, Suite 18
Kent, WA 98042
253/630-6908

ISBN-1-878631-18-7

Replaces
TEACHERS MAKE THE DIFFERENCE

In Chapter 4, characteristics exemplifying each of the seven intelligences
by Thomas Armstrong are reprinted by permission of The Putnam
Publishing Group from *In Their Own Way* by Thomas Armstrong.
Copyright ©1987 by Thomas Armstrong.

TABLE OF CONTENTS

Dedication   i

Welcome From the Author   ii

Introduction   **vii**
    Curriculum: Birthplace of Change   vii
    Mismemes in Education   viii
    New Memes for Education   xvi
    Toward a New Meme-Based Curriculum   xx
    Where to from Here?   xxi
    Welcome to Integrated Thematic Instruction   xxiv

Chapter 1 — The Model   **1**
    The Yearlong Theme   4
    Key Points and Inquiries   9
    The Road to Integration   10
    Creating Necessary Support for Implementing ITI   13
    Brain Research—The Basis for Change   16

Chapter 2 — Absence of Threat   **17**
    The Triune Brain Goes to School   20
    Structuring Teacher-Student and Student-Student
        Interactions   20
    Lifelong Guidelines   25
    LIFESKILLS   29
    Guidelines for Creating Absence of Threat   33

Chapter 3 — Meaningful Content   **35**
    Learning from Real Life   37
    Dependence upon Prior Experience   38
    Learning Clubs   40
    Age-Appropriateness   41
    The Brain As Pattern-Seeker   46
    The Brain As a Self-Congratulator   51
    Guidelines for Building in Meaningfulness   52

Chapter 4 — Choices   **53**
    Choices—The Ultimate Determiner of Success   53
    Providing Choice for Students: Seven
        Intelligences   56
    Providing Choice for Adults   65
    Guidelines for Providing Choice   66

Chapter 5 — Adequate Time   **67**
Time for Pattern-Seeking   68
Time for Program-Building   70
  Just What Is a Program?   70
  Making Time for Program-Building   74
Guidelines for Providing Adequate Time   76

Chapter 6 — Enriched Environment   **77**
The 19 Senses   79
The Teachers' Environment   85
Guidelines for Creating an Enriched Environment   86

Chapter 7 — Collaboration   **87**
Structuring Effective Collaboration   89
  Curriculum Design   89
  Flexible Student Grouping   92
  A Touch of Common Sense   95
Outcomes of Working in Group Settings   96
Guidelines for Encouraging Collaboration   97

Chapter 8 — Immediate Feedback   **99**
Building in Immediate Feedback   101
  Change the Curriculum   101
  Change the Instructional Materials   101
  Change the Structure   102
Eliminate Delayed Feedback   104
Guidelines for Providing Immediate Feedback   105

Chapter 9 — Mastery   **107**
Meaningful Curriculum and Application   109
Implementing Lifelong Guidelines and
  LIFESKILLS   110
Eliminating Grading and the Bell Curve;   110
  Setting Standards for Mastery: The "3 Cs"   115
Implementing Assessment Based on Mastery   116
Steps in Designing Assessment for Competence   117
Guidelines for Implementing Competence
  Assessment   119

Chapter 10 — Curriculum: What's Worth Learning?   **121**

What Is Brain-Compatible Curriculum?   122

Characteristics of Brain-Compatible
Curriculum Tools   122

New Tools for Creating Brain-
Compatible Curriculum   124

Sample Science Continuum of Concepts   125

The Bottom Line: Why Curriculum?   131

A Warning to All   131

The ITI Rubric   132

Chapter 11 — Creating a Yearlong Theme   **139**

Construction Terminology for Building a Theme   141

Step A: Determine Your Starting Point   142

Step B: Rethink What Students Are to Learn   143

Step C: Select Physical Locations and Human Issues   144

Step D: Identify Your Organizing Concept
(Theme) and Rationale   145

Step E: Selecting Monthly Components and
Weekly Topics   148

Pattern Shapers List   150

How to Use *Pattern Shapers*   151

Step F: Dream a Theme Title   159

Criteria for Evaluating Your Theme   160

Inside the Mind of a Teacher   161

Chapter 12 — Identifying Key Points   **171**

What Is Essential?   171

Thinking Steps for Developing Key Points   174

Characteristics of Good Key Points   178

Examples of Key Points   179

Using Key Points   183

Importance of Multiple Resources   184

Chapter 13 — Developing Inquiries   **189**

Refining the Essential Content to Be Learned   190

Writing Inquiries   191

Inquiry Builder Chart   192

Examples of Inquiries   195

Getting a Little Help From the Kids!   198

Criteria for Evaluating Inquiries   198

How to Use Inquiries   199

Evaluating Student Work on Inquiries   199

Chapter 14 —Integrating the Basic Skills   **201**

   The Classroom of the 21st Century   202

      Reading   203

         Comprehension   205

         Reading Skills   206

         Vocabulary   208

      Writing   209

         Writing Skills   210

      Math   212

         Math Skills   214

      A Day in the Life of   215

   Orchestrating a Concept-in-a Day: Long Division   219

      Overview of the Day's Activities   220

      Format at Each Station   221

      Methods of Orchestrating Learning   222

         Maximize Input to the Brain   223

         Patterns for the Day   223

         Choices   223

   "Anchor" Math   225

      Three Levels of Math Language   225

      The Concept of "n-Ness"   226

      Introducing "Flexing"'   227

   Real Writing Experiences   229

   Research Skills   232

Chapter 15 —Transitions   **233**

Appendix A—Celebrations of Learning   **235**

   The Making of a Celebration   235

   Basic Ingredients for a Successful Celebration   238

Appendix B— The Discovery Process   **239**

Appendix C— Communicating with Parents   **249**

   Parent Packet   250

   Glossary   269

   Notes   275

   Bibliography   279

   Index   281

DEDICATION

The growth of the Integrated Thematic Instruction (ITI) model into a nationwide, even worldwide, movement is the result of dedicated classroom teachers who persevered in their search for better learning experiences for students—teachers whose convictions pushed them to advocate for all students, whose courage lead them to challenge the system. It is their work pioneering the application of brain research to the classroom which has carried ITI throughout the United States, Canada, and Europe. It is their work which gives me hope that the system can be changed, that schools can be made to serve the needs of our democracy and the demands of life in the 21st century.

This book is dedicated to all who dare to make a difference and especially to those whose challenges are extraordinary.

Barbara Pedersen
a Lebanon, Indiana, educator of incredible strength and dedication continuously modeling truth and personal best so that teachers and students can learn without fear!

Sr. Patt Walsh
our tireless ambassador to Slovakia commuting each month from Pennsylvania for ten days of coaching and training in our four ITI schools.

Lori Helman
who has, with her two children and husband, lived in Bratislava, Slovakia for one year, coaching and training our ITI teachers.

Stephany Hrivñáková
a visionary for her country whose commitment to a new school philosophy for a country freed from 45 years of communism has never wavered, who brought the ITI model to Slovakia, and whose translation skills make the work of Sr. Patt and Lori possible.

Jo Gusman
whose deep insights into children and the human condition enriches the ITI team and model.

ALL TEACHERS
who are willing to risk in order to provide an education that equips students to become contributing members of society.

I thank you, your fellow educators thank you, and, most importantly, the children and grandchildren who are to follow thank you.

WELCOME FROM THE AUTHOR

Integrated Thematic Instruction was originally conceptualized twenty years ago during the era of programs such as Gifted and Talented, Mentally Gifted Minors, Extended Learning Programs, accelerated learners, etc. In California, the basic premise of the Gifted and Talented Program (GT) was that gifted students needed to have additional opportunities to use their talents, to spend time with others who were quick to conceptualize and synthesize. In short, because of their special gifts, such students were entitled to a "qualitatively different" learning environment. Clearly, the gifted students were bored with the usual fare of the regular classroom and were not profiting by it and something had to be done about it.

In pursuit of the "qualitatively different," the byword for gifted programs became "higher levels of thinking" or multiple thinking skills, an innovation based upon Bloom's Taxonomy of Cognitive Objectives. Although developed originally to guide the design of questions on exams at the college level, Bloom's Taxonomy took on a life of its own at the elementary school level; the "process verbs" at each of the six levels became guides for developing curriculum that promoted a different kind of learning experience, and, adding to that, challenge and excitement.

Achieving the legislatively mandated rule that gifted programs must be "qualitatively different" from the daily fare of the regular classroom was not difficult on two counts: first, teachers who chose to be GT teachers were frequently those chaffing under the constraints of the textbook-driven regular classroom and looking for something different from the typical classroom requirements; and second, they were, for the most part, classroom teachers who had already acquired sufficient curriculum development skills to do many exciting firsthand and hands-on activities.

It was agreed by many parents and educators in general that gifted students shouldn't be bored and that most classrooms were not sufficiently stimulating and challenging to keep their attention or direct their interests and energies. On such a premise, state legislatures across the country poured forth millions of dollars.

I was firmly committed to all of this until a personal experience forced me to question the policy foundations of GT education and the entire educational system. Of my three children, two were identified gifted and one was not. The questioning began.

The genetic theory of intelligence leaves many unanswered questions. If the parents were the same, why wouldn't all the children of that union be the same? Or, if you believed that environment was the determinant, then why weren't the three children who were raised in the same environment within 40 months of each other, all be identifiably gifted? Clearly, the answers within the GT program movement were too simple, too pat. And, I came to realize, rather elitist.

So, what does this say about those who are identified as gifted and how the GT program would further augment their intellect? Again reflecting on the GT programs, from my experience, a mainstay of the program was hands-on and firsthand. There was money for field trips and for special equipment to enable the learner to expand his/her horizons. There was no need to use textbooks—at least not until the Advanced Placement classes in high school—and worksheets were limited to exciting, divergent thinking activities and input about topics that weren't in the textbook.

I believed that what I was doing as a GT teacher was right, necessary, and mandatory, for we simply had to save some children from the drone of the average classroom. Why not start with the identified bright!

What changed my mind and forced me to confront my beliefs was a statement from my 14-year-old, unidentified GT son while he accompanied me during a model teaching week for the gifted in middle America. During dinner one night with the GT coordinator, and after listening to her extolling the needs of gifted students for 45 minutes, effusive about their progress, my son leaned across the table and asked her in a most direct manner, "Do you really believe that the only kids who want a great teacher and something exciting to learn are those kids who score the right number on a one-hour test?" Her shocked response was that he seemed a little hostile. His response, "Yes, my brother and sister get all the good teachers and I get the leftovers!"

Ah, not being able to see the forest for the trees! If the GT students were only getting 200 minutes a week of enriched learning through the GT program, who were their teachers the rest of the time, and what was the expectation for them in their so-called "regular" class? AND WHAT ABOUT THE "REGULAR" KIDS IN THE "REGULAR" CLASSROOM? They, too, were waiting for something to challenge and interest them. Did we not care about them? By national and state policy was it not important to ensure they had a program that was engaging and worthwhile?

Haven't your own children longed for an exciting class and a dynamic teacher? Do you recall the dread you felt when your child came home from school early in September and said, "Mom, my class is really a bore; all we do is read the textbook and answer questions at the back of the chapter. I hate school this year!" Think back to your own school experiences as a student. Remember those teachers who changed your life? How many were there? Twenty? Probably not. Ten? Not likely. Five? Perhaps. Three? Or one?

Since that personal revelation sparked by my son twelve years ago, my goal has been to push for programs which represent the best we know about learning, about teaching strategies that allow all learners equal access to mastery, and about curriculum so relevant and exciting that it has students resisting summer vacation because school is so exciting. It is too late for my son, but hopefully not too late for his children!

In 1983 I read a book that changed my life, *Human Brain and Human Learning* by Leslie A. Hart. Based on the explosion of brain research in the late sixties through early eighties (and confirmed by later research), we now know what elements make for a "brain-compatible" learning environment, and which make for a "brain-antagonistic" and less productive learning situation. Interestingly, the research confirms much of the intuition good teachers have held over the years. The power, however, of an articulated, thoroughly integrated theory of learning is that it allows one to construct a completely new vision of learning and teaching using some old practices, some altered approaches, and some completely new methods. Most importantly, it involves knowing which practices to leave behind. Today, through training and acknowledgment of our own personal learning capabilities, we can have all teachers aware of and practicing brain-compatible strategies.

Today when I look at an audience of teachers, I know change is possible and, in every audience, a percentage of teachers will hear the message and move forward. Surprisingly, such change can occur in two very different sets of circumstances: when supported and encouraged by their peers and administrators, or when completely ignored by them. Anything in between with negative messages and frontal or subtle undermining is almost always fatal. But changing one teacher is not enough; I can no longer bear the pleas of children for relief from the constant "potluck" they get in schools. For example, a letter from a seven-year-old, written to his second grade ITI teacher while he was in the third grade, stated:

> "I miss you very much. You know you found my brain last year and taught me how to make it work. This year I'm not happy. I can't use my brain in school. I have to wait until I get home and use it. I go to my room and create all kinds of things. I can still hear you say, 'Jeff, you are so creative.' I told my new teacher, but she said, 'Sit down.' I won't let my brain die, but I wish you were my teacher."

At least Jeff could put into words what he knew was missing. Most children think that something is wrong with them or believe they have no right to expect better in their classes. Or worse, they have never had a teacher who touched their mind and soul, changed the course of their lives—a teacher they would remember forever.

A letter received from a high school sophomore sounds the same alarm.

Dear Susan,

> Hello! It is your favorite Bridey. I'm here at Martha's house. I wish I could have seen you this trip. How are you doing? I'm doing just fine. I've been really busy with school and church. I just finished *'Sound of Music'* at school. I was a nun (not the biggest role, but they can't do the show without nuns).

> School seems to be ok for me. Oh, the joys of tenth grade. At least the year is almost over.

Susan, you have to do something about the math situation! High school algebra and geometry are a joke. It's what's ruining my perfect report card. I have all *A*'s and a *B*. It's quite sad. I am really just getting the grades so I can get into college. Yes, I know. The wrong reasons.

Susan, please do something with the high schools. Get rid of the teachers that were boring and useless when my mother was at my school. I want to do anything I can to help. I know I'm young, but if there is anything I can do, please tell me. I want to help and make a difference, too.*

Love always,
Bridey

We have an opportunity in the beginning of the last decade of the 20th century. The opportunity is to seek the best we know about learning and determine that less than the best is unacceptable—in the classroom and throughout the system. What is needed is a revolution of spirit, of goals, of believing in our power to change for the benefit of all of us—democracy is a very fragile system. It needs informed and capable citizens!

April, 1994
Kent, Washington

---

* At the end of the 1992 school year, Bridey elected to "home school" using curriculum from Brigham Young University, Utah! In 1994 she was accepted as a full-time student at Brigham Young University.

INTRODUCTION

So where do we start and how do we change a system? As you progress through this book and review the brain-compatible components, changes will be necessary at the state, district, school, parent, and classroom level. If change does not occur at all these levels simultaneously, then there will be no momentum to institutionalize lasting change. Karen Olsen, with her twelve years with the California State Department of Education, observes that she has never seen a transformed school stay transformed for more than six years; schools always "go back" to the way it's always been. Given how hard change agents try and how much money is spent on staff development, it is an embarrassment when asked "How far have we come?" The painful but truthful answer is that we have not changed at all in over a hundred years. The curricular, instructional, and structural features of the American School (high school and elementary) are still virtually identical to the Prussian model brought back from Europe by Horace Mann in 1840, whose instructional traditions stemmed from cadet corps training of a highly regimented military tradition and whose curricular modeling goes back to the catechism of the medieval church (one right answer from a single source, single point of view).

A question never asked is "Why do we choose to maintain and perpetuate a Prussian model of education when what we need is a model appropriate to the processes and philosophies of a democracy?" Why, indeed?

CURRICULUM: BIRTHPLACE OF CHANGE

It is my belief, and one concurred with by many observers of failed reform efforts over the past 70 years*, that the reason such reform efforts have failed is primarily because we have never abandoned our notions about subject area "disciplines" and the belief that

---

* I recommend the following books as "must read" analyses of what ails the American public school system and the schooling it provides: *What's Worth Teaching? Selecting, Organizing, and Integrating Knowledge* by Marion Brady and *The Predictable Failure of Public School Reform* by Seymour Sarason.

the purpose of schooling is mastery of identified content based upon a world view forged during the middle ages, a time of limited understanding of our world. It therefore should not surprise us that students have difficulty seeing the relevance of what they are studying to their lives. As twentieth century life has pulled ahead of us, with all its multiple and complex changes in daily living, we continue to give our students curriculum content of a bygone era rather than for surviving and thriving in daily life in the 21st century.

MISMEMES IN EDUCATION

So, let us ask ourselves again, how is it that our schools have remained unchanged for over a hundred years? How can so many well-intentioned (and well financed) reform movements come and go without leaving even the smallest permanent dent?

A useful metaphor for examining this queer blindness is that of "memes," a neologism invented by Richard Dawkins. Dawkins, while emphasizing the importance of genes to cells, argues that memes exercise the same kind of control in the mind. It is memes, not genes, that have been shaping the force of our culture. Building on Dawkins' discussion of memes, Richard Bergland, in his book *Fabric of Mind*[1] makes the following comments: "The genetic distinction of Beethoven or Einstein is lost in three or four generations; their splendid genes, once poured into the extraordinarily large vat of the human genetic pool, are lost forever. But the memes of Beethoven and Einstein, their good ideas, are passed from one generation to another and have an eternal significance. All animals are gene dependent. But the evolution of our culture, of our civilization, is meme dependent."

"Genes are body shapers, actually cell shapers, which may infect the cell; once inside, they cause it to 'selfishly' replicate more and more identical genes. Memes, Dawkins contends, are mind shapers, which pass from brain to brain like an infectious virus. Not all of the ideas that pass from one brain to another brain, however, are good ideas; some are mistakes. These I call 'mismemes.'"[2]

The power of mismemes is well illustrated by the following two stories.[3] Originated with the Pythagoreans, given the ring of authority by Plato, two powerful mismemes shaped scientific thinking for two centuries. One was the idea of the universe as a perfect sphere centered around the earth and the stars moving in perfect circles. No other mismeme has had the impact of this false notion. Although Copernicus knew for certain in 1510 that the sun, not the earth, was the center of our universe, he dared not publish his discovery. Thirty years later, the book was published in the year of his death, 1543. Nearly a century later, Galileo supported Copernicus but was forced by the church to recant his support of Copernicus in 1633 because : ". . . it had been notified to me that the said doctrine was contrary to Holy Scripture." Thus, "the circular movement that Plato gave to the stars took on a scientific, philosophical, and religious significance that held thoughtful people in intellectual chains for 1,900 years." **

Plato's belief in the perfect sphere led him to another strongly held mismeme—the perfect sphere must be the residence of "the divinest part of us." Thus, the brain (located in the spherical skull) must be the source of genetic material for new life; ergo, the brain was a gland that produced semen.

Two centuries later, Leonardo da Vinci's anatomical drawing illustrates a continuous pathway that could carry sperm from the brain, through the spinal cord, and through a fictitious tube into the penis of a copulating male and into the female vagina. This in spite of Leonardo's extraordinary powers of observation. Despite what he saw, he altered his drawings to reflect the anatomical beliefs of the church.

As Bergland comments, "This mismeme gave the female brain no role at all and regarded women only as flower pots for male seeds. The acceptance of this paradigm led to the exclusion of women from

---

**The trial and condemnation of Galileo by the Inquisition has long been recognized as one of the watersheds in Western intellectual history. Three hundred and fifty years later, the Galileo affair still haunts us and remains the subject of controversy. According to Maurice Finocchiaro, author of *The Galileo Affair: A Documentary History*, the questions it raises involved the nature of science and religion, their relationship to politics and society, individual freedom, institutional authority, and the conflict between conservation and innovation.[4] Not until 1978 did the church agree to formally study the issue and consider exonerating Galileo and then it took 13 years to publicly acknowledge their errors. Tradition dies hard.

the governance of academic, religious, and governmental institutions for 2,000 years or longer. This is perhaps the best evidence that the form of our culture and our civilization can be shaped—or misshaped—by the scientific views concerning the brain."[5]

You may be laughing now . . . "How quaint," you say. Downright silly of them. The church no longer controls thought in our society. In the Decade of the nineties we are a society of free thinkers. Think again. Education is enormously tradition-bound. Recent findings of psychology and sociology have created but the thinnest of veneers over centuries-old curriculum structures and content, changing our rationales but not the substance. Issues of tradition are not easily changed. For example, official apology and retraction of Galileo's condemnation for views that clashed with biblical verses and pontifical interpretations did not occur until October, 1992, and that after thirteen years of study. Along similar lines, when will the hue and cry for "Back to Basics" be re-examined?

Mismeme 1: All Students Learn in the Same Way

How about the mismeme "All students learn the same"—patently wrong, you say? Flatly contradicted both by recent brain research, personal experience, and common sense? Yes, we agree. But . . . look at the very structure of our schools. Same textbook for all, students of the same age grouped together or, even more dramatically, tracked so that they can be treated alike, same instructional procedures for all students (the time of year may vary). The only possible explanation for such structures and practices is a belief—the mismeme—that all students learn the same—take the same amount of time to learn the same amount of content, process it in the same way. We have used time as the determiner of learning—180 days, 45 hours, two semesters, six weeks, 47 minutes, etc. All students are subjected to this type of schedule and if, during that allotted time learning does not take place, it is *always* someone else's problem!

Mismeme 2:
Yesterday's Curriculum Is Good Enough for Today

"If it was good enough for Grandpa, it's good enough for Tommy," goes the maxim. Not so. To each his time. In the 1920s, only 20 percent of the population graduated from high school. And today, that same 20 percent finds ready success in our secondary schools; 80 percent do not.[6]

Our old notions of what is important to learn remain embedded in structures set during the days of the medieval universities. The study of the natural world was part of a course in philosophy until the quantity of known facts grew too large, at which point it became a separate course. When natural science became too big to study all in one clump, it was broken down into biology, physics, and alchemy. When biology got too big, it was broken down into zoology and botany. And these structures remain with us.

This piecemeal, patchwork stuff—arms' length from a modern world view of knowledge—leaves students unprepared for our fast-paced world. Not only does it get in the way of understanding the interconnectedness and interrelationship of critical issues such as unemployment, pollution, transportation, and overpopulation of the planet, but it simply does not match adult living and experiences. Jobs called biologist or physicist are now almost extinct. Today's occupations are microbiologist, biochemist, biophysicist, and nuclear physicist. Such titles are more than a reflection of specialization, they speak of a degree of integration needed to address real problems of the real world.

In similar fashion, in the area of history/social studies, it is no longer possible to study European history or history of the Far East as a backdrop for understanding one's community. Further, studying Vietnam or China will not necessarily enable students to predict the cultural beliefs and values of the Vietnamtown or Chinatown within one's own city. Nor did the study of history of the former USSR allow us to predict the rapid disintegration of the communist empire. *Classical education is backward-looking*; study of the past through old perspectives will not enable one to anticipate and handle day-to-day living in the future. Only study of the present, with the past as a reference (not a beginning) point, will prepare students to handle the future.

Mismeme 3: Words Create Knowledge

Every culture has its maxim that describes humankind's experience with teaching its young. The Chinese voice it well: "Tell me, I forget; show me, I remember; involve me, I understand." In the United States we are so sure of this that we have an idiom which attempts to divert attention from the power of the truth: "Do what I say, not what I do." In the staff development world, our research about what we learn and retain is quite precise. We learn and retain as follows:

10 percent of what we hear

15 percent of what we see

20 percent of what we both see and hear

40 percent of what we discuss

80 percent of what we experience directly or practice doing

90 per cent of what we attempt to teach others.[7]

Piaget's work seventy years ago reached the same empirical conclusions and recent brain research substantiates the fact that learning occurs best when it begins with the concrete, then moves to the symbolic, and lastly to the abstract. Traditional curriculum and instruction, to the contrary, typically begins with the abstract or symbolic and hopes that students might intuit how it applies to the concrete, real world.

And yet, despite all the axioms of our language, and those from other cultures around the world, despite research within our own educational community, despite the brain research described in this book, despite our direct experience as parents, education continues to cling to the tradition of telling as the primary medium to convey knowledge.

Truly, we know better and it is time to make our actions bespeak what we know.

Mismeme 4:
Acquisition of Knowledge and Skills Is the Goal of Education

Acquisition of knowledge and skill is wholly inadequate as a goal for education in the 1990s. First, it carries with it the implication that knowledge can be quantitatively measured by the pound like a commodity on a dry good shelf, purchased by the uniform currency of "seatwork." Second, in our "Age of Information," an era of exponential expansion of knowledge, particularly in science and technology, and rapidly changing major events such as the fall of communism, it is a cruel joke to send students out into the real world believing that what they have squirreled away in their knapsacks will be sufficient to the challenges they will face.

Our national goal for public education ought to be learning how to learn from a dizzying array of sources and formats and mastery in applying what is learned. Definitions from *Webster's* dictionary are useful here; they have the correct denotations and connotations.

> **Mastery:** "act of mastery; state of having control over something; superiority in competition; victory; eminent skill or thorough knowledge"

> **Application:** "the act of applying or putting to use"

Mismeme 5: Textbooks Equal Curriculum and Instruction

For most Americans, textbooks are *the* symbol of education. As Marion Brady comments in his book, *What's Worth Teaching? Selecting, Organizing, and Integrating Knowledge*, "Some measure of their perceived importance is indicated by the action and attitudes of our society related to them. Parents demand that they be brought home from school. Many teachers won't start classes without them. Academic departments will adopt new textbooks and then spend weeks reorganizing courses, as if the change in books had somehow altered the field of study. Administrators sometimes think that all books for a class should be the same, and that all classes using textbooks should be on approximately the same page on the same day. Elaborate and expensive procedures are devised to select them. Angry crowds sometimes burn them and, not infrequently, the courts are asked to make judgments about them. Obviously, textbooks are thought to be very important."[8] How rare! We have obviously confused the tools of schooling with educating and education.

More than a mismeme, Brady suggests that "traditional textbooks are a major, perhaps *the* major obstacle to the achievement of educational excellence."[9] Yet like Galileo's stipulation that the sun, not the earth, is the center of the universe, this criticism of textbooks will seem to many to be nothing less than heresy. As Brady says, "It's acceptable to find fault with textbooks, to criticize the uninspired writing, the 'dumbing down' of vocabulary, the concern for comprehensiveness at the expense of depth and clarity, spiraling cost, the usual several years' lag behind current knowledge, the dreary sameness stemming from publishers' attempts to duplicate the current best-seller. But to suggest that, in most disciplines, the textbooks actually stand in the way of major educational improvement is to risk being labeled as too eccentric to be taken seriously."[10] I firmly believe that textbooks, and their organization of content is the tack that nails one shoe of school reform to the floor, limiting vision and action to a small circle, one already explored and already proven ineffective and deadening for students.

According to Brady, textbooks offer students only a "kind of residue of a discipline,"[11] a compilation of decades or centuries of thought, argument, exploration, criticism, organizing, and reorganizing. The result is but a thin gruel of what John Gatto calls "prethought thoughts."[12] He identifies two problems with textbooks: 1) the assumption that what's basically a reference book is a proper tool for instruction—which it is not; and 2) because the content of the conventional expository text is primarily a compendium of conclusions, all significant thinking has already been done. "It's very much like giving the student a vast crossword puzzle with all the blanks filled in. There's nothing left to do except perhaps memorize it—a task not likely to generate enthusiasm or sharpen the intellect."[13]

According to Brady, textbooks should be used as a primary instructional tool only when it is impossible to touch the real thing, or its tangible residue.[14] And, of course, "filling in the blanks" should be eliminated entirely.

Mismeme 6: Changing One Aspect of the System is Sufficient

"If only the teachers would be better trained," or "if we had a different principal," or "if there were more money," or "if the Board of Education were more competent" . . . the litany goes on and on.

We hold the shimmering belief that "if only x, then everything would be better." Nonsense.

What you will find in this book is a reflection of hard lessons learned over the past thirty years, i.e., change in one area or even two or three, however significant and well-founded, is insufficient. The entire system must be changed simultaneously, or what is not changed will undo what is done. This is to say, the system must be totally reinvented from whole cloth simultaneously, or else the unchanged pressures that surround a school (community, district office, school board, etc.) and the culture within the school continue to exert the same forces that molded the school originally. The bottom line here is that the same forces applied to a school—from within and without—produce the same predictable results, faith replication of the past.

Thus, significant, long-term change is not possible without significant change in all four areas (shown in the following diagram) and *change in all four areas simultaneously at the district and school levels.*

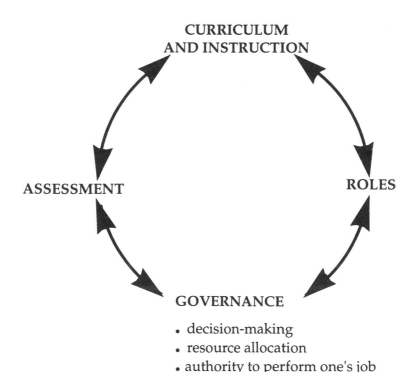

**CURRICULUM
AND INSTRUCTION**

ASSESSMENT

ROLES

GOVERNANCE

- decision-making
- resource allocation
- authority to perform one's job

NEW MEMES FOR EDUCATION

Life in the 21st century and the ITI model demand new memes or foundational premises which are consistent with brain research and the developmental characteristics of children. We suggest the following:

- **The purpose of public education is the perpetuation of democracy**
- **Real life is the best curriculum for children; the curriculum for the 21st century must be based on reality, not on "disciplines" and textbooks**
- **Learning is a personal affair**
- **Curriculum should consist mostly of concepts, skills, and attitudes/values which students can experience through** *being there*
- **Instructional strategies should provide students choices which allow for their unique ways of learning**
- **Curriculum should be framed so as to reduce "telling about" and be based upon exploration, discovery, and application of concepts to the real world**
- **Assessment should be reality-based**

New Meme 1:
The Purpose of Public Education Is the Perpetuation of Democracy

I wholeheartedly accept the statement made by Carl Glickman, author of *Renewing America's Schools* and professor of educational leadership at University of Georgia, "the one primary goal for American public schools: to return to its essence and prepare its students to become productive citizens of our democracy."[15] As Glickman points out, "The value that unites Americans as a people, regardless of religion, culture, race, gender, life-style, socioeconomic class, or politics, is a belief in 'government of the people, by the people, and for the people.' Public education is the only institution designated and funded as the agent of the larger society in protecting the core value of its citizens: democracy."[16] Furthermore, says Glickman, "What difference does it make if we graduate 100 percent of our students, or if SAT scores rise twenty points, or if our students beat other countries in achievement in science when they have not learned how to identify, analyze, and solve the problems that face their immediate and larger communities? Our country would be better served by schools that produce caring, intelligent, and wise citizens who willingly engage in the work of a democracy than by schools that produce graduates who do well on isolated subgoals."[17] Glickman also postulates that "if our schools were to focus on the main goal of citizenship and democracy and show students how to connect learning with the real issues of their surroundings, then more students would learn how to write cogent compositions, would learn basic skills, would use higher-order thinking, would learn aesthetic appreciation, would excel in academics, and would graduate."[18] The most critical aspect of the ITI model lies in the belief that students who *understand* what they are learning will have the capacity to solve real problems—in their classroom, school, community, and beyond. Education for citizenship is at the core of ITI. Teachers need to orchestrate learning to provide opportunities for doing the real work of a community. Content is the brain's basic need and a belief in democracy demands that all individual are competent decision-makers

New Meme 2: Real Life Is the Best Curriculum for Children; the Curriculum Must Be Reality-Based

The curriculum of the 21st century must be based in reality, not in subject area "disciplines" and textbooks. We believe the only way to achieve that goal is to teach students about real life—not life in the America of thirty years ago, but **now**; not the life of the disappearing cowboy of the Wild West, but **here** in one's neighborhood—the street where one's house sits, as well as the neighborhood of a world economy. **The here and now of real life in the 1990s.**

While we often argue that reality, like beauty, is in the eye of the beholder, we define reality as the slice of life directly experienceable by students at, around, or through their school's location or outreach capacity. The brain is genetically designed to learn from real life—our survival as a species in climates around the world fully attests to that fact. We should use that marvelous capacity rather than wall it off by closing the classroom door.

New Meme 3: Learning Is a Personal Affair

That every brain is unique, having its own way of gathering information, extracting meaning, processing, storing, and using what is learned, is firmly and irrefutably established by recent brain research. Therefore, curriculum must be personalizable—for and by individual students. Choices for students must be built into the curriculum in order for students to steer their own course between too difficult (thus resulting in failure), and too easy (thus resulting in boredom),[19] and to better engage the entire brain and the seven intelligences described by Howard Gardner.

There must also be a range of choice for teachers. Curriculum simply cannot be made teacher proof—so fully described that it stands alone and immune to teacher influence. That has been repeatedly proven. Thus, developing curriculum scope and sequences which are overly prescriptive is, first of all, futile as a management tool and, second, suffocating and stifling for teachers in the classroom. The balance to be struck here is quite delicate. For the students' sake, there must be schoolwide agreement among teachers regarding what is to be studied and when, in order to prevent repetition and gaps for students. Yet, detailed prescriptions are counter productive. In our opinion, a one-page outline of concepts developed by each teacher or team is about the right level of detail to serve as a schoolwide planning guide. More detailed planning then occurs teacher by teacher.

New Meme 4: Curriculum Through *Being There*

Curriculum should consist almost entirely of concepts, skills, and attitudes/values which students can experience through *being there*—out in the real world where what is being studied can be experienced in action, in its natural context, e.g., studying real frogs in a real pond. The rationale for curriculum which allows students to "be there" is undergirded by brain research—what happens to the physiology of the brain when all 19 senses are activated—and by the characteristics of the student who thrives on active learning and interaction with peers and important others.

New Meme 5: Instructional Strategies Should Provide Students Choices That Allow for Their Unique Ways of Learning

Sameness and uniformity are killers for students and staff. On the other hand, choice opens doors to alternative ways of learning and expressing what is learned, to greater commitment to a task as personally meaningful, to higher motivation to persist on tasks, and many other pluses. In a word, choice in how students go about learning builds power into the curriculum.

Most importantly, it allows the learner to sit in the driver's seat—experiencing both freedom to be oneself and the responsibility of becoming one's own person, capable and contributing. Like a muscle, the skills necessary to become effective lifelong learners are developed only through use.

New Meme 6: Curriculum Should Be Framed so as to Reduce "Talking About" and Be Based on Exploration, Discovery, and Application of Concepts to the Real World

Traditional curriculum consists primarily of factoid statements—statement of facts, dates, definitions, rules—all divorced from a larger context of meaning. From the students' point of view, they are things to be memorized but provide no help in understanding the world around them or their future. Instead, curriculum should be stated in conceptual terms, bottom lines which assist students in understanding events around them and into the future. Furthermore, instructional strategies must include collaboration and much opportunity to apply and practice using what is being learned.

In ITI classrooms, the goal is to limit teacher presentation and lecture to 11 to 16 minutes per hour. This is essential for several reasons. The importance of this meme stems from our earlier discussion about how the human brain learns, especially the program-building processing of the mind. Information that we use is embedded in programs; conversely, information which does not get loaded up into a mental program is typically unretrievable. Programs are built by applying information in real world settings. (See Chapter 5 for a discussion of developing *mental programs*.)

New Meme 7: Assessment Must be Reality-Based

Demonstration of mastery of curriculum should be through application of relevant knowledge, skills, attitudes and values, situations, and settings, in accordance with standards typical of adult living or the work place. Focus should be placed on real life problem-solving and/or on producing a product which has real life usefulness and standards. Paper and pencil testing should be used sparingly, and only when no other means of assessment are possible. (See Chapter 9 for a discussion of assessment and evaluation.)

Common sense is needed when considering assessment. Renate and Geoffrey Caine suggest that there are at least four relevant indicators which should guide evaluation:

- the ability to solve real problems using the skills and concepts
- the ability to use the language of the discipline or subject in complex situations and in social interaction
- the ability to show, explain, or teach the idea or skill to another person who has a real need to know[20]
- the ability to perform appropriately in unanticipated situations

The key to authentic, reality-based assessment is that the curriculum it measures must also be reality-based.

TOWARD A NEW MEME-BASED CURRICULUM: THE CURRICULUM OF HERE AND NOW

It is one thing to criticize the old; it is quite another to provide a sufficiently clear picture of the new that pioneers can hitch up their wagons, strike out with a destination in mind, confident that they are mentally prepared and amply outfitted for the journey. The purpose of the next pages of this chapter is to describe the destination of a new meme-based curriculum using the ITI model.

Webster's Dictionary defines "the here and now" as: "this place and this time; the present." What a recipe for making the school experience relevant for students! And what a recipe for ensuring that students will be successful after they leave school.

To base curriculum in "this place, this time, and in the present" marks a radical departure from our current subject area disciplines-based curriculum. Conceptually, the contrast is as follows:

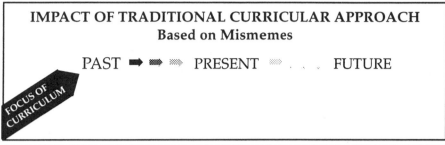

IMPACT OF TRADITIONAL CURRICULAR APPROACH
Based on Mismemes

PAST ➡ ➡ ➤ PRESENT ⋯ ... FUTURE

FOCUS OF CURRICULUM

IMPACT OF HERE AND NOW CURRICULAR APPROACH
Based on New Memes

PAST ⬅ PRESENT ➡ ➡ ➤ FUTURE

FOCUS OF CURRICULUM

WHERE TO FROM HERE?

At this point in my career, after thirty years of working within the educational establishment, after training thousands of teachers K–12, I firmly believe that the focus of compensatory, special focus programs and budgets spent on students who don't "fit" the regular classroom image needs to be rethought. I believe such resources should be redirected and used to train *all teachers* to be gifted teachers, sufficiently gifted to do the job of teaching *all students*. Every penny spent on compensatory education programs, reading specialists, math specialists, disability specialists, Chapter 1 specialists, resource specialists, gifted specialists, etc., is *tacit agreement that the regular classroom is failing our students.* I believe the fix is not to spend money around the edges of the classroom, but rather to invest in the classroom—to invest in massive teacher training and *support* so that regular classroom teachers can do the job right the first time.

In business circles, a book titled, *If You Haven't Got the Time to Do It Right, When Will You Find the Time to Do It Over?* is self-explanatory. Not to us in education. We never raise the question, "If we don't have the tools and training to do it right the first time, why will doing more of the same make a difference?" Furthermore, as my son pointed out, what makes us presume that all students don't want a learning experience that is exciting, challenging, fun, and firsthand? Or that all students wouldn't prefer that the regular teacher take time to find out where they are stuck and why they have trouble understanding something?

We are misusing our funding. Recently, a colleague worked with a school district to develop a New American School Development Corporation (NASDC) proposal for a yet-to-be-built school in the district. Using the budget of a similar school within the district, they found that all of the following could be purchased within the special monies budget at the school (those which could legally be used in other ways): extend the student year by twenty days; the teacher year by forty days; change the school calendar so that after every thirty-five or forty-five days of teaching, teachers would get two weeks off—one for holiday, one for paid professional development time (inservice training and/or curriculum development); reduce class size to twenty students, provide an extended day program from 7:15 to 5:15 for all interested students, and more! All within existing monies.

Starting Point. Brain research, the basis for the ITI model, is a very hot topic these days, finally capturing the attention it deserves. The cover of *Newsweek*, March, 1992, announced the strides we have made in understanding the human brain of normal, healthy people when faced with challenging activities from real life. This under-standing is made possible with new technology that allows us to lit-erally look inside the brain while it is functioning. Likewise, the September, 1992, issue of *Scientific American* is devoted entirely to the mind and the brain. Freed from the behavioral psychologists and their research with rats and pigeons, we can now move from reward and punishments as controllers and begin to direct our activities toward the way the brain actually does work.

There is much to choose from; new publications about the brain are coming off the presses at a dizzying rate. Authors such as

Armstrong, Buzan, Caine, Cohen, Elkind, Feuerstein, Gardner, Hart, Healy, Keirsey, Lazaer, Lowery, Montessori, Restak, Russell, Smith are people who have written understandable and very useful books on the subject of the human brain and how it learns.

In analyzing this information, our task was to translate how it could be applied in the classroom—how it would look, how it could be done. There are eight implementation elements needed to create a brain-compatible environment in which performance for both children and adults can be improved.

These eight brain-compatible elements are:

- **ABSENCE OF THREAT**
- **MEANINGFUL CONTENT**
- **CHOICES**
- **ADEQUATE TIME**
- **ENRICHED ENVIRONMENT**
- **COLLABORATION**
- **IMMEDIATE FEEDBACK**
- **MASTERY (APPLICATION)**

Every successful learning experience you completed had as its core three or more of these components. As parents, when your children were learning to walk, talk, and interact with the world, you automatically assisted them with immediate feedback, collaboration, and absence of threat, until they had achieved MASTERY!

The Journey. The ITI model as discussed here is not finalized. It will never be. As we learn more, we will continue to synthesize and adjust. There is no such thing as "complete and finished" in education. In a world of 5.1 billion individuals, and with that number doubling in the next forty years, we dare not stand still when it comes to problem-solving. America is not, and will never be, isolated from the rest of the world. Currently, we are the largest immigrant nation in the world—a country where people are willing to die just to risk coming to the "land of opportunity." In the field of education, our greatest opportunity is the call for change. Are we up to the challenge? Do we care enough about tomorrow to take a risk today?

WELCOME TO INTEGRATED THEMATIC INSTRUCTION

This is the best of times to be an educator. Everywhere there is a call for change, a sense of urgency born of crisis. For the Chinese, the symbol for "crisis" is twofold: danger and opportunity. The danger is that we would lack the courage to move quickly and decisively to completely reconceptualize and rethink the system, and that we fail to see the opportunity that human brain research has given us.

CHAPTER ONE

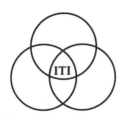

THE MODEL

I believe that schooling should impact students' lives in such a way that they are willing and able to become contributing members of our democratic society. I am not willing for schools to be a holding pen for adolescents nor a cheaper form of day care for young children. I feel an obligation to make it clear to youngsters why the knowledge and, more importantly, the actions of an educated person are essential to sustaining a democratic society. Consequently, the Integrated Thematic Instruction (ITI) model always stresses problem-solving and decision-making.

This philosophy is what determines and influences the selection of significant content around which to organize a year's worth of study. Not unexpectedly, my choice for organizing curriculum for elementary students is first, science—the understanding of how the natural world works and the implications of man's interactions with it—and, second, social studies—the study of the needs and expectations of groups, communities, and societies.

The ITI model is designed on three interlocking, interdependent principles. First, that human brain research has given us a window on learning never before realized in the history of civilization and that this knowledge must become the basis for all decisions made to improve student and teacher performance.

Second, that teachers' strategies or ability to orchestrate learning in a classroom is both an art and a science. It is poetry in motion when a teacher can work with thirty students, all

1

with different backgrounds and needs, and introduce curriculum that motivates while at the same time makes them potential contributors to society. It is the best of applied science to take the enormous array of brain research findings, ferret out their implications, synthesize them, and implement them in the classroom. To apply such art and science, teachers MUST constantly update their knowledge and skills.

And third, curriculum development cannot be mandated by text-book publishers from afar but must be developed at the classroom level from the knowledge and understanding only the classroom teacher can bring to bear—an understanding of the learners and the communities in which they live. This is not to suggest that teachers begin from scratch and "make up" their curriculum. Rather, the district/school must agree on a continuum of concepts that all children should understand and then allow each school the opportunity to select the content that best supports and extends the concept. If learning is to come alive, curriculum must be a creative act of the teacher, a modeling of what it is to be a learner, to possess an absolute passion for lifelong learning.

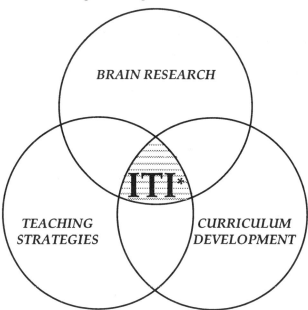

*Integrated Thematic Instruction

Integrated Thematic Instruction is the vehicle for bringing these three areas together, a way of conceptualizing and implementing a "brain-compatible"* learning environment for students and teachers. It is based upon the development and orchestration of one unifying yearlong concept and all its ramifications through which all content and skills are woven. The theme acts as a pattern for organizing ideas, materials, and actions for both teacher and students.

While the notion of thematic units is not a new one, purposefully using the theme to enhance the pattern-seeking operation of the brain is.** The entire ITI model—curriculum development and instructional strategies—has been selected and organized with great care to fit how the brain learns. As a result, all aspects of the classroom operation must be rethought.

The purpose of the remainder of this chapter is to define the ITI model and describe a possible time line for implementation.

A Word about ITI as a Model

The effectiveness of any model is how the parts and pieces are interwoven. The eight brain-compatible elements are key to the effectiveness of this model. I have seen school districts select the elements they feel comfortable with and ignore the others. It doesn't work! The elements are an inseparable whole—a learning environment which is brain-compatible for all. The absence of even one element shatters the whole.

---

*"Brain-compatible" learning is a phrase coined almost two decades ago by Leslie Hart, a pioneer in translating the implications of brain research to school and classroom settings. Hart uses the term to describe a classroom whose curriculum and instruction fits the way the human brain learns, i.e., allows the human brain to operate as it does naturally and thus most powerfully.

**See Chapter 3 of this book for a discussion of the brain as a pattern-seeker.

THE YEARLONG THEME

The yearlong theme is the heart and soul, the inner engine of the ITI classroom. It is the source of curriculum development and sets the direction for instructional strategies. The yearlong theme is a "big idea" with a "kid-grabbing" twist to it. As the following mindmap suggests, the yearlong theme is the organizer for the components (which last roughly a month) from which spring the weekly topics (again, "weekly" is a rough estimate).

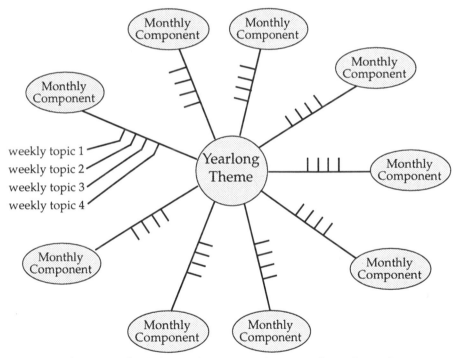

(See Chapter 11 for information on creating a yearlong theme.)

Because the theme is so critical to brain-compatibility, its selection deserves careful thought. The criteria for selecting a yearlong theme are as follows:

1. It must have substance and application to the real world

The theme should

- provide a snapshot of reality, a *here and now* quality, a slice of life, a time, a place, an event, a question

- engender student recognition of the application and value of what is studied outside the classroom

- impact one's life and the way we relate to the world around us

As Marion Brady, author of *What's Worth Teaching? Selecting, Organizing, and Implementing Knowledge*, comments, "the primary purpose of schooling should be to help students understand their world."[1] And, of course, children's world is the world of here and now—which *Webster's Dictionary* defines as "this place and this time; the present."

A key feature of *here and now* curriculum is that it is immediately recognized (by the student) as being relevant and meaningful, a prerequisite condition for brain-compatible learning. Content which is here and now also activates at least fourteen of the 19 senses, thereby enhancing the taking in, processing, storage, and retrieval of learning (see Chapter 6). Furthermore, it purports to teach our young about their world and the skills necessary to act within and upon it, thus preparing themselves for living the fast-paced changes of the 1990s and beyond.

Here and now curriculum is grounded not in the traditional subject areas but in

- **physical locations** in the locale of the school or community, accessible for study and frequent visiting by students

- **human issues** that students are experiencing or can experience in the physical locations identified above

For younger students, K-4, physical locations and the science that goes with them, are the best sources of curriculum for a yearlong theme. Older students can begin to lean more toward human issues. For a discussion of using here and now as the basis for developing a yearlong theme, see Chapter 11

2. It must have readily available resources

Given what we know about the pattern-detecting ability of the brain and the necessity of huge quantities of input, the theme must be one whose reality you can recreate in your classroom—an environment or situation that begins to deliver some of the impact that would be felt if you were having a firsthand, being there experience.

3. It must be age-appropriate

While it is unquestionably true that the brain grows best when it is challenged and that high standards for children's learning are important, it is also true that curriculum needs to be considered in terms of age-appropriate challenge.

The notion that the human brain unfolds in predictable developmental stages goes back to Maria Montessori ninety years ago and to Jean Piaget seventy years ago. While the details of their work have been debated endlessly, recent brain research has confirmed most of their basic premises. The application of their work to today's curriculum and textbooks reveals that a large percentage of the concepts identified for elementary students is, in fact, beyond what students can understand at those ages; they may be able to memorize and parrot them back but that does not indicate a real *understanding*. This is particularly true in science. For example, solar system as a subject for second or third graders is wildly age-inappropriate. The concepts are highly abstract and not experience-able—the ground on which we stand is spinning at hundreds of miles an hour and the distances between planets are computed in millions of miles or even light years, a measurement that most adults can't relate to.

David Elkind, after lengthy studies of the effects of stress upon children, preschool through high school, suggests that pressure on students to learn things that their minds cannot comprehend may in fact be harmful to the brain, causing it to organize itself to do memorization instead of seeking understanding.

Yes, dinosaurs are fascinating, but how do you connect a happening of 250 million years ago to today? Dinosaurs have been dead and gone for sixty-five million years. We are not talking relevancy. To quote Dr. Larry Lowrey, professor of science education and the staff at the Lawrence Hall of Science, UC Berkeley, "Do not confuse enthusiasm with understanding." Because students are enthusiastic about something does not mean that they understand it or that it has relevance or value in terms of helping them understand their world. This is not to say you can't have an extracurricular Dinosaur Club for those who are interested or that it wouldn't be a fascinating subject for the students to develop at home with their parents and siblings.

Something that is age-appropriate for students means that they can and do make meaning of what they are studying and can apply it in their real, away-from-school-worlds. For the young child, this usually results because of *being there* experiences, not from lecture or second hand presentation of abstract concepts.*

4. It must be worthy of the time spent on it

Nobody really has any more time than anyone else. We have each day and the minutes in that day; the significant difference among people is how they *use* their time. Most teachers work very hard to create learning experiences for students and the amount of paperwork that needs to be done at the end of the day is legendary. The question, therefore, is: *"Is what you are doing worthy of your time?"* You must choose carefully when selecting content so that the time you spend enhances who you are and what you are capable of doing. Will it expand your knowledge base? enable you to make new and interesting connections? meet new people and visit new places?

---

*For more information about age-appropriateness, see *Thinking and Learning: Matching Developmental Stages with Curriculum and Instruction* by Larry Lowery.

Curriculum development takes time. It is labor-intensive but fruitful for both students and teachers. The extra effort produces powerful learning and memorable moments. I have often been asked how effective it is to team-teach with each teacher on the team taking one month's curriculum and then sharing it. I don't discourage it when asked because, if teachers are asking, hopefully they already have a working relationship they trust and it might work. My suggestion, however, is to try it and evaluate with your students how effectively the month you *didn't* create was orchestrated. Was it as powerful for students as the curriculum you created? Unfortunately, there are few shortcuts to developing powerful curriculum for your students. On the other hand, teachers and principals alike report that teachers who regularly share their experiences of implementing the model with a colleague make the quickest progress.

5. It should flow—from month-to-month and back to center

> F — footbridge between components
> L — linking the months
> O — opening doors to generalizations
> W — weaving the components together

A significant advantage of one yearlong theme is the capacity to provide the foundation for making generalizations and connections in the content. Less is best and less is more. This is not about covering the material, but about understanding the concept and being able to apply it in the real world. The link "back to the center" allows you to continue to build and support the concept of your yearlong theme.

6. The title should be a kid-grabber

A promise, a commitment, a challenge, a wow! Let the title speak for the action of the year, capturing students' imagination as well as reflecting the big idea or concept being studied, e.g., "You Can't Fool Mother Nature," "The Time Bomb," "What Makes It Tick?"

KEY POINTS AND INQUIRIES

Once the theme is created, one can proceed with defining what every student is expected to learn. Key points delineate the essential core of knowledge and skills all students are to master each week, month, and year. They are conceptual rather than factoid (isolated bits of information that don't contribute to the overall concept being addressed) and encourage exploration rather than lecture.

Inquiries structure the activities needed to enable students to use knowledge and skills they have learned, to learn how to apply them to the real world, and to develop *mental programs* for their long-term retention and application.

The yearlong theme is not lockstep; it encourages active participation and questions from the learners. At any point within the theme, students may add extra key points or expand the monthly components.

See chapters 12 and 13 for a discussion of how to identify key points and develop inquiries.

CHAPTER 1: THE MODEL

THE ROAD TO INTEGRATION

Full implementation of ITI does not occur overnight. Three to five years is the typical period of time to reach full integration of all content and basic skills through a single yearlong theme. So . . . be gentle with yourself! Start slowly and be thorough. Each year it is becoming more and more obvious that students are coming with fewer and fewer social skills. DO NOT neglect the opportunity during the beginning months of school to address this issue; until there is an absence of threat (among the students and between you and the students), learning with understanding is not possible.

Take the time to model and practice the Lifelong Guidelines:

- TRUSTWORTHINESS
- TRUTHFULNESS
- ACTIVE LISTENING
- NO PUT-DOWNS
- PERSONAL BEST

See Chapter 7, "Collaboration," for more details on what these Lifelong Guidelines should look and sound like.

The ITI model and the integration of content is powerful when the brain-compatible elements are understood and practiced by everyone in the class. The purpose of the next eight chapters is to explain each of these elements:

- ABSENCE OF THREAT
- MEANINGFUL CONTENT
- CHOICES
- ADEQUATE TIME
- ENRICHED ENVIRONMENT
- COLLABORATION
- IMMEDIATE FEEDBACK
- MASTERY (APPLICATION)

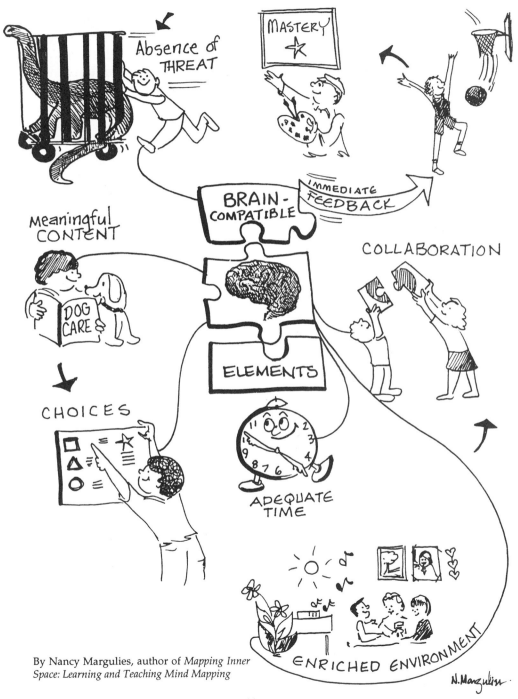

By Nancy Margulies, author of *Mapping Inner Space: Learning and Teaching Mind Mapping*

Another major focus of ITI is the look of your room. What impact does it have on your students? Does it enhance learning or detract? Add plants and lamps; create one whole wall that displays your theme; create bulletin boards that are interactive; and organize your room for positive traffic flow and accessibility to interest centers. When designing bulletin boards, use only two or three colors, including white, to frame interest areas (think of your living room at home and the tone you have created there).

Wherever you are doing direct instruction, have an uncluttered backdrop. When the president speaks, he doesn't have a cluttered wall/ceiling behind him. You shouldn't either. Also, when using your overhead projector, ALWAYS use increased letter size. All of this attention to detail creates an unforgettable learning environment.

As you travel down the road to integration, remember that it is best to do things slowly and well, to build a secure foundation, to become confident with the vocabulary, and to "see" the natural integration of the skills so the model does become one's own.

For a travelogue of the ITI journey, see the ITI Rubric, pp. 132-38.

CREATING NECESSARY SUPPORT FOR IMPLEMENTING ITI

To create an environment in which significant change can succeed on a long-term basis, all parts of the system must be re-thought and restructured. To support a brain-compatible learning environment for both students and teachers, the following actions are needed:

State

- develop legislation and policy directives that require all curricular and instructional planning for federal and state monies be based on current brain research

- eliminate curricular improvement cycles at the elementary level which require focusing on a different subject area each year in favor of an improvement effort which acknowledges that truly significant change in a content area requires three to five years

- review existing policies, directives, criteria, etc., of the State Board and Department of Education and update them to eliminate contradictions (e.g., requirements for content that is not age-appropriate, time requirements that do not allow for the development of *mental programs*)

District
school board

- state the intent and goal of the district to provide all students with a brain-compatible learning environment. Identify the key sources of brain research and parallel learning theory upon which this will be based

- review existing policies, directives, etc., and update them to reflect the above policy and to eliminate policies and directives supporting brain-antagonistic elements (e.g., use of assertive discipline, use of textbook monies for a single adoption with a book for every student)
- develop new policies to encourage implementation of specific brain-compatible elements and structures

district office

- revise district scope and sequences for all subjects in order to ensure age-appropriateness, focus on fewer, more conceptual notions rather than factoids, and encourage curriculum based in the *here and now* rather than in traditional subject areas ("the way it's always been")

- refocus all staff development monies on brain research and how to implement this information in the classroom; eliminate one-shot events in favor of on-site, whole staff trainings consistent with a comprehensive school plan

- eliminate curricular improvement cycles at the elementary level which focus on a different subject each year, thus expecting mastery of significant change in a curricular area within only one year (which never works!)

School
staff

- acquire a thorough understanding of current brain research and its implications for your classroom and school

- visit other "brain-compatible" schools to develop a clear picture of what your goal is—what is possible and how to make it happen

- examine the structure of the "system" and determine which structures and past practices are truly brain-antagonistic; develop a time line for targeting and eliminating each one

- set a feasible schedule for implementation, realizing that it will likely take three to five years to achieve a fully integrated program

- identify the old practices of the system and your own *mental programs* that must be left behind so that you can move forward

- involve staff in comprehensive restructuring planning for the school level (and involve your district level staff in your processes)

- revise homework policies to reflect less busy work and more real life application

- re-allocate all monies available for staff development use for schoolwide, concentrated training on brain research, its implications for the classroom and implementation strategies

parents

- acquire an understanding of current brain research and why a brain-compatible ITI learning environment is effective; learn to judge new practices and features of a classroom in relationship to this new knowledge

- offer support—tangible and moral—to your child's teacher as he/she transitions into ITI

- understand that an ITI classroom "changes the rules of the game" and that your child's initial reaction is likely to be one of complaints and even anger (this is especially true for older students who have gotten by without ever achieving mastery)

- anticipate that ITI will change the nature of your child's "homework"; make an effort to find out the purpose of the assignments and allocate time to work with your child to show real life applications for what he/she is learning

CHAPTER 1: THE MODEL

BRAIN RESEARCH—THE BASIS FOR CHANGE

Given the incredible complexity of the brain, one might think that it is all beyond the purview of the regular classroom teacher; some might argue that it is irrelevant to the act of teaching, that it belongs in the science laboratory. The truth lies somewhere in the middle. I don't expect classroom teachers to become experts on the human brain and all its intricacies. But I do expect each and every teacher—preschool through adult education—to understand how to implement a learning environment that is brain-compatible and to know how to orchestrate curriculum so that each and every student can learn to a level of application.

The following chapters will present the eight elements of a brain-compatible learning environment, their bases in brain research, their implication in the classroom, and the how-tos for implementing them. The appendices will provide examples of curriculum.

CHAPTER TWO

ABSENCE OF THREAT— CREATING A TRUSTWORTHY ENVIRONMENT

The human brain is staggeringly complex in its structures, chemistry, electrical signals, and functions. To view it in three basic "chunks" is admittedly a vast oversimplification, yet a useful one when examining how the brain functions and implications for classroom application. As first theorized by Dr. Paul MacLean, NIMH, Bethesda, Maryland, the brain can be thought of as three brains in one, each with specific responsibilities essential for human survival and growth, each constantly assessing the needs of the situation at hand to determine the most appropriate response. Dr. MacLean coined the term "triune brain": the brain stem, limbic system, and cerebral cortex.

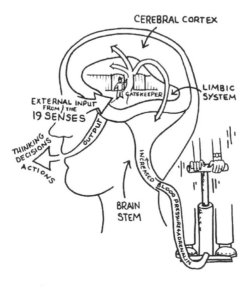

CHAPTER 2: ABSENCE OF THREAT

The limbic system—The limbic system is composed of several interconnected structures, ranging from the size of an olive to a walnut, that emerge out of the cerebral cortex. It is our brain's principal regulator of emotions and it also receives sensory data coming from the 19 senses, sending it along a fast track through the amygdala, if the data suggest possible threat or arousal of intense emotion, or along a slow track through the hippocampus, for analysis and "thinking about" in the cerebral cortex.[1] Thus, the limbic system can be thought of as our mental gatekeeper. Its role includes:

- converting information that the brain receives into appropriate modes for processing, constantly checking information relayed to the brain by the senses and comparing it to past experience

- directing information to the appropriate memory storage areas of the brain. (This function is needed because memories are not stored in one specific place, but rather are distributed throughout the brain in the areas functionally associated with the nature of the memory to be stored. Words, numbers, and visual images, for example, are stored in areas associated with the language center, the calculation center, and the visual cortex, respectively.)

- transferring information from short-term to long-term memory[2]

The limbic system also regulates eating, drinking, sleeping, waking, body temperature, chemical balances such as blood sugar, heart rate, blood pressure, hormones, sex, and emotions and is the focus of pleasure, punishment, hunger, thirst, aggression, and rage."[3] A busy place!

The early view of the triune brain from MacLean's work left the impression that the cerebral cortex is the most important and controlling structure of the brain and that the normal state is to be "in" the cerebral cortex processing in logical and rational ways. The latest research says not so. The new news about the limbic system is that it is powerful enough to override other rational thought and innate brainstem response patterns. In short, as Dr. Robert Sylwester of the University of Oregon points out, we tend to fellow our feelings.[4]This gatekeeper role in learning has far-reaching implications—both for teachers and students—because the limbic system is key to what gets processed and how, and in determining what gets stored for later recall and use. Boredom and frustration shut down the brain; curiosity and enthusiasm open the doors. Positive emotional engagement is essential; perceived threat is brain antagonistic. Until 1995, discussions about how to apply the triune brain theory in the classroom placed emphasis on the importance of preventing "downshifting" from the cortex to the limbic system so that academic learning could occur. It now appears the conversation needs to be reversed; since we live in the limbic system, the question is how to get students to "upshift" and remain processing in the cerebral cortex.

The cerebral cortex—The cerebral cortex has been with us for only a few million years. In evolutionary terms, a very new item indeed. It is a multi-modal, multi-path system that, per minute, can process thousands of bits of information picked up through the 19 senses and forwarded via the limbic system. Given the volume of such information, it understandably is the slowest of the three levels of the brain. The cerebral cortex can reason, solve problems, analyze, create, synthesize, and handle a multitude of complicated tasks. This is the home of academic learning. This is the part of our brain which handles language, symbols, and images for learning Shakespeare, exploring the complexities of science, studying ancient history, writing an essay, or contemplating the issues and problems of the future. It is the part of the brain that students must be in if cognitive learning is to take place. Consequently, the first step toward brain-compatibility in the classroom is creating an environment with an absence of threat and curriculum that is truly engaging to students.

The brain stem—The oldest part of the brain, over 200 million years old, is often referred to as the reptilian brain. The existence of our species attests to the success of this part of the brain. It is thought to control genetic/instinctual behaviors such as hierarchies of dominance-submission, sexual courtship, defending territory, hunting, bonding, nesting, greeting, flocking, and playing.[5] Always on the alert for life-threatening events, it is the part of the brain we "downshift" to when responding to situations perceived as physically life-threatening—physical life and death occurences. This process has the effect of overriding input to and from the more slowly processing cerebral cortex. The brain stem has no language. And while this brain utilizes visual input, it typically does not store it. Storing things in memory takes time, a luxury, which the human organism under life-threatening attack cannot afford. Action is needed NOW.

Recall an all too common experience: a car ahead of you going out of control. As it suddenly swerves into your lane, you experience great fear and react swiftly to avoid the oncoming car. The fear is gut-wrenching, things happen in slow motion. You brace yourself for the crash. Seconds later you "come to" and find yourself parked safely at the side of the freeway but have no visual memory of how you missed the car in your lane or got safely to the side of the freeway and came to a stop. These are everyday examples of the effects of "downshifting" to the brain stem when threat is extreme and considered life-threatening. No time here for learning long division! When this ancient brain goes to school, it does not shut off. It remains on the alert for any threats—real or perceived.

The implications of the triune brain for the classroom are simple and startling. As the teacher responsible for orchestrating the total learning environment for students, your first task is creating an environment in which students can remain upshifted. If you fail at this, nothing else matters—academic learning at the level of creating *mental programs* cannot occur. The environment—schoolwide as well as in the classroom—must eliminate all real and perceived threat between teacher and students and among students. Next, the teacher must engineer and nurture a sense of trust and trustworthiness.

STRUCTURING TEACHER-STUDENT AND
STUDENT-STUDENT INTERACTIONS

Given the nature of the triune brain and the disruption of learning caused by emotional override, teacher-student and student-student interactions must be structured with great care. There are three important areas of classroom operation which provide the context for classroom interactions. The teacher controls all three:

- relationship
- classroom management
- behavior guidelines

Relationship

The quality and nature of the relationship between the teacher and his/her students is the keystone for all else in the classroom. My best advice is to frame it carefully and model it always.

Perhaps the best model of relationship and the social skills and actions that go with it is to consider the classroom as your living room, your students as neighbors and friends. If you were to invite neighbors to your home, how would you go about it? Remember, you are modeling. And what you want to model for students is not the indifference of a large bureaucracy but skills for life, the adult interaction skills for successful living.

Just remember that you never get a second chance to make a first impression. So, prior to the the first day of school, every student should receive a phone call or postcard from their teacher inviting them to their new class, asking them to bring something appropriate to the first day of school (given theme and grade level). Make sure you tell them that you are looking forward to the year.

As your students arrive the first day of school, greet them at the door, exchange a word of welcome with them, share a personal observation, e.g., "Welcome to our classroom. I'm excited about your being in this class."

As you would at a sit-down dinner, invite them to find their name tag and tell them where to sit, where to put their personal belongings, what they can do to settle in and feel comfortable. Preparation says that you care, you value their coming. On the first day name tags and binders with student names should be at the seats.

Have soft music on to set the tone. Each folder should have an agenda to allow the students to anticipate what you have planned for them for the day. They should also have a schematic of where things are located in the classroom—this is a beginning step in map reading. For K-1 students, use pictures or have a helper there to assist on the first day.

The room speaks for you. Just as our homes get their most thorough cleaning when company is coming, the classroom must be inviting—clean, yet not institutionally bare, rich without being cluttered, focused without being sterile. The classroom itself will speak to your students as they come through the door of your classroom. What message do you want your classroom to give to your students?

Functionally, the room must offer areas for specific purposes, such as a work area for groups and for individual quiet time, a place for materials, an area for a resource center and for direct instruction, teacher space, personal space, and spaces for personal belongings. There should be order and symmetry whenever possible, allowing for movement and organized flow within the room.

The walls should herald the content students will experience this year. The yearlong theme should occupy one whole wall and be colorful, easy to read, and as three-dimensional as possible. Skills should be written on sentence strips in different colors and placed around the ceiling to be there for all to know what is expected in this class this year.

CLASSROOM MANAGEMENT

Classroom Management

Your management style and procedures in the classroom are a major means of sculpting teacher-student interactions. Are you so spontaneous students are forever anxious and feeling off-balance? Or, so predictable they're bored? You must demonstrate yourself worthy of being trusted before you can ask your students to be trustworthy.

According to Pat Belvel of the Training and Consulting Institute, good classroom management consists of four elements. In the ITI model they are:

- you have **powerful** curriculum all planned and ready to go—meaningful, useful, relevant, with opportunities to be creative and emotional

- the **prerequisites** are in place—teacher and students are in relationship with each other, as are students with students

- the **parameters** are clear at all times—general and specific ground rules, procedures, and directions

- **participation** is expected and nurtured (students are actively engaged and on task; direct instruction provides for student involvement)

ITI will provide your powerful curriculum. Prerequisites—relationship—must be worked at daily at both group and individual levels. Procedures to set parameters are discussed below. Tools for framing participation are discussed later under Lifelong Guidelines and LIFESKILLS.

Procedures are another means of ensuring understanding, consistency, and personal responsibility. By posting in clear terms the steps necessary to do particular activities in the classroom, you get away from the temptation to take short cuts and make spur of the moment decisions which all too often invite chaos. Procedures should be on chart paper on an easel and tabbed to facilitate ready access. Also, each child should have a list of frequently used procedures in his/her binder to refer to in order to proceed independently without hanging on the teacher for direction every step of the way. Procedures should be established for such frequently performed tasks as:

- labeling papers
- turning in homework
- using classroom resources
- doing a group activity
- selecting inquiries (more about this in the curriculum chapter)
- working on a research project
- what to do when the substitute comes
- how to be a host or hostess to room visitors
- how/when to go to the office, the nurse, recess, assemblies, etc.

Although such procedures may sometimes seem to constrain the class, realize that they are also an important element of consistency, allowing everyone to be "safe" by knowing what is expected. Not everyone is an auditory learner and verbal directions leave so much to remember.

When giving direct instruction, I recommend such sessions be limited to not more than eleven to fifteen minutes (and with appropriate props in hand for both the teacher and the students); when students are presenting, there should be no more than seven minutes of visually supported talk. Videotape yourself and your students to provide direct feedback on how one's presentation style comes through. Note elements such as tone of voice, eye contact with the audience, connection with the audience.

Lifelong Guidelines

The behavior guidelines of the ITI learning environment, called Lifelong Guidelines, are :

- TRUSTWORTHINESS
- TRUTHFULNESS
- ACTIVE LISTENING
- NO PUT-DOWNS
- PERSONAL BEST

The Lifelong Guidelines are consistent with brain research, based upon respect for others and self and, when consistently followed, ensure that students can remained "upshifted" for learning.

To implement the Lifelong Guidelines, modeling is the best form of teaching them. The second best way is acknowledging others' use of them on a daily basis. This allows students to see what the guidelines look and sound like, to observe firsthand what behaviors contribute to a sense of workability in life, not only in the classroom but in real life, now and as an adult.

The Lifelong Guidelines are literally the social outcomes we set for our students *and* for our fellow educators. There must be consistent parameters and expectations for how to perform and what to expect from others. For the adults in a school, this is an opportunity to "walk our talk," to model the behaviors we expect students to master. The skills are critical components of the model and the foundation *all* youngsters need to master and apply as they master the academic work that lies before them.

Trustworthiness. To act in a manner that makes one worthy of confidence. Do you remember that adult who was worthy of your confidence? The day in, day out sense of fairness, no surprises, no tantrums, no misplaced anger, unflagging joy of learning—a person you could rely on. If a teacher models this behavior, it is possible to develop a sense of trust in the class which will enable students to seek help, ask questions, deal with difficult situations, and generally look forward to being at school.

Trustworthiness is created by consistent modeling and expecting and insisting upon trustworthiness in others.

Truthfulness. Telling the truth is about personal responsibility and mental accountability. It is an important motivator behind rigorous intellectual pursuit—to "get it straight," to fully understand. And, in terms of relationship in the classroom, it is a fundamental cornerstone.

This is not to say that one should always blurt out what one thinks; tact is an important social skill to learn. Absence of threat rests heavily upon knowing that people around us are truthful with us—we know where we stand with them and we know what to expect.

Active listening. Listening with intention involves more than just hearing. It is the greatest gift we can give another. Think for a moment, who listens to you, really listens? who *hears* you—what you are saying and feeling, who you are?

EAR

YOU

EYES

UNDIVIDED
ATTENTION

HEART

Chinese verb, "TO LISTEN" Source: TRIBES Training

Some years ago, during a TRIBES training (see Chapter 7 for more information on collaboration and TRIBES), we were given the Chinese symbol for "to listen." The symbol means listening with your eyes, ears, and heart—and undivided attention—a perfect description of active listening. It is useful in the classroom because it identifies for children what the skills of listening are.

So many of our students are being bombarded by television programming that makes no mental demands on them and by commercials that assail their senses in order to gain their loyalty. Neither asks for active listening or intelligent responses. We should not be surprised that students come to us without listening skills, yet such skills are critical to success in school.

Teaching students to listen and to be able not only to understand but to ask thoughtful questions in return is worthy of our time and energy.

This symbol also provides good direction for speakers as well—say something that is worthy of being listened to!

No put-downs. A put-down is a way of saying, "I am better than you, richer than you, smarter than you, have more options than you." The goal is to elevate the speaker to a position of being noticed, controlling the behavior of those around them, undermining the relationship between people, sidetracking the real issues, promoting him/herself by creating a laugh at someone else's expense. Teachers and students need to learn how to handle put-downs and how to prevent them from controlling their lives.

Violence is the ultimate put-down and, in homes across America, students are exposed to more hours of television before they are five than they'll spend getting a B.A. degree in college. An article by

Thomas Radecki, a practicing psychiatrist and the research director of the National Coalition on Television Violence, reported in 1989 that:

> "The average American child with pay cable TV or a VCR in the home will watch 32,000 murders, 40,000 attempted murders and a quarter million total acts of violence by age eighteen. Even with a VCR or cable TV, 40 percent of all television and film entertainment contains high levels of physical violence, usually in a glamorized or exciting format. Other concerns include the transmission of inappropriate sexual values, unrealistic attitudes toward drugs and alcohol, an exaggerated worship of entertainers and entertainment, a neglect of nonfiction and educational material, and a neglect of reading in general."[6]

Since that report in 1989, our students have witnessed a blow-by-blow, minute-by-minute account of the Gulf War and have seen the Los Angeles riots, the worst in over a hundred years.

The behaviors and language students are exposed to find their way into the classroom. Every put-down finds a place to roost inside our brain. If we hear enough of them, especially about our character, our intelligence, or our work habits, we eventually become them! Who puts you down the most? Can you still hear the voice?

Put-downs are everywhere. Listen in the faculty room, the home, the grocery store, etc. The classroom must become an island in the storm, a place where students can sort out what is true about themselves and what is not.

Personal best. Can we still aspire to expect personal best? Who decides what best is and how it is measured and supported? Why is it necessary to make it a guideline? Education has been the business of evaluation, of determining by subjective and objective measures what is acceptable, what constitutes passing and who gets the *A*'s. Personal best says it is not the teacher alone who determines success, but rather students are given guidelines to evaluate their own performance against some rather telling criteria. For this purpose, we we have created the LIFESKILLS chart and subsequent list. This list is not intended to be complete; it is a beginning of what ITI teachers around the country have seen as valuable tools for establishing a model for personal best including skills and attitudes.

LIFESKILLS

The purpose of the list of LIFESKILLS is to provide parameters that help students evaluate their own performances—to guide them, individually and in groups, to an understanding of which social behaviors will enhance their success. Which of these descriptors you use may depend on your students—their age and their personal skill levels. We would hope that by at least eighth grade all can be identified, explained, and modeled by the students and that, more importantly, they have become part of students' persona—who they are and how they act upon the world.

The LIFESKILLS appear on the next page.

LIFESKILLS

INTEGRITY: To act according to a sense of what's right and wrong

INITIATIVE: To do something because it needs to be done

FLEXIBILITY: To be willing to alter plans when necessary

PERSEVERANCE: To keep at it

ORGANIZATION: To plan, arrange, and implement in an orderly way; to keep things orderly and ready to use

SENSE OF HUMOR: To laugh and be playful without harming others

EFFORT: To do your best

COMMON SENSE: To use good judgment

PROBLEM-SOLVING: To create solutions in difficult situations and everyday problems

RESPONSIBILITY: To respond when appropriate, to be accountable for your actions

PATIENCE: To wait calmly for someone or something

FRIENDSHIP: To make and keep a friend through mutual trust and caring

CURIOSITY: A desire to investigate and seek understanding of one's world

COOPERATION: To work together toward a common goal or purpose

CARING: To feel and show concern for others

COURAGE: To act according to one's beliefs

PRIDE: Satisfaction from doing your personal best

LIFESKILLS

The LIFESKILLS are easy to use—merely label examples of behavior that occur: "John and Jim were using the LIFESKILL of *cooperation* so well that they have completed their project. They have created a better project than if each had done it by himself." "Emily took *responsibility* for herself by moving to a part of the room where she could complete her assignment." "Your *patience* while waiting for me is appreciated. Thank you." Secondly, ask your children to brainstorm which LIFESKILLS they will need to be successful when completing a particular assignment, group or individual. Then ask what those behaviors would look and sound like, given the context of that assignment. When they have the needed skills and attitudes clearly in mind, have them proceed. Lastly, always give them time to debrief, sharing what behaviors worked and which didn't, and how they would go about such a task in the future.

Notice that when labeling examples of behaviors we have dropped the "I" statement that many of us were taught in school, e.g., "I like the way so and so is doing such and such." "I feel . . . , I notice . . . ." We've done so because we began to see that they can easily become "bondage statements." Such comments can send the message that pleasing the teacher is the primary goal for behavior. In contrast, children need to become responsible for themselves and know what that looks like and sounds like.

The Lifelong Guidelines and LIFESKILLS are examples of mental parameters in a learning environment. By posting them and using them daily, they can become your silent partner in creating an environment which enhances learning.

A trusting environment demands consistency and forethought. Consistency in daily interaction and expectations allows the children and you to concentrate on the work at hand. From the temperament of the teacher to the format of the day, the human brain looks for a pattern of action that is non-threatening. Forethought is about planning, both daily, weekly, and long-range. To have thought through the activities, class movements, and scenarios that will best support powerful learning is the "gift" you give your students.

CHAPTER 2: ABSENCE OF THREAT

If change in classrooms and schools is to occur, the "absence of threat" must be uppermost in our minds, not only for our students, but at every level of a system that seeks to control and direct our every move. Just as teachers must remove threat from the classroom for students, administrators must remove threat from the schools for teachers.

A number of key issues surrounding the teacher are critical to making this happen. First, does the teacher feel/know that he/she is working in a trustful environment? Has someone provided him/her with the tools and support needed to get the job done? Second, does the teacher have the knowledge in relation to the content, skills, and methodologies of teaching/learning that create a sense of competence?

It is essential to create a threat-free environment at all levels of education—classroom, school, and district—if we are to move forward to create an educational system worthy of students who must learn to survive and thrive in the 21st century.

Take the opportunity presented by the nationwide call for reform and restructuring to build a solid, schoolwide base that eliminates threat.

GUIDELINES
FOR CREATING ABSENCE OF THREAT
IN THE CLASSROOM

- insist that students leave the language and attitudes of television sit-coms at the door; create the classroom as a place where thoughtful human beings work together

- make the students feel honored as important and worthwhile people to know and to be in relationship with

- do group-building activities regularly, at least once a week throughout the year (intensely at the beginning of the year until trust has been created)

- don't assume students come with social skills and LIFESKILLS; teach them

- through consistent offering of meaningful curriculum to the students, develop the expectation that, if you're offering it, it is do-able and, best of all, worthy of their time and careful consideration

CHAPTER THREE

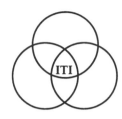

MEANINGFUL CONTENT

What is "meaningful" content? The answer lies in answers to other questions:

- Why do we go to school?

- What does it mean to live in the Age of Information? What is the purpose and impact of "the textbook" in such an era?

- Are we really in a post-literate society? (How many of our friends/peers read at least two nonfiction books a month?)

- If television is the primary means of communication, are we teaching our students to be critical audiences?

- If our economy is undergoing a massive reorganization, are we preparing students to be problem-solvers of real world problems, powerful decision-makers (starting with their own lives)?

- And . . . just what should the end product of thirteen years of public education be?

These questions are troubling, for they seem to pull us from the comfort of familiar curriculum content and lead us to the inescapable admission that the content of our current curriculum is, for the most part, meaningless in its content, and boring in its delivery. And yet, curriculum content has remained virtually unchanged for over a hundred years. If you don't believe it, go to an antique store and pick up some old textbooks. The foreword to the teacher in the Silver-Burdett reading series of 1897 reads like that of the reading series of the 1990s—teach reading through literature. Try a sixty-year old science text; it recommends teaching through hands-on strategies, the same content that our current science textbooks suggest teaching through hands-on. Sound familiar?

How would one describe meaningful content? That's a tricky question for an educator because, in fact, it is not the educator's question to answer. Just as beauty is in the eye of the beholder, so is meaningfulness determined by the learner. And yet, it is a question that must be answered because meaningful content is the most powerful brain-compatible element. It digs deeply into the learner's pool of intrinsic motivation and provides focus for the ever active brain, harnessing its attention and channeling its power. Fortunately, we can now do a better job of surmising what the learner beholds than ever before, if we look to recent brain research.

Although what constitutes "meaningfulness" is unique to each learner, there are several factors which help provide significance.

Meaningful content

- is from real life, the natural world around us
- depends heavily upon prior experience
- is significant to membership in a "learning club"* in which the learner holds full membership
- is age-appropriate and thus understandable
- is rich enough to allow for pattern-seeking as a means of identifying/creating meaning
- can be used within the life of the learner
- does not involve an external rewards system. The brain is a self-congratulator

---

* Frank Smith's definition of a learning club is "a group whose goals we adopt and whose membership adopts us."

REAL LIFE

LEARNING FROM REAL LIFE

The cerebral cortex is a four-million year old structure. It is programmed to learn from the natural world—to make sense of it and to act upon it to ensure survival. In other words, our genetic neural wiring makes us natural scientists—research and application. The survival of our species is abundant proof of its effectiveness. The brain seems to have "pay attention" triggers attached to input from the real world and an innate capacity to process that input and take meaning from it.

In contrast, reading, writing, and mathematics are very new to the human brain. We have no built-in wiring for these tasks; we have to learn how to learn them and then how to use them in our daily lives. Consequently, we could greatly enhance learning—motivation to learn and ability to extract meaning—if we focused our curriculum in subject areas that the brain is already genetically wired to perceive and understand e.g., science. Science provides the most powerful context for learning all the other subject areas and basic skills, math, language arts, art, music, history, social studies, etc. The advantages of studying the real world of science are numerous:

- the brain is already "tuned to that channel"
- the skill differences among students are the least (as compared to reading and writing where the differences among learners are the greatest and consequently social status problems begin to creep into the classroom)
- firsthand, being there experiences can be provided in your school and community
- it is possible to gather local resources
- a content area provides the playground for exercising all the basic skills, thus making integration natural for students and possible for the teacher
- application of what is learned in real life situations—the purpose of schooling—is built into the curriculum

CHAPTER 3: MEANINGFUL CONTENT

DEPENDENCE UPON PRIOR EXPERIENCE

It is often said that 80 percent of reading comprehension is based on prior knowledge. For example:

> *"Cayard* forced *America* to the left, filling its sails with 'dirty air,' then tacked into a right-hand shift. . . .That proved to be the wrong side. *America*, flying its carbon fiber/liquid crystal main and headsails, found more pressure on the left. *Cayard* did not initiate a tacking duel until *Il Moro* got headed nearly a mile down the leg. . . . *Cayard* did not initiate a jibing duel to improve his position heading downwind and instead opted for a more straight-line approach to the finish."[1]

We can assume this paragraph has something to do with sailing and we could answer questions such as these:

1. Who forced *America* to the left?
2. What kind of air filled *America's* sail?
3. Which boat had carbon fiber liquid crystal main and head sail?

The larger question is, "Does answering the questions successfully mean you *understand* what the paragraph is stating? Ninety-nine percent of my audience answers *no*—and why, because they have never been sailing.

This passage could be understood with teacher explanation and the use of a dictionary but arrival at the level of comprehension and ability to apply this understanding in new situations is highly improbable because my brain has no prior "being there" experience with sailing and therefore no mental patterns or programs. Prior experience is not a luxury; it is a prerequisite for the action! According to Jane Healy, there is much brain research to explain this familiar phenomena. In her book, *Endangered Minds: Why Our Children Don't Think*, she explains, "Experience—what children do every day, the ways in which they think and respond to the world, what they learn, and the stimuli to which they decide to pay attention—shapes their brains. Not only does it change the ways in which the brain is used (functional change), but it also causes physical alterations (structural change) in the neural wiring systems."[2] Prior experience based on being there experiences literally builds neural wiring which becomes the base for new learning

The following diagram illustrates how powerful, brain-compatible learning occurs. The brain readily learns (makes meaning) and applies (builds a *program* for using) information learned in this sequence.

BEING THERE   APPLICATION
EXPERIENCE ➡ CONCEPT ➡ LANGUAGE ➡ TO REAL WORLD

In contrast, conventional schooling starts with language and definitions *about* things. Basing instruction on "the textbook" when there is no prior experience makes it difficult or impossible for the brain to understand and learn. The following sequence illustrates this:

LANGUAGE ➡ CONCEPT ⸱ ⸱ ⸱ APPLICATION

Experience, those "being there" opportunities, is the prerequisite for understanding. Reading comprehension and actual understanding are two very different concepts!

If we went sailing we would understand the CONCEPT is "catching the air," the language needed to do that is clearly related to that specific event, right-hand shift, tacking duel, jibing duel. The language explains how to best accomplish our goal at any given moment—how we could sail again or go on another type of sailboat and be able to assist and/or understand.

With the sailing example in mind, consider the vast difference in levels of understanding and ability to apply knowledge that occurs when learning begins with being there experiences as opposed to hearing the teacher lecture about it.

Words (symbols for something for which there is no prior experience) rarely evoke an accurate understanding of their concept and therefore their application is impossible. A good example of the weakness of this approach is illustrated in the video "A Private Universe," which depicts Harvard University graduates being interviewed in their caps and gowns. The question put to them is "Explain the reasons for the seasons." Over 80 percent of the randomly selected students *and faculty*—despite their high school and university science classes—give the "stove is hot" theory, i.e., in the summer the earth is much closer to the sun and is therefore hotter. In fact, the earth's orbit is nearly round; distance from the sun is not a factor. This despite the amount of formal teaching received—varying from none to classes in advanced planetary motion!

Therefore, meaningfulness for elementary students must begin with firsthand, *being there*, here and now experiences. They provide the mental scaffolding for the words which represent the concepts and definitions of things they have experienced. The number of "experiences" must continuously increase so that students will have a basis for relating and applying new information.

LEARNING CLUBS

Frank Smith, in his book *Insult to Intelligence: The Bureaucratic Invasion of Our Classrooms*, points out that the bulk of life's learning occurs in "clubs"—a group whose goals we adopt and whose membership adopts us.[3] Examples of learning clubs include the language club of our family from whom we master our mother tongue, the neighborhood club with whom we pal around while exploring, riding bicycles, playing games, climbing trees, and our best friends club.

When we choose to join a learning club, we choose to be like its members and we go about "becoming" like the other members.

What the learner can picture him/herself doing, the skills and knowledge exhibited by members of the club becomes meaningful learning material. The motivation is intrinsic, the learning empowered through constant modeling, trial and error, and immediate feedback.

On the other hand, says Smith, when a learner is rejected by a potential learning club (because of race, socioeconomic status, being new to the neighborhood, etc.), that learner then makes the decision to be unlike the members of that club—in fact, the opposite. Thus, for example, low status children make the decision to reject the goals of the group that rejects them ("I don't want to be in that dumb ol' reading group anyway! Who cares about writing . . . only sissies do it! Math? That's for school boys, not us!")

An ITI classroom presents a comprehensive picture of a learning club going about the business of meaningful learning. Teachers receive immediate feedback of classroom effectiveness, both from high daily attendance and from low incidence of behavioral problems—a definite vote of confidence that students want to participate.

AGE-APPROPRIATENESS

A young child's brain is not just a "junior" version of the adult brain, an adult brain with less information in it. It processes differently. As mentioned in Chapter 1, the human brain unfolds in predictable developmental stages. Each stage is like an ever more complex template laid over the top of the previous one. At each of these stages, the brain is capable of more complex thinking, comparing, and analyzing. Incoming information that requires a level of processing not yet acquired by the brain results in lack of understanding, inability to "get it." When things are "ungettable," students give up and resort to memorization. Over time, when too many things are "ungettable," students slowly learn not to try to understand but merely to memorize and parrot back.

This is a serious issue because it undermines students' confidence in self as well as teachers' expectations. Worse, it absolutely kills the joy of learning.

Following is a brief overview of developmental stages based on the work of Larry Lowery, as reflected in presentations to administrators and teachers of the Mid-California Science Improvement Program (MCSIP) and in his book, *Thinking and Learning: Matching Developmental Stages with Curriculum and Instruction.**

CHAPTER 3: MEANINGFUL CONTENT

Age Three to First Grade:
Comparing the Known to the Unknown

During this stage of life, children learn to understand more words (and the concepts behind them) than they will for the rest of their lives. The child does this through one-to-one correspondences, putting two objects together on the basis of a single property and learning from these comparisons more than was known before. According to Lowery, the child constructs fundamental concepts about the physical world and its properties (similarities and difference comparisons based on size, shape, color, texture, etc.), about ordinal and cardinal numbers (one-to-one correspondence of varying degrees), about all measures (comparison of known to unknown), and about the use of symbols to stand for meaning (word recognitions).[4]

The major mode of operation at this stage is trial and error. Often, adults mistakenly try to "help" the child in an attempt to reduce or eliminate error or reprimand the child for making an error. This is unfortunate, because the important point here is that the child learns from the situation *in either case*—erroneous or correct. Whether putting puzzle shapes into the wrong space, learning to dress oneself and getting the shoes on the wrong feet, or falling off a tricycle. For the child, a "no" provides as much information as a "yes."

An important characteristic of this stage is that the child does not yet have the ability to group objects using more than one property simultaneously.[5] For example, pairings made on the basis of size, color, shape, texture, speed, using one property or characteristic to pair them. The three- to six-year-old may also arrange objects by chaining, i.e., the third object in the chain shares an important

---

*Used with the permission of Midwest Publications, Inc.

characteristic with the second object (which was initially chosen to pair with the first object) based on a different characteristic:

This stage is variously described as: ability to put two objects together on the basis of a single property[6] or learning by one-to-one correspondence. Piaget's description: *pre-operational stage.*

If you take the time to put this information to use and analyze your district's scope and sequence or current textbooks, you're in for a genuine shock and complete surprise. You will find that there is a high percentage of material that is wholly inappropriate. Examples of age-inappropriate topics from a popular, state-adopted science textbook for first grade include: earth as it looks from space, landforms around the world, how water shapes the land, air, and much more!

Second Grade to Third Grade:
Putting Things Together, Taking Things Apart

At this stage a child develops the capability to group all objects in a set on the basis of one common attribute (as compared to putting only two objects together on the basis of a single property). This capacity begins at about age six (late) and is established for most youngsters by age eight.

According to Lowery, "for the first time the student's mental construct is comprehensive and has a rationale or logic to it. . . . Simple rules can be understood and generated by the student if given the opportunity."[7]

At this stage students do less trial and error exploration and are more thoughtful about the actions they impose upon their environment; they create an internal mental structure of those manipulations.[8] An important aspect of students' actions is the rearrangement of the materials with which they work. Students also have the capacity to do things in reverse direction without distorting the concept, e.g., 3 + 2 = 5; 5 - 2 = 3. This is one of the powerful aspects of thinking at this stage.[9]

From an adult's perspective, there is a correct and an incorrect way to put things together or take them apart; the child at variance is thus seen as having done the job "incorrectly." Rather than just judging the task, however, adults should also examine the reason why the student chose that particular response and then focus on the quality of the understanding that is revealed in the answers given.

This stage is variously described as: ability to put all objects together on the basis of a consistent, single property rationale or putting things together and returning things to the way they were.[10] Piaget's term: *early concrete operations*.

Again, examples of age-inappropriate content from a popular science textbook include the following. For second graders: prehistoric animals and climate changes creating extinction, matter, magnets, light waves, heat transfer, air and air in water, rotation of the earth. For third graders: photosynthesis, particles in matter, changes in matter, forces (gravity, magnetism), energy (work, earth core, earthquakes), forces which shape the land (weathering, water, wind), tilt of the earth produces weather changes, and the solar system. Such topics require an ability to think abstractly which is not possible until the pre-frontal lobes are developed.

Fourth Grade to Sixth Grade:
Simultaneous Ideas

At about age eight to ten, children develop the capacity to mentally coordinate two or more properties or concepts at a time. According to Lowery, when this capacity is in place—which may occur as early as age eight or as late as age ten—students can comprehend place value in math, the need for controlling variables in a science experiment, the use of similies and multiple themes in literature, and can begin to understand the relationships that exist in free trade in social studies.[11] According to Lowery, "as with earlier capabilities, this new one integrates with those preceding it much like a new map of greater abstraction that can be overlaid upon other layers of maps."[12]

At this stage, students enjoy puns and can easily learn about homonyms. In their writing they shift to using multiple descriptors: "an old, bent, tired man." They shift from trial and error thinking to contemplating the effects of comparing two or more situations under different situations.[13] Arrangement of objects now indicates the intersection of multiple properties.

Piaget refers to this stage as late concrete operations; Lowery's term is simultaneity of ideas.

Examples of age inappropriate content from the same popular science textbook (distributed 1985) are mind boggling. For fourth grade: heat as particle activity, how fossils are formed, ocean floor, causes of tides, ocean currents around the world. For fifth grade: atoms, elements, compounds, molecules, chemical bonding; nuclear fusion; light energy waves; and many other topics which should be moved to junior and senior high. For sixth grade: virtually all areas should be moved to junior and mostly senior high levels.

The irony here is that, for all of America's glorification of youth and childhood, our traditional school curriculum treats elementary students as young adults. Yet for our young adults—high school students—the curriculum for the non-college bound is a re-run of what students were given in elementary school and, thus, is unchallenging and often boring.

So, what does all this mean for an ITI classroom? It means that the closer the curriculum is to the real world, the more likely it will be age-appropriate rather than abstract and calling for mental processing students don't yet possess.

Note. The idea of age-appropriateness is certainly not new. Montessori, Piaget, and countless others have addressed the issue quite clearly. Yet, it just gets pushed aside by tradition when textbooks and state frameworks are being created. A glance through textbooks from the past several decades shows tradition at its most mindless and blind adherence to "the way we've always done it."

The purpose of looking at what is appropriate at each age level is to make thoughtful decisions for less is more. Notice, in particular, the age at which each capacity comes into place. And bear in mind that there will be some students on both ends of each predicted age group. If the mental scaffolding doesn't exist for learning a particular concept, content must be changed to match the stage of intellectual development of individual students. Thus, teachers need to be cognizant of content that relies on this scaffolding that just doesn't exist. Because some students can understand something doesn't mean that all students at that age can, nor does it mean that such students are less capable.

THE BRAIN AS PATTERN-SEEKER

In catching up with the 1990s, the California State Language Arts Framework states that "recent discoveries about learning have revealed that schools have often neglected young people whose dominant mode of learning is not linear."[14] This quote provides an apt introduction to our discussion of the brain as a pattern-seeking device. Recent brain research has shattered our previous ideas about how learning takes place and new definitions of learning are emerging. According to Hart in his book, *Human Brain and Human Learning*, "no part of the human brain is naturally logical while it is learning,"[15] i.e., making meaning. (This is in contrast to its ability to *use* information already learned in a "logical" or sequential way if the situation so requires.) Instead, the brain learns by sifting through massive amounts of input, processing thousands of bits of information per minute arriving through all 19 senses. Obviously, and fortunately, this information is processed in a multi-path, multi-modal way. Imagine if the brain processed only one set of information at a time, e.g., first vision, then hearing, then bodily-kinesthetic, etc. If such were our processing, our ancestors would have been devoured and half digested by the saber-toothed tiger before their brain ever concluded danger lurked nearby.

Hart, in his book, *Human Brain and Human Learning*, defines a pattern as:

> "An entity, such as an object, action, procedure, situation, relationship or SYSTEM, which may be recognized by substantial consistency in the CLUES it presents to a brain, which is a pattern-detecting apparatus. The more powerful a brain, the more complex, finer, and subtle patterns it can detect. Except for certain SPECIES WISDOM patterns, each human must learn to recognize the patterns of all matters dealt with, storing the LEARNING in the brain. Pattern recognition tells what is being dealt with, permitting selection of the most appropriate PROGRAM in brain storage to deal with it. The brain tolerates much variation in patterns (we recognize the letter *a* in many shapes, sizes, colors, etc.) because it operates on the basis of PROBABILITY, not on digital or logic principles. Recognition of PATTERNS accounts largely for what is called insight, and facilitates transfer of learning to new situations or needs, which may be called creativity."[16]

As the brain attempts to make sense out of the chaos which surrounds each of us, it constantly searches for patterns that can impose meaning on the input received. Its "aha's" arise from detection of a recognizable (from the learner's perspective) pattern or patterns. This pattern detection propensity is seen in the operation of each of the senses. The ear registers every sound wave within its perceivable frequency, but it attends only to those which provide a meaningful pattern. Sounds of traffic or workshop chatter are ignored and only the presenter's voice is "tuned in" or noted as a pattern to attend to. Similarly, the eye "recognizes" a chair; be it a three-legged milking stool, a church pew bench, part of a student desk, a log in the forest when one is tired, or the more common no frills chair at the kitchen table; it does so by looking for the pattern of typical attributes necessary for something to be a chair when one wants to sit down.

CHAPTER 3: MEANINGFUL CONTENT

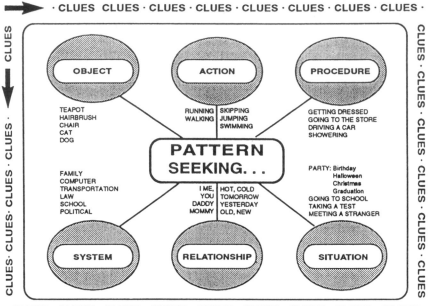

From the time we are born until we die, the brain takes in these patterns as they present themselves, sorting and categorizing down in an attempt to make sense out of our complex world. Learning takes place when the brain sorts out patterns using past experiences to make sense out of input the brain receives.

According to Hart, learning is "the extraction, from confusion, of meaningful patterns." In real life settings, information comes at the learner in a way that can best be described as rich, random, and even chaotic.[17] Over the millenniums, the brain has perfected learning within such an environment.

This pattern-detecting aspect of the brain can be clearly seen in the brain's mastery of one of its biggest accomplishments: learning the mother language. Watch mothers just home from the hospital with their newborns (or even listen to them talk to their child in utero!). Mothers know how to teach language. They do not "dumb down" their language to the infant to single syllable communications. Instead, mothers discuss the everyday happenings of life and share their hopes and dreams for their little one—"When you grow up, you'll go to Stanford and become an astronaut. You'd like that very much, I think. Very, very exciting occupation." "Oops, in thirty minutes your father comes home from work; we'd better get dinner started. Let's see, mother's milk for you and hmmm . . . oh, oh, I forgot to buy something for the main course tonight. Be sweet and charming, little one, when Daddy comes through the door!"

Such a barrage of sounds coming at the child in real life fashion would at first seem a hopeless environment in which to master language. But an environment similar to the one previously mentioned—rich, random, even chaotic—gives large amounts of input to the child, and thus provides his or her mind with the opportunity to search for patterns. As educators, we have been carefully and logically taught that such an environment would make the task of learning a language impossible. Consequently, we teach English as a second language logically and carefully, "This is a pen. What is this? This is a _____." Unfortunately, the human brain does not learn well from such logical, tidy, greatly restricted input because it is so antagonistic to the learning methods the brain has perfected over the ages.

In short, the mind is genetically designed to learn from the natural complexities of the natural world. To the extent that schools oversimplify, or make logical, or restrict the world's natural complexity is the extent to which schools inhibit the natural workings of the mind and restrict a student's ability to learn. Input from the real world, as described before, is "rich, random, even chaotic." Logical, sequential curricula delivered in logical ways are highly brain-antagonistic. Comments Hart, "Perhaps there is no idea about human learning harder to accept for people familiar with classroom schools than this: that the ideal of neat, orderly, closely planned, sequentially logical teaching will in practice, with young students, guarantee severe learning failure for most."[18] Patterns are the building blocks of meaning, the heart of curriculum development.

Stripping a learning situation of its real life richness also robs the child's mind of the possibility of perceiving pattern and thus making sense of what is in front of him/her. Ironically, we do this consistently with students who need special help. If they are slow, conventional wisdom has dictated that the task be broken into smaller and smaller pieces. We've now achieved pieces that are so small and so "easy"—only one item to focus on—that there is no longer any pattern to perceive. Consequently, Chapter 1 students with their finely chopped, oversimplified diet say "I don't get it" which confirms to us that they are "slow." However, most Chapter 1 students are adept learners from real world input. They come to us having learned their mother tongue and a wide range of skills for coping with life. For example, the immigrant child who is the translator for the entire family, the ghetto child with street savvy, the migrant child with flexibility and resourcefulness to "figure out" each new setting from town to town.

The amazing flexibility of the brain in its pattern-seeking is apparent in its ability to recognize the pattern of the letter *a*; we recognize it amid an amazing range of fonts, sizes, shapes, positions. This speed and flexibility can occur because the brain naturally works on a *probabilistic* basis. The brain does not add up, for example, all the parts of a cat until all parts are perceived and accounted for: four legs, a tail, fur, meows, purrs, etc. Rather, the mind "jumps to the conclusion" that the pattern "cat" applies when only one or a few characteristics have been noted. While this jumping to conclusions sometimes gets us in trouble, it is crucial to rapid completion of myriad actions minute by minute. The rapid reader, for example, does not see every letter before deciding what the word is. Context clues or the mere outline of the word are used, in probabilistic fashion, to jump to conclusions.

In the example of our infant learning its mother tongue, language pours around the child for hours and hours a day. The more input, the more readily the child learns. The first patterns perceived are those that are most meaningful—the child's name and then the name of mom and dad. Patterns are at first quite gross, i.e., "Dadda" means any man in trousers. As the snickers erupt, the child's mind is alerted to a problem with the pattern and, over time, with continued rich input, the patterns become more and more refined until, finally, the educated adult ends up with a vocabulary of 10,000 plus words with subtle shades of meaning and used with considerable precision.

The entire structure of language is based on pattern. Plurals mostly end in *s* except for mice, moose, fish, etc. Past tense ends with *ed*. Words ending in *ing* are a real thrill for most children. When they first grasp the "*ing*" pattern, everything is jumping, leaping, hitting, running, etc., for several days until another "pattern" of language is discovered. Every noun and verb in our language is a pattern.

What is one learner's pattern is another learner's hodgepodge. This is to say that we cannot predict what any one particular child will perceive as a pattern, because so much depends upon prior knowledge and the existing neural networking of the brain used to process the input. A common mistake of public schools is stripping down the input to a small amount of "stuff" so the "right" answer seems inescapable. **This does not work**. Instead, the brain demands large gulps of input which flow from the 19 senses which it processes by categorizing down in a multi-path and multi-modal way, far outstripping the most sophisticated version of computer artificial intelligence to date.

THE BRAIN AS A SELF-CONGRATULATOR

We are born virtual learning machines. We become our environment and our brains are a recording of what we have done, and where we have been literally becomes who we are. Humans are born with a keen drive to understand and act upon their world. When information is identified by it as "meaningful," it jumps into high gear. Taking a chemical perspective of the brain, Paul Messier states that the brain, using neurotransmitters, "rewards itself and the entire organism with feelings of well-being when new meaning and comprehension are achieved."[19] Along a similar vein, Smith maintains that learning is its own reward, no coercion is needed. External rewards are unnecessary.

CHAPTER 3: MEANINGFUL CONTENT

In short, when students are bored and turned off, something very wrong has occurred. A great majority of the time, that "great wrong" is meaningless curriculum. In ITI classrooms, more than 95 percent of the discipline problems disappear when meaning comes back into the curriculum.

GUIDELINES
FOR BUILDING IN MEANINGFULNESS

- provide *being there* interaction with the real world
- ensure that curriculum is age-appropriate, comprehensible by the student, given his/her stage of brain development
- do not assume/require experiences which the student does not have
- offer content that excites the interest of both students and teacher
- make sure the curriculum meets the CUE criteria, i.e.,

  – it is Creative (and thus memorable)

  – it is Useful (logged into the brain under several "addresses," one for each way in which the learner believes it will be useful; this usefulness greatly enhances the "retrievability" of the information)

  – it creates an Emotional bridge between the teacher and the learner (and thus there is sufficient epinephrine to carry the learning from short-term memory to long-term memory)

CHAPTER FOUR

"You have brains in your head. You have feet in your shoes. You can steer yourself any direction you choose. . . ."
—Dr. Seuss, *Oh, The Places You'll Go*

CHOICES

If the reader is counting the ways in which our antique school system is brain-antagonistic rather than brain-compatible, then you have recognized that its biggest crime is its assembly line sameness. The unspoken paradigm underlying the current system is that all children learn the same way. Yet clearly, all children do NOT learn the same way. Parents know that and so does every teacher. But the system seems to be impervious to truth and reality.

Thus, we put age-mates together (in spite of the fact that age is one of the least powerful predictors of what a child's learning needs and processes will be), we make all students read the same textbooks, do the same pages in the workbooks, receive the same curriculum year by year. Even if we have three reading groups (bluebirds, redbirds, and sparrows), all that varies is the time of year they hit a particular textbook. In the end, the same reading instruction is applied to all children. Teachers will try whatever is in vogue at the moment—look/say, phonics, language experience, whole language—there is always the hope that one method will be best for all. It never has been and simply never will be.

CHOICES—
THE ULTIMATE DETERMINER OF SUCCESS

Webster's defines choice as "the act or power of choosing, the thing chosen, alternative, preference, the best."

CHAPTER 4: CHOICES

I especially like the phrase "power of choosing" because it pinpoints the essential characteristic of the lifelong learner. "Preference" acknowledges what brain research tells us over and over again: every brain is different and, therefore, each individual learner has preferred ways of learning which that individual knows to be more effective and reliable for him/her. In an ITI classroom, students have a choice of *how** to go about learning, which inquiries they would like to do, or any number of ways to go about something. This is essential because, as Smith notes, "the most difficult kind of thinking is that which is imposed on us by someone else."[1]

According to recent brain research, choice is critical because it

- increases the likelihood that the learner will be able to detect similarity to or relationships between new information/situations with existing patterns and *mental programs* in their brain

- provides a variety of inputs and thus a variety of possible patterns to recognize (brain as pattern-seeker)

- prevents downshifting as a result of stress or frustration due to boredom or failure (triune brain)

- allows the learner to select, organize, and experience input in preferred ways, resulting in more learning. As illustrated by Jung, Meyers-Briggs, and Keirsey-Bates, personality preferences with which we are born affect ways of taking in information (details vs. theory), decision-making (thinking vs. feeling) lifestyle (highly organized vs. spontaneous), and orientation to others (extrovert vs. introvert)

- increases epinephrine by heightening interest (epinephrine is a necessary chemical in the brain that shifts learnings from short-term to long-term memory)

---

*In implementing the ITI model, it is important to make a distinction between *what* and *how* students learn. The what, or content, to be learned is the responsibility of the teacher in conjunction with the school and district. It is a vital set of decisions which should be reached before curriculum development for ITI begins. On the other hand, how to most effectively go about learning is highly individualistic and a requisite skill for lifelong learning; students should begin early to experiment with what works best for them.

- allows the learner to steer his/her own ship and establish his/her own level of challenge (controlled risk)

- lets the learner utilize tools/materials/situations which would be most effective in individual problem-solving (seven intelligences)

- permits the learner to build independence as a learner by providing ample opportunity to create and/or select learning processes and situations which are meaningful for the learner and, in so doing, builds confidence and competence

Montessori, over one hundred years ago, recognized the powerful learning drive of all children. Her model of education was grounded firmly on the learner's ability to choose and the fact that the learning itself must be intrinsically interesting. Some of the ideas, techniques, and materials used by Montessori to illustrate this include:

- "the 'ungraded' class in which children are grouped by interest and ability rather than age and in which there is individually paced instruction; the child is given the freedom to proceed at his/her own rate—grading the material the children have access to but not arbitrarily grading the children

- the judgment that real learning involves the ability to do things for oneself, not the passive reception of a body of knowledge

- that the things that teach—the child's learning materials— should be intrinsically interesting and self-correcting and should train the senses in the perception of and therefore in the ability to deal with reality

- the right of every child to develop his/her own fullest potential and the idea that the school exists to implement that right

- the idea that the school must be part of the community and involve the parents if education is to be effective"[2]

CHAPTER 4: CHOICES

In 1990 Jane Healy was alerting us in even more forceful language:

"If we wish to remain a literate culture, someone is going to have to take the responsibility for teaching children at all socioeconomic levels how to talk, listen, and think. If we want high school graduates who can analyze, solve problems, and create new solutions, adults will have to devote the time to showing them how. And they had better get at it before the neural foundations for verbal expression, sustained attention, and analytic thought end up as piles of shavings under the workbench of plasticity.

"It appears that schools will have to assume a larger share of this responsibility. Students from all walks of life now come with brains poorly adapted for the mental habits that teachers have traditionally assumed. In the past, deep wells of language and mental persistence had already been filled for most children by experiences at home; an educational priming of the pump made learning flow with relative ease. Now teachers must fill the gaps before attempting to draw 'skills' from brains that lack the underlying cognitive and linguistic base."[3]

Why do we wait? What is the overwhelming pull toward sameness? What will it take to make schools wake up? Yesterday is gone and today is almost over—someone must *demand* that change happen now . . . perhaps the children will lead us.

PROVIDING CHOICE FOR STUDENTS: THE SEVEN INTELLIGENCES

Providing choice for students in the classroom is possible, thanks to the theoretical work Howard Gardner has done regarding multiple intelligences; it is now readily within the classroom teacher's grasp to create meaningful choice. Say good-bye to dependence on your textbooks because they are the antithesis of choice and the nemesis of the Age of Information. It is time to strike a blow for freedom of the brain to learn, to strike out in new directions!

SEVEN INTELLIGENCES

In his book, *Frames of Mind: The Theory of Multiple Intelligences,* Gardner suggests that we each have at least seven intelligences. He describes intelligence as "a set of problem-solving skills, enabling the individual to resolve genuine problems or difficulties that he or she encounters and, when appropriate, to create an effective product; it also entails the potential for finding or creating problems, thereby laying the groundwork for the acquisition of new knowledge."[4] Gardner theorizes that each of these intelligences is relatively independent of the others, with its own timetable for development, peak growth, and a sensitive period. Each operates from a different part of the brain. Each is valued in ALL cultures.

Writing ITI curriculum using the seven intelligences ensures choice for learners. There are many ways to problem-solve. Allowing students to choose their best way is a victory for both student and teacher because what is being learned is the same; it is *how* it is learned that varies.

To grasp the power of this theory, one must make a distinction between how students take in information through the senses (what in the past has been referred to as the visual, auditory, kinesthetic, and tactile modalities) versus how students process information once inside their brain to first make meaning of the input and then to use the meaning to act upon the world. Gardner's focus, and ours, is how information—which comes in from all nineteen senses gets processed.

(Note: Please keep in mind that these seven intelligences are sets of problem-solving capabilities, not merely gateways through which information passes to reach the brain. Do not equate modalities with these intelligences. Our previous preoccupation with the "modalities" has, as yet, no brain research to substantiate it.* We in education "made up" a theory to fit our observations.)

---

*According to Healy and Hart, there is as yet no brain research which corroborates the assumptions about modalities made by educational researchers and practitioners.

CHAPTER 4: CHOICES

The seven intelligences identified by Gardner are:

- logical-mathematical
- linguistic
- spatial
- bodily-kinesthetic
- musical
- intrapersonal
- interpersonal

Logical-mathematical intelligence—(left hemisphere, front and back of both sides of the brain)

The core function of this intelligence is the confrontation with the world of objects—ordering and reordering them, assessing their quantity, comprehending numerical symbols, appreciating the meaning of signs referring to numerical operations, and understanding the underlying quantities and operations themselves.[5]

Logical-mathematically talented children

- compute arithmetic problems quickly in their head
- enjoy using computers
- ask questions like, "Where does the universe end?" "What happens after we die?" and "When did time begin?"
- play chess, checkers, or other strategy games, and win
- reason things out logically and clearly
- devise experiments to test out things they don't understand
- spend lots of time working on logic puzzles such as Rubik's Cube[6]

This intelligence appears early and the most productive work is done by age forty if not by age thirty. The basis for all logical-mathematical forms of intelligence spring from the handling of objects; later these become internalized ("done in one's head"). One proceeds from objects to statements, from actions to the relations among actions, from the realm of the sensori-motor to the realm of pure abstraction—ultimately to the heights of logic and science.

The classical description of the development of this intelligence, the home of science and math, is that by Piaget; his work remains an extremely accurate description of the logical-mathematical intelligence, *but his work does not describe development of the other six intelligences.*

Linguistic intelligence—(predominantly left hemisphere—temporal and frontal)

Linguistic competence is the most widely and most democratically shared across the human species. ". . . one could not hope to proceed with any efficacy in the world without considerable command of phonology, syntax, semantics, and pragmatics."[7]

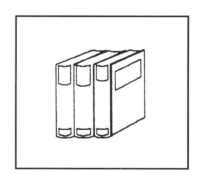

Linguistically gifted children

- like to write
- spin tall tales or tell jokes and stories
- have a good memory for names, places, dates, or trivia
- enjoy reading books in their spare time
- spell words accurately and easily
- appreciate nonsense rhymes and tongue twisters
- like doing crossword puzzles or playing games such as Scrabble or Anagrams[8]

CHAPTER 4: CHOICES

Without question, high linguistic intelligence is over 80 percent of the formula for success in traditional schooling. Without it, schooling is painful and frustrating, if not a failure, despite competence in the other intelligences.

Spatial intelligence —(right hemisphere)

The core operation of this intelligence depends on the ability to image. It also involves the capacity to perceive the visual world accurately, perform transformations and modifications upon one's initial perceptions, and recreate aspects of one's visual experience, even in the absence of relevant physical stimuli. The mind's link to language is 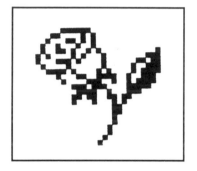 through pictures, not sound. This intelligence is as critical as linguistic intelligence because the two are the principal sources of storage and solution of problems.[9]

The problem-solving function of the spatial intelligence is the processing of information received, not just the avenue for bringing in information. Spatial intelligence is a collection of related skills. The images produced in the brain are helpful aids to thinking; some researchers have gone even further, considering visual and spatial imagery as a primary source of thought.

For many of the world's famous scientists, their most fundamental insights were derived from spatial models rather than from mathematical lines of reasoning. Einstein once commented: "The words of the language, as they are written and spoken, do not play any role in my mechanisms of thought. The psychical entities which seem to serve as elements in thought are certain signs and more or less clear images which can be voluntarily reproduced or combined. . . .The above mentioned elements are, in my case, of visual and some muscular type."[10]

Children strong in spatial intelligence

- spend free time engaged in art activities
- report clear visual images when thinking about something
- easily read maps, charts, and diagrams
- draw accurate representations of people or things
- like it when you show movies, slides, or photographs
- enjoy doing jigsaw puzzles or mazes
- daydream a lot[11]

Bodily-kinesthetic intelligence—(left hemisphere dominance in right-handed people)

Characteristic of this intelligence is the ability to use one's body in highly differentiated and skilled ways for expressive as well as goal-directed purposes (e.g., mime, actor, athlete, tradesman) plus the capacity to work skillfully with objects, both those that involve the fine motor movements of one's bodily motions, and the capacity to handle objects skillfully.[12]

Children who excel in bodily-kinesthetic intelligence

- do well in competitive sports
- move, twitch, tap, or fidget while sitting in a chair
- engage in physical activities such as swimming, biking, hiking, or skateboarding
- need to touch people when they talk to them
- enjoy scary amusement rides
- demonstrate skill in a craft like woodworking, sewing, or carving
- cleverly mimic other people's gestures, mannerisms, or behaviors[13]

CHAPTER 4: CHOICES

Involving the rest of the body in any learning event increases the neural activity of the brain and increases the flow of adrenaline (which aids transfer from short-term memory to long-term memory).

Musical intelligence—(right hemisphere)

This intelligence is the earliest to appear and is the most separate from the other intelligences. Core functions include pitch, melody, rhythm, timbre (tone), and pattern.

Students who are unusually high in musical intelligence and relatively low in linguistic intelligence will use their musical intelligence skills to "translate" language into rhythmic patterns. An example of this type of student is the one whose body begins to jive and tap the instant the teacher begins to speak, stopping the second the teacher stops talking, restarting with the next burst of speech—all in rhythm with the teacher's words. Content in rhyme can be readily absorbed by these students while the same information in an uninspiring lecture or in the stilted prose of a science textbook can be completely indigestible. Monotone speakers have particularly deadening effects for the highly musical students.[14]

Musically gifted children

- play a musical instrument
- remember melodies of songs
- tell you when a musical note is off-key
- say they need to have music on in order to study
- collect records or tapes
- sing songs to themselves
- keep time rhythmically to music[15]

SEVEN INTELLIGENCES

Intrapersonal/interpersonal intelligence—Both of these intelligences are far more diverse and culturally dependent than the previous five. For example: extreme circumstances such as times of war, subjugation, famine, disaster in general, recession/depression, life or death situations, and death itself. All of these circumstances make demands for action that are unpracticed by most people. They are one-time or seldom experienced events. Cultural premises demand that these events be responded to and expressed differently, depending upon locale, age, status in the community, etc. In short, these are problem-solving situations requiring problem-solving intelligences. Although not so dramatic, daily living requires the same kinds of problem-solving from us.

Intrapersonal—examination and knowledge of one's own feelings. "Sense of self"—the balance struck by every individual and every culture between the prompting of inner feelings and the pressures of "other persons."

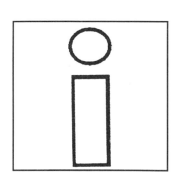

The core capacity is access to one's own feeling life—one's range of affects or emotions; the capacity instantly to effect discrimination among these feelings and, eventually, to label them, to draw upon them as a means of understanding and guiding one's behavior.[16]

Intrapersonally talented children

- display a sense of independence or a strong will
- react with strong opinions when controversial topics are being discussed
- seem to live in their own private, inner world
- like to be alone to pursue some personal interest, hobby, or project
- seem to have a deep sense of self-confidence
- march to the beat of a different drummer in their style of dress, their behavior, or their general attitude
- motivate themselves to do well on independent study projects[17]

Interpersonal—looking outward toward behavior, feelings, and motivations of others.

The core capacity is the ability to notice and make distinctions among other individuals and, in particular, among their moods, temperaments, motivations, and intentions.[18]

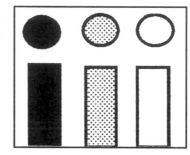

Interpersonally gifted children

- have a lot of friends
- socialize a great deal at school or around the neighborhood
- seem to be "street-smart"
- get involved in after-school group activities
- serve as the "family mediator" when disputes arise
- enjoy playing group games with other children
- have a lot of empathy for the feelings of others[19]

In an advanced form, interpersonal knowledge permits a skilled adult to read the intentions and desires—even when those have been hidden—of many other individuals and, potentially, to act upon this knowledge, e.g., by influencing a group of disparate individuals to behave along desired lines. We see highly developed forms of interpersonal intelligence in political and religious leaders (Mahatma Gandhi or John Fitzgerald Kennedy), in skilled parents and teachers, and in individuals enrolled in the helping professions, be they therapists or counselors.

Do the activities within each category strike a familiar chord? They should. Each of us is born with all of these intelligences but individuals tend to develop those valued by their culture (home, school, church, community). It is the goal of the ITI classroom to make sure that all intelligences are used and developed on a daily basis.

How to use Gardner's seven intelligences as a guide for developing your ITI curriculum is described step-by-step, with examples, in Chapter 13.

PROVIDING CHOICE FOR ADULTS

Today there is much talk about "choice" schools within districts and outside the public school districts. The idea of establishing a magnet or focus for a specific school within a district for parents and students is hardly new. It receives the spotlight during times of high criticism of the public schools but has made no significant impact on changing the system.

Choice outside the system has likewise existed for years, although in limited but growing numbers. Parochial and private school have been choices, albeit additional financial responsibility. In my work with parochial schools, especially in parts of New York and Pennsylvania, I have always been aware of the difference in tone in the school building: the commitment to be there (students' and teachers'), the desire and commitment to achieve, the quality output with such scarce financial resources. That such schools survive over the years, struggling through tight money times, is mute testimony of the power of choice as foundation of commitment and motivation.

In a similar vein, we must let the choice concept include the teacher's ability to choose so there will be a sense of everyone working toward the same goals. My experience with change is that it must engage *all* members of a staff in an agreed upon goal; furthermore, it must happen school by school; otherwise it is not cost or time effective and the old "this is the way we were taught" will persist.

CHOICE demands commitment, agreement, and constant reevaluation regarding goals and time lines. This is true for parents, students, and teachers; it is at the core of what democracy is all about—freedom to choose and to be responsible about one's choice!

GUIDELINES FOR PROVIDING CHOICE

- the choices should be genuine—truly varied (based upon childhood's why and wherefores, seven intelligences, levels of Bloom's Taxonomy, etc.)

- each choice should do the job of moving students toward mastery of the identified key points; choices are not a collection of unrelated "fun" activities or trivial pursuits

- whenever possible build in playfulness; remember CUE. (The brain will respond to a presentation that is Creative, Useful, or that creates an Emotional bridge between the teacher/content and the learner.)

- choice offered to students should immerse them in real life and *being there* experiences

CHAPTER FIVE

ADEQUATE TIME

It was Einstein who said that man invented the concept of time and has spent the rest of his life being controlled by it! It seems all the more true today when technology has literally added 20 percent to our working week, mainly because we take on larger and larger undertakings due to computers, fax machines, cellular telephones and instantaneous worldwide communication through satellite. This deluge of high technology has produced a new ailment: information anxiety.

> "Information anxiety is produced by the ever-widening gap between what we understand and what we think we should understand. It is the black hole between data and knowledge, and it happens when information doesn't tell us what we want or need to know."[1]

Due to the increased knowledge that accumulates daily, it is essential that we constantly re-evaluate what we "believe" students should know in order to become contributing members of society. Too often I hear history teachers say they never get past World War II, leaving me to wonder when we will be willing to drop the details of past events, trotted out in chronological sequence, and instead look to the important concepts represented by such events. Perhaps then we could better understand our present and face our future with confidence.

To understand the power of this brain-compatible element, it might be helpful to apply it to our own lives first.

CHAPTER 5 : ADEQUATE TIME

For example, how many of us would sit down to complete our income taxes on a short weekend, knowing that the task will take at least three to four days of uninterrupted work? Or how many of us are eager to take a two-hour task out of our in-basket when we don't have a two-hour time block and we know that, with interruptions, it will end up taking us six hours? Answer: a very rare few. Lack of completion, time wasted in "figuring out where we were" on the last round, frustration and disappointment in having to drop something just when we were "getting into it"—these are all side effects of inadequate time.

A New Definition for Learning

Sage and wise as he is, Leslie Hart draws our attention to a new, two-part definition for learning.

> **Part one**: Learning is the extraction, from chaos, of meaningful patterns (see Chapter 3, Meaningful Content).
> **Part two**: Learning is the acquisition of useful programs.

Thus, pattern-seeking is the process of meaning-making or arriving at understanding of what is being learned; program-building is the process of putting what we know into action and practicing ways of using it, in real life situations, until it becomes locked into long term memory, ready for retrieval years later when needed.

Both parts of the learning equation take time. Neither can be rushed without forcing the learner into trading understanding for rote memory and useful application for multiple choice or fill in the blank dittos.

TIME FOR PATTERN-SEEKING

As discussed in Chapter 3, the brain is a persistent pattern-seeker in its pursuit of meaning. Think back to the incredible attention span young children have when engaged in something that has meaning to them. Then think back to the frustration that occurs when there is a rush to complete a task and time runs out before it can be completed. Remember the satisfaction that comes from doing a job well from beginning to end, the enjoyment of doing it when there is time to "go with the flow" while learning something new, the pep and energy that comes from confidence in succeeding if we just "stick with it."

In short, we know from our own experience that lack of adequate time is a killer; it inhibits comprehensive understanding. In terms of brain research, the anxiety and frustration trigger down-shifting (triune brain) and spawn shoddy work, low standards, and, eventually, apathy.

Adequate time is needed to get the job of learning done well, to accomplish mastery (the ability to use the concept/skill in real life settings), to fully understand the connections among prior learnings and learnings yet to come. And yet . . . in old practices and new, we violate what we know. Examples abound: using fragments of time—20 minutes for this, 40 minutes for that—we guarantee a low degree of meaningfulness and high failure rates. Even worse is the recent trend toward departmentalization in elementary schools.

This worrisome change hides under the guise of better serving the students through specialization or of better using teachers' areas of expertise. Time frames become more rigid, children get shuffled from place to place, tracking is pushed yet lower—and adequate time for concept attainment and mastery are lost in the shuffle.

This trend toward departmentalization contradicts brain research conclusions. As Frank Smith points out in his "Learner's Manifesto," "learning is incidental," i.e., children learn from the totality of their environment, not just from the content of the lesson at hand. So what are the incidental learning messages that students receive when sent from class to class on such short periods of time? Some are explicitly stated, some are implicit: "It's not important, don't expect to finish, don't get too involved—understanding isn't the goal in this class; Mr. B. is big on meeting deadlines . . . that's what's important in this class. The clock is more important than the learning, the students, or the teacher." So where in one's life do effort, perseverance, personal best, and learning to the level of application fit in?

TIME FOR PROGRAM-BUILDING

Just as processing input to arrive at understanding rather than memorization takes time, so does the program-building for mastery. Think back to a time when you were learning to tie your shoes, ride your bike, skate, collect bird eggs, skip stones, fish, hunt, water-ski, cook, snow ski, drive, all the things you've learned that you value. Remember how you hated to be stopped or pulled away? Each new endeavor was an effort to make meaning from a new pattern and then to create a mental program appropriate for that pattern. Your natural inclination was to "do it" until you learned how to use it, i.e., until you had developed a mental program for using what you had learned.

Just What Is a Program?

Our behavior, and that of our fellow human beings, has long been one of life's greater mysteries. Behavior—its building blocks and why specific building blocks are chosen at any one moment in time—must be understood if we are to create schools which foster real learning.

According to Hart, the key to understanding behavior is "the realization that we act very largely by *programs* . . . a fixed sequence for accomplishing some intended objective." In other words, to carry on activities, one must constantly select a *program* from among those stored in the brain and put it to use.[2]

Hart defines a *program* as:

"A sequence of steps or actions, intended to achieve some GOAL, which once built is stored in the brain and 'run off' repeatedly whenever need to achieve the same goal is perceived by the person. A program may be short, for example giving a nod to indicate 'yes,' or long, as in playing a piece on the piano which requires thousands of steps, or raising a crop of wheat over many months. A long program usually involves a series of shorter sub-programs, and many parallel variations that permit choice to meet conditions of use. Many such programs are needed, for instance to open different kinds of doors by pushing, pulling, turning, actuating, etc. Language requires many thousands of programs, to utter each word, type it, write it in longhand, print it, etc. Frequently used programs acquire an 'automatic' quality: they can be used, once selected, without thinking, as when one puts on a shirt. Typically, a program is CONSCIOUSLY selected, then run off at a subconscious level. . . . In general, humans operate by selecting and implementing programs one after another throughout waking hours."[3]

To understand the power of Hart's statements, consider some everyday examples. Simple ones are such things as a procedure for putting on one's shoes. There are the "right-foot-right" people and the "good heavens, no—the left first" folks. Same with putting on a coat. For high good humor, watch someone in a restaurant offering to help another with their coat. Of course the assistant offers the coat in the manner that *they* would put it on . . . to the left or right, low or high; and the recipient of this assistance struggles and struggles to accept the assistance. How about the shower? Your favored hand grabs the soap and that ole' soap knows just what to do and zip! you're done with the shower. But, if for some temporary reason that hand can't get wet, the soap no longer remembers what to do. The result is a shower that takes much longer, frustration, and the feeling of not being quite as clean and refreshed as usual and you can hear your mother's voice asking, "Did you wash behind your ears?" Sound familiar?

Another example, how many of us have driven for miles with absolutely no recall of the journey? A little scary! Or, after being reassigned to a new school, we find ourselves one morning in the parking lot of our former school. How did that happen!

On a more serious note, children, who "misbehave" as a result of wanting to attract the teacher's attention, reach into their mental bag of programs and, as unconsciously a the driver sitting in the wrong parking lot, automatically pull out a behavior that makes the teacher furious. In their mental bag of programs, they have too many of the "wrong" behaviors/programs and too few of the "right" ones.

Equally somber is the child-grown-adult who has no program for using multiplication for real-world application such as computing mortgage payments or figuring the real cost of an item they've let ride on the VISA charge card.

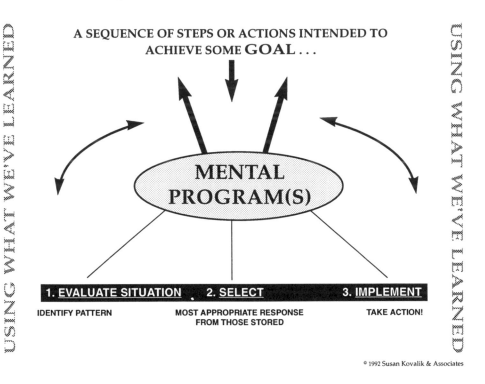

© 1992 Susan Kovalik & Associates

The basic cycle in using *programs* is:

1. **Evaluate** the situation or need (detect and identify the pattern or patterns)
2. **Select** the most appropriate *program* from those stored
3. **Implement** the *program*

For example:

> *Situation:* You're invited to a party

> *Selection:* Is it a birthday, graduation, holiday, costume, or office party? (Each party demands certain consideration, appropriate dress, gifts, etc.)

> *Implementation:* Once you have selected from your store of *mental programs*, you'll *take action!* If it's a birthday party, you pull up your *program* for going to a birthday party—send an RSVP, buy a present, wear party clothes, and expect to eat cake

As the previous example notes, the first step in the learning process is detecting pattern. Once a situation has been analyzed, and if action is required, the brain scans its repertoire of stored *programs,* selecting the one that is most appropriate or by calling forth two or more and using them in fresh combinations. Such capacity to "use old *programs* in fresh combinations" seems to underlie what we call creativity.[4]

Successful implementation of *mental programs* are their own reward, accompanied by feelings of accomplishment and increased satisfaction. Aborting a *mental program* that doesn't work is emotionally unsettling because it leaves us unsure of what to do next and decreases our sense of self confidence.[5] When orchestrating your curriculum, provide the time and experiences that allow youngsters to master new information and add it to prior knowledge in a meaningful way, thereby creating new *mental programs.*

Hart, in fact, defines learning as "the acquisition of useful *programs.*" "Learning" which does not result in acquisition of a *program(s),* such as getting an *A* on a paper/pencil test, is not learning from Hart's perspective because it doesn't stick. Says Hart, information that does not become part of a *program* is usually unretrievable. For example, recall your sophomore college days and the traditional western civilization class. The characteristics of this stunning

CHAPTER 5 : ADEQUATE TIME

experience: yearlong, 99.9 percent lecture, and an enormously fat textbook. For the mid-term and final exams, you used the ubiquitous blue book. Weeks later when the blue book was graded and returned, you glanced inside. To your total shock, there were paragraphs of stuff you didn't even recognize—never heard of before! A classic example of information which never became part of a *program* and, thus, is unretrievable and often even unrecognizable, even a bare three weeks later. In other words, most information that we *use* is embedded in *programs*; the corollary is: information which is not used is also not retrievable and, if truth be told, was probably never "learned" in the first place. Thus, "covering information" is a colossal waste of time for both students and teachers.

The implications for the classroom of the 21st century are obvious—we need to do less and do it better and more in-depth, giving students time to "use" the information again and again in varying settings until the information is recallable in a useable form, i.e., a behavior, a *program*.

It should be noted that *programs* and subskills are not identical and have little in common. A *program*, while it can be enormously complex, such as driving a car, is a sequence for accomplishing some end—a goal, objective, or outcome—an end with meaning to the learner. Subskills such as the blend "ch" or the short "i" are not a sequence for accomplishing some end; they are experienced as isolated, fragmented pieces. In contrast, the *program* to be attained is the act of reading.

Making Time for Program-Building

I remember my daughter asking when she was in the eighth grade how could they go ahead in the math book if the class didn't understand the last chapter? What is the answer to that question? How, indeed. Any sensible answer would call into question the mindlessness of the system. No pattern was found. No program was made. Nothing exists on which to base the next months learning. Real learning, that is, pattern-seeking and program building, cannot take place without adequate, uninterrupted time.

TIME FOR PROGRAM-BUILDING

At elementary grades, a similar and equally disturbing trend surfaces when I ask elementary teachers how many of them have at least two uninterrupted hours each day when NO children leave their classroom. From the "You've got to be kidding!" responses, I am assured that movement in and out, from hither to yon, is to be expected. One teacher commented that she had seventeen different "specialists" come through her room in one week, each taking children out for one thing or another. The only time she had all the students together was for the first fifteen minutes of the day when roll call was taken. Another example: a district coordinator stated that in each of the thirty-six elementary schools there were more specialists than teachers! This amounted to at least $500,000 *per school*. That money could buy considerable time and expertise to enable the classroom teacher to be able to work effectively and efficiently with a range of students.

It is irresponsible to continue adding layer after layer of "specialists" to a system that is unclear of its mission. Currently, at the elementary level, we have these categories of specialists:

- reading
- resource
- learning disabled
- English as a second language
- music
- speech
- gifted
- vocal music

- math
- Chapter 1 teacher
- special education
- art
- computer
- physical education
- instrumental music
- counselors

What competencies does a K-6 credential represent? There needs to be a comprehensive revision of coursework not only at the primary and secondary levels, but also at the colleges of education across the country. In order to be aware of the problems in schools such as the layering of specialists, professors need to be people who have worked *successfully* in the elementary educational system within the last five years!

CHAPTER 5: ADEQUATE TIME

And yes, I know it is a catch-22—"If the classroom teachers had better training . . .," "If the class size were smaller . . . " "If students were better prepared when they came. . ." But the question remains the same: "Do students have adequate time to learn new *mental programs* to the level of application in their everyday world?"

If a student needs a specific mental program, the specialist should take a solid block of time to orchestrate a way the student can develop one. Twenty minutes twice a week or even daily is *rarely* adequate to do the job.

GUIDELINES FOR PROVIDING ADEQUATE TIME

- eliminate "regular schedules" with their specified time blocks

- make yourself slow down—plan at the conceptual rather than factoid level; this will give you less to do so it can be done more thoroughly

- build in time for "opportunities to manipulate information" and apply what is learned in real world settings before you move on to the next time block

- don't be afraid to allow a lesson to take on a life of its own, to take advantage of the so-called "teachable moment" and open the windows of opportunity when children are truly engaged. Their interests and excitement will take them on side excursions, adventures into the land of "what's this to me, what's it good for?" Learning to learn, learning how to steer one's own learning takes time

---

CHAPTER SIX

ENRICHED ENVIRONMENT

Think of your favorite restaurant, vacation site, thinking space at home, favorite childhood memory . . . what locations and situations come to mind? Describe it to yourself—the sights and sounds, the feelings, the intangible impressions . . . the thoughts.

It should not come as a surprise that what you describe is a location with situations that drew input from all 19 senses (yes, *19*). An enriched environment is one which awakens the entire nervous system, one which is stimulating, curiosity feeding, capable of answering many questions and engendering more, a setting which is alive with resources, reflective of real life, bursting with non-print materials such as experts in their fields and samples of the real McCoy.

In contrast, a typical classroom is often barren, sterile, unpleasant in its institutionality, and greatly restrictive or overstimulating in its input to the nervous system. Classically, classroom input consists almost entirely of print and lecture. And, yes, I have been in some very stunning school buildings with big assembly rooms, large gyms, cafeterias that hold 800, auditoriums that hold 1,500; an overall physical plant that could hold 2,500, technology centers that could send specific video, database or CD-ROM into every classroom with a person hired to do just that, carpeting in all rooms, and spacious classrooms with equipment as up-to-date as the purchase order that requisitioned it. And yet, . . . underneath the glitter, the ubiquitous textbook remains as the students' main resource.

CHAPTER 6: ENRICHED ENVIRONMENT

Perhaps the most pernicious aspect of our current curriculum and related materials—textbooks, workbooks, skill packs, dittos, etc.—is their poverty of input to the nervous system and brain and their artificiality. As noted earlier, the brain is always in search of meaning. The detection of *patterns* (identification of elements related in a way that has meaning to the perceiver) and the development of *mental programs* through application and use of knowledge and skills in real life contexts depends heavily upon a learning environment being rich and real, lifelike. Remember, the brain is designed to learn from the complexities of real life.[1] The artificial simplicities of textbooks and "seatwork" are highly brain-antagonistic.

When creating an enriched environment, it is important to keep in mind the extent and kind of experiences with the *natural world* that your students bring with them to school. The key here is to balance that experience, not replicate it. For example, if students come to you long on TV, videos, Sesame Street, and secondhand sources (books and pictures), then the classroom must provide the REAL stuff—not books about, videos about, pictures about, replicas of, models of, but the real thing!

If we are to have truly brain-compatible learning environments, we must heed what brain research tells us about the physiology of learning. Intelligence is a function of experience rather than immutable genetics. Immersion in an enriched environment causes the electrical/chemical soup of the brain to wake up; the result is an enlargement of neurons and the growth of dendrites (nerve fibers which sprout from the neurons). Physiologically, this build-up of dendrites and enlargement of neurons results in a denser brain, a heavier brain; intellectually, this build-up results in a greater ability to problem-solve which in essence is intelligence!

As dendrites grow and branch, each neuron can communicate with up to 600,000 other neurons. This physiological capability to make connections underlines our common sense definitions of intelligence: the ability to see connections between things, observe subtle similarities and differences, use metaphors that are useful in understanding how things work and how they can be used in new settings or for new purposes.

THE 19 SENSES

The key question here for the classroom teacher is how to elicit maximum activation of students' brains. What kinds of input will produce maximum dendritic growth? Answer: when all 19 senses are engaged and processing incoming data.

THE 19 SENSES[2]

SENSES	KIND OF INPUT
Sight	Visible light
Hearing	Vibrations in the air
Touch	Tactile contact
Taste	Chemical molecular
Smell	Olfactory molecular
Balance	Kinesthetic geotropic
Vestibular	Repetitious movement
Temperature	Molecular motion
Pain	Nociception
Eidetic imagery	Neuroelectrical image retention
Magnetic	Ferromagnetic orientation
Infrared	Long electromagnetic waves
Ultraviolet	Short electromagnetic waves
Ionic	Airborne ionic charge
Vomeronasal	Pheromonic sensing
Proximal	Physical closeness
Electrical	Surface charge
Barometric	Atmospheric pressure
Geogravimetric	Sensing mass differences[2]

Does this surprise you? Nineteen, not five. There is an interesting history here. Robert Rivlin and Karen Gravelle in their book, *Deciphering Your Senses*, present the scientific evidence underpinning the 19 senses and give an historical perspective explaining why the mistaken notion of the five senses has persisted for so many centuries despite the scientific evidence to the contrary.

". . . according to the Medieval philosopher Cornelius Agrippa, arguing Plato's philosophy, 'Divinity is annexed to the mind, the mind to the intellect, the intellect to the intention, the intention to the imagination, the imagination to the senses, and the senses at last to things. For this is the bond and continuity of nature.'

"There was, in fact, a divine relationship between the senses and the world they sensed. And, like many things in God's divine plan for the universe, the senses were seen to occur in fives—a prime number with considerable symbolic significance. How convenient, then, to think of the body as having five senses, corresponding roughly to the sensory organs (eyes, ears, nose, tongue, and skin). That the skin could feel both temperature and touch, to say nothing of pain, was somehow conveniently overlooked in order to align the essential unity of the human body with a metaphysical plan of the universe; to say we had eight or eighteen senses simply wouldn't do."[3]

Consider for a moment "experiences" you have had which engaged your 19 senses. Chances are you were camping, hiking, visiting a foreign country, experiencing a snowstorm or earthquake, or taking part in a cultural ceremony different from your own. Or perhaps it was one of those special moments from childhood, e.g., at age eight, whiling away a lazy summer afternoon with an older brother; engaged in the thoroughly hopeless but intriguing task of attempting to dam up the creek; sunshine on our backs; bare feet scrunching in the pebbly gravel; the tepid, slow moving water with darting minnows disturbed by our rearranging of rocks and shovels full of smelly mud; our laughter rippling across the creek; my brother's nearness; his patience with a little sister who "never stayed home like the other girls did" . . . the lessons of that day, the wonder of the creek, the beauty of family relationships, will never be forgotten.

Such moments of acute sensory awareness stay with us always. Imagine if every school day produced memories of such power! Can the school have such impact on learners? I believe the answer is a resounding "Yes!"

"Yes," if our curriculum and instructional strategies are based upon *being there* input extended by *immersion* and enriched with *hands on of the real thing*. In contrast, learning based on secondhand input—print with some video—is inherently brain-antagonistic because it severely restricts sensory input. The fewer senses involved, the more difficult the task of learning becomes as illustrated on pages 82 and 83.

The six kinds of input are the following:

For examples of each level, see page 84.

CHAPTER 6: ENRICHED ENVIRONMENT

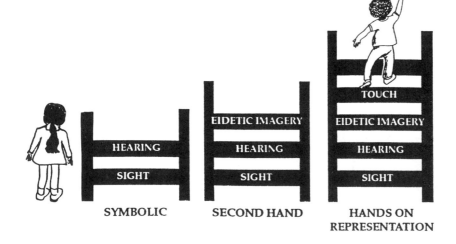

SYMBOLIC   SECOND HAND   HANDS ON
                                       REPRESENTATION

THE 19 SENSES

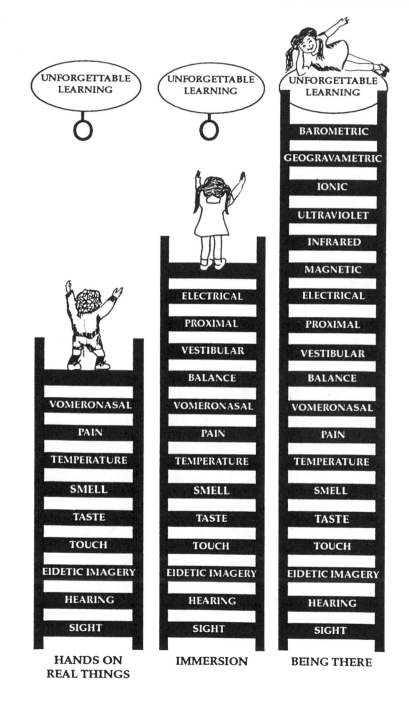

HANDS ON
REAL THINGS

IMMERSION

BEING THERE

For example, suppose the topic is glaciers. Imagine three scenarios:

- spending seven days *on* a glacier—climbing, camping out, observing, preparing food, and dealing with your basic needs
- seeing slides of someone doing the above
- reading a book describing the scientific explanation for glaciers

It is obvious which scenario would have the greatest impact and result in the most learning—and it would be easy to do if your school was located near a glacier. If not, however, you still have options available to you in the classroom which can make learning come alive.

being there—is just what it says! Go visit a glacier!

immersion—in the classroom, students make three-dimensional cutouts of glaciers to scale, paint them glacier blue; create a classroom pond filled with ice water and ice cubes; make papier-mâche animals to scale. Resource people who have been glacier climbing bring in their climbing and camping equipment, huskies and dogsleds, and their slides. Play sound-tracks to recreate the sounds of parts of glaciers breaking off and of animals native to the area

hands on of the real thing—show the students camping equipment, climbing gear, ice; let them meet a resource person from the zoo who will share items from the Alaska exhibit

secondhand—show movies, videos, pictures, books

hands on of representational things—a bag of books to represent the weight of the gear the climbers carry, an ice cube to represent the cold that must be endured, or a towel folded to show how many layers of clothing are needed to keep warm

symbolic—teach scientific formulas for the formation of glaciers and the mathematical equation for their size and movement

As the ladder graphic on the previous pages makes clear, there is simply no substitute for the real thing. The secondhand and symbolic tools provided by the system are wholly inadequate to the task of creating learning of consequence.

The moral to the story is, "Dittos don't make dendrites!" That is to say, neither dittos nor the textbook or workbooks create an enriched environment which activates the brain at the level of powerful learning. In other words, every minute spent on what students experience as boring, or as "seat work," is a minute spent NOT building intelligence.

THE TEACHERS' ENVIRONMENT

The more personal experience a teacher has, the richer the pool of ideas he or she has to draw from. We recommend every teacher experience an Earthwatch* adventure. Each year Earthwatch, a worldwide nonprofit organization, coordinates over a hundred scientific expeditions providing volunteers an opportunity to assist scientists at a variety of locations throughout the world in their study of specific animals, plants, environmental problems, and archeological sites. This powerful learning experience has great carry-over into the classroom because now the classroom teacher also has had a *being there* experience.

Additional national organizations include World Wildlife Fund, Sierra Club, and The Audubon Society plus many local and statewide organizations.

---

* EARTHWATCH: annual membership is $25.00 which includes subscription to their monthly magazine. Contact:

Earthwatch Expeditions	West coast office:	Fellowship
P.O. Box 403	Linda Knight	information:
Watertown, MA 02272	100 Wilshire Blvd.	Dane Trusdale
	Ste. 800	1 (800) 776-0188
	Santa Monica, CA 90401	

CHAPTER 6: ENRICHED ENVIRONMENT

GUIDELINES
FOR CREATING AN ENRICHED ENVIRONMENT

- immerse students in reality; use firsthand sources

- next, and only after all available firsthand resources have been exhausted, use only those secondhand experiences which allow for hands-on of real items (not plastic replicas)

- only use books and other print materials, video, and pictures as supplementary extensions of what is taught through firsthand resources

- provide each class with a broad based reference library; trade books, current encyclopedias, CD-Rom video discs

- make the environment body-compatible

- eliminate clutter; avoid distraction and overstimulation

- change bulletin boards, displays and materials frequently; always stay current with what is being studied at the moment. Put away the old except for a few items (e.g., the mindmap for the component) which will jog recall

- consider not purchasing class sets of textbooks. Buy only a few for teacher resource and spend the money on *being there immersion,* and hands-on (of the real thing) materials for students

- have regularly scheduled guest speakers to support content

- increase input by at least ten times what it is today— and that's just for starters

CHAPTER SEVEN

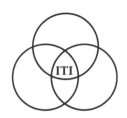

COLLABORATION

The history of the United States has been the enshrining of individualism—the spirit of Frank Sinatra's "My Way." In schools, students work alone at their work, no sharing (no cheating), no talking (learning occurs when everything is quiet), competition (get graded on the bell curve). While such a picture fits Hollywood's notion of how the West was won, it belies the reality of day-to-day living. The pioneers relied heavily on each other for their very existence. And today, real work of significance (landing a person on the moon, designing the user-friendly mouse for computers) is also a collaborative venture. In short, our schools, with their Prussian ancestry, are out of step with the real world.

In 1989, the U.S. Department of Labor released its commission report entitled, "Investing In People." An entire chapter is devoted to what education needs to do in order to improve the quality of the American work force. This is one of its observations:

> "Business can make additional contributions by providing schools with the information that they need to develop course content and instructional methods that meet the current and emerging needs of the work place. Increasingly, employees will have to work in cooperative groups, be able to make decisions about production problems and processes, and develop the ability to acquire new skills and behavior on the job. We urge schools to adjust their instructional methods to match more closely the situation students will later face in the workplace."

CHAPTER 7: COLLABORATION

The requisite skills for running one's own business, a farm, a home or being an inventor or a businessperson (even as a shoe shiner or newspaper deliverer) have always been *problem-solving, decision-making,* and *the ability to communicate with peers and those of all ages.* The majority of one's neighbors are employees, not entrepreneurs. Significant numbers of children are growing up in homes where the work of the parents or other adults is not known to the child and the standards for success in business (drive to master skills and provide quality customer service) are rarely practiced with a sense of consequence to the survival of the business or to one's personal reputation in the community. Further, today's home as a model for collaboration has a 50 percent chance of falling apart. Children learn what others do. Where are the models for working together toward a common goal, using give and take to achieve eventual success?

In addition, there is great generational segmentation in our society—great rifts in understanding and appreciation between retired citizens, youth, and the working adult. The school, with its rigid age-gradedness, reinforces this sense of segmentation and is out of step with the needs of today's students and society. Segregation by age is an enormous mistake. Teaching students the skills to successfully collaborate in the classroom will assist them in becoming effective members of society as adults.

Another, more powerful, rationale for collaboration comes from brain research. Hart talks about the need for great quantities of input to the brain; Smith stipulates that a learner needs "much opportunity to manipulate information."[1] Talking with others in a work group is an effective way to manipulate information. According to both authors, one teacher facing a classroom of thirty brains, each with very different ways of learning, is insufficient to the task. Collaboration—students teaching each other and providing a sounding board for each other—is an essential element in a brain-compatible learning environment.

What Is Collaboration?—The choice of the word "collaboration," rather than cooperation or cooperative learning, is deliberate here. In *Webster's Dictionary* it means: **"to work in association with, to work with another."** Collaboration means working together toward a common goal. The common goal in an ITI classroom is achievement of mastery and competence of skills and knowledge that have application in the real world, not a short-term goal of completing a worksheet.

In the ITI model, it is irrelevant which approach to cooperative learning a teacher may choose so long as the teacher philosophically believes in collaboration and the end result is achieved—that of students working together productively to enhance learning. In other words, collaboration is a desired means to an end, not an end in itself, and the means may vary.

STRUCTURING EFFECTIVE COLLABORATION

Structuring effective collaboration in the classroom involves two areas: the design of the curriculum and flexible grouping of students for different purposes. There are many sources available today which address how to organize a classroom for collaboration. My favorites are *Designing Groupwork: Strategies for the Heterogeneous Classroom* by Elizabeth Cohen, which provides a clear analysis of the peer social norms which a teacher must alter if low status students are to succeed plus some how-tos for multi-ability classrooms as well as bilingual classrooms; and *TRIBES: A Process for Social Development and Cooperative Learning* by Jeanne Gibbs, a wonderfully practical book, with lots of ready-to-go activities for developing a sense of group through the creation of a sense of inclusion, influence, and affection.

Curriculum Design

Cohen points out that collaboration, or "groupwork," is the appropriate vehicle for achieving outcomes in three areas:

- cognitive or intellectual goals
- social goals
- solving common classroom problems

CHAPTER 7: COLLABORATION

Cognitive Goals. Collaboration is especially powerful in promoting conceptual learning, practice with creative problem-solving, the learning of language, and the improvement of oral communication. In contrast, Cohen points out that putting groups together for other cognitive tasks, such as the infamous seatwork ditto, is a complete waste of time. Student response to such assignments is quite predictable: let the smartest kid do it and then everyone else copies.[2]

ITI inquiries developed for collaborative work must be designed with care. Two criteria to follow: 1) the outcome should be something that even the most capable student can't do alone, and thus everyone's contribution is needed, and 2) the work should be engaging, reflective of real life.

Social Goals. In real life, each of us is a member of many groups: family, extended family, close friends, peer acquaintances, neighbors, fellow workers, clients, car pools. The contribution to our learning from each group is different and greatly enriched by the diversity in ages, experience, and points of view. If we could only belong to one group, our experiences would be severely restricted. So it is in the classroom. An enormous mistake in the system is segregating students by age. True brain-compatibility in the classroom will not be achieved until multi-aged grouping of students occurs (a minimum age span of three years) and there is frequent interaction with experts from outside the classroom.

The truth is that we live our lives in groups and much of the satisfaction (and dissatisfaction) in our lives comes from our level of success at being group members. According to Brady, "most personal needs are met, most problems are solved, most public goals are attained by *organized collective action*."[3] Yet nowhere do we get formal training in how to be successful group members. If our parents do not have those skills to pass on to us, we have to resort to trial and error; the pain level for failure is high, the time line for learning long.

EFFECTIVE COLLABORATION

We owe it to our students, and to ourselves, to learn how to be successful group members. Therefore, we need to develop curriculum which uncovers the concepts and skills of group membership. The content focus for the first two to three weeks of the school year should be on understanding one's own learning processes and on the nature of groups, group development, and how to be a group member.

The basic building blocks for collaboration in an ITI classroom are the Lifelong Guidelines described in Chapter 2: trustworthiness, truthfulness, active listening, no put-downs, and the LIFESKILLS that assist one in doing one's personal best.

In our move to collaboration, behaviors need to be modeled and labeled for others to see what the Lifelong Guidelines and LIFESKILLS really look like, sound like, feel like, and how they affect the outcomes we achieve. Depending on the level of the social skills of your students, it may take a month or so of being consistent as a whole class before you move to groups.

Solving Common Classroom Problems. Again, one of the best resources we have found to build the necessary inclusion, influence, and affection between individuals is *TRIBES*.* The premises upon which the *TRIBES* Program is based are:

- Children who maintain long-term membership in supportive classroom peer groups will improve in self-image, behave more responsibly, and increase their academic achievement

- Teachers will spend less time managing student behavior problems and have more time for creative teaching

---

*TRIBES is an eminently practical book, containing more than a hundred pages of activities which can be used as is or can be adapted to incorporate content from subjects being studied. Also, many of the activities can be used with adults. We recommend that group-building activities be built into each staff meeting and that the entire staff consider being trained as a group in the *TRIBES* process.

- Schools, organized into the *TRIBES* system, will create a positive climate for learning

- Parents will report a carry-over of positive statements and attitudes from their children into the home environment[4]

Flexible Student Grouping

Among the lessons needed to operate effectively in a group is the willingness to be flexible, patient, and to believe that collaboration is beneficial to the whole as well as to each member of the group. If this is firmly in place and applied daily, students will not have difficulty moving from group to group in the classroom or in real life.

As mentioned above, learning in real life settings occurs through a multitude of groups. It is probably not too great an exaggeration to say that the difference between a country cousin and a city cousin, between a parochial perspective and a world view, is the number and variety of learning groups encountered in life. Similarly, assignment in school to one collaborative learning group for the year is restrictive. For maximum brain-compatibility, we recommend using at least three groupings: family, skill, and interest.

The family group. This is the basic membership group through which students learn how to be group members, handle most conceptual learning inquiries, write in their journals, and record the daily agenda. In the true sense of family, the family group is the context in which students come together daily, checking in, asking for advice, getting assistance, and generally "touching base."

Family groups should be heterogeneous and multi-aged; the ideal size is four to five students. The family group is together all year and meets daily.

GROUP FORMATS

Skill groups. These groups operate "as needed" on a short-term, ad hoc basis. No one group has a membership that is permanently assigned; groups are formed by the teacher as the need arises in order to provide opportunities for acquiring specific skills or concepts. For example, three students needing to master the use of semicolons or learn how to avoid run-on sentences Students shift from skill group to skill group as mastery is attained.

Groups can (and should) vary throughout the day depending on what is to be learned; most do not last more than a week or two weeks maximum.

Interest groups. Like skill groups, these groups are short-term, ad hoc, very spontaneous. They are appropriate when creating projects, doing specific inquiries, planning a closure (see appendix A), working on research, or sharing common interest regarding a long-term project. They change from day to day, week to week. They are very loosely knit, largely autonomous. Their success requires a high degree of cooperation by each member and high commitment to the task at hand because the groups typically operate with minimal supervision by the teacher.

Care should be given to see that membership, whenever the groups are established by self-selection, is done with content in mind rather than merely current friendship. This can usually be done by simply restating the criteria for the groups' formation—they are *work* committees—and identifying the requisite LIFESKILLS and knowledge needed within the group.

The above group structures are used for organizing all students around learning tasks. Yet another group, the work group, involves only a few students at a time.

The work group. The above group structures are used for organizing all students around learning tasks. Yet another kind of group, the work group, involves only a few students at a time. The work group is a practical response to the teacher's need to get the business of the day accomplished for the classroom. These groups may be for the moment, the day, the week, the month. Because such a group usually consists of not more than two or three students and produces tangible, easily measured results, it provides a good opportunity for developing leadership skills. Examples include cleaning cages, setting up a display, making a bulletin board, improving skills, or working on a project.

The work group is also a vehicle for an individual student when he/she needs to accomplish a personal task. Just as adults understand who to contact when they need to undertake a specific project, students learn to choose the partner needed for a specific activity. Listing the specific tasks with the needed skills on a bulletin board or job list assists students in selecting a partner who would best assist in getting the job done well and on time. Similarly, having a chart inside each student's binder listing the student's talents, and added space to write the date when the talents have been tapped, helps students focus on who they are becoming and what they have to offer others and the world. The important lesson here is that we all have very specific areas in which we are competent and are willing to assist others. Commitment to contribute to one's community, not just take, is an essential value to teach all students in a democratic society.

Name	Talent	Date used
Mitchell	• working with others • drawing	
Kathryn	• building structures • oral reading • solving problems	
Sarah	• math problems • writing essays • making graphs	
Emily	• poetry • dance • game strategies	
Philip	• working with clay models • creative writing • building dioramas	

COMMON SENSE

The committee of one. One of the common mistakes in implementing collaboration is the assumption that if a little is good, then lots must be terrific. Under this mistaken notion, teachers attempt to have students in groups all day long, day after day. Three reasons to consider not having groups all day everyday are, first, the sameness is boring. Second, group environments are not the best context for some assignments and tasks. Third, the classroom should nurture development of intrapersonal intelligence and provide quiet time for introverts as well as develop group skills.

A Touch of Common Sense

Don't be rigid in your scheduling of group work. Be flexible. Choose collaboration, whole class work, individual work, pairs, or other configurations **based on what is the most appropriate vehicle for the purpose and content of the moment.** The bottom line is common sense. Don't get tied into something that is unworkable and formula-driven. Always be willing to discuss with the students the effectiveness of the working arrangement.

Collaboration as a structure is not an end in itself. It exists for three reasons:

- to substantially increase manipulation of information
- to help students learn group skills which are essential to success in life
- to serve as the instructional vehicle for carrying out a particular activity or inquiry when a group context is best

Most importantly, collaboration is not just a tool for the classroom, it is a way of life—a philosophy and a system of values.

CHAPTER 7: COLLABORATION

OUTCOMES OF WORKING IN GROUP SETTINGS

During the early stages of implementing collaboration, it is not unusual to panic about the amount of time it takes: "When will I ever get to my subject content? I can't afford to delay getting to what my principal expects me to be teaching." The pressure to give it up will become extreme. Just know that those before you had the same worries. And you, as they, will discover that, once the family groups have developed a sense of group and learned the skills of working together, cognitive learning is speeded up enormously. Students will learn far more—in breadth and depth—once they have handled the social and personal issues in the classroom.

Work habits and skills learned through working in groups include the LIFESKILLS plus the following:

- *thoughtfulness*—assisting others when it is needed
- *follow-through*—knowing the rest of the group is depending on you
- *respect*—being able to act in a way that allows others the confidence to do their best
- *creativity*—seeing new ways to solve problems and enhance projects
- *planning*—learning how to structure an activity within a time frame
- *leadership and followership*—learning when and how to lead and when and how to follow others' leadership

GUIDELINES
FOR ENCOURAGING COLLABORATION

- remember the Lifelong Guidelines and LIFESKILLS; they are the cornerstone of interpersonal skills

- plan on at least a month of practicing working together before your family groups are officially selected

- do not use groups as reward and punishment; groups are the way the world works

- the information processed during collaboration must be meaningful from the learner's point of view and provide real life problems to be solved, not contrived worksheet exercises

- it is important to make a distinction between two or more students sharing the same assignment together vs. true collaboration in which there is a sense of group built and maintained by attention to process and to the development of requisite group and social skills

- if students have low peer status, teachers must make every effort to *alter their social standing* within their group(s) and in the class as a whole in order to prevent the pygmalion effect from shutting down their learning

CHAPTER EIGHT

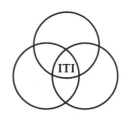

IMMEDIATE FEEDBACK

Immediate feedback is a necessary element in the learning environment—both for pattern-seeking and for *program-building* (see Chapters 3 and 5). In all learning environments except the school, it is present in abundance. Consider, for example, when children first begin to talk. Each time they say something incorrectly, we immediately give them the correct word, usage, and pronunciation. Imagine letting all their mistakes pile up during the week and correcting them on Friday!

When children learn to walk, we give support for the smallest step and then we provide something to hang onto and give them a little more space until they have established what it takes to be balanced. Good parenting, like good teaching, is the process of providing immediate feedback, feedback which is appropriate, consistent, and delivered with loving care.

Think back to the time you learned to drive a car. Feedback was instantaneous and continuous. If you returned home with no dents and no tickets, your parents knew you had a fairly successful time! Similarly, when learning to play a game or sport or beginning a hobby, feedback is built in, immediate, and continuous. In such cases, either the learning materials or the conditions themselves provided the immediate feedback, or your "teacher" or fellow adventurer interpreted your approximation toward mastery. This is a far cry from the classroom setting with the often asked question, "Is this right, teacher?" "Teacher, is this the way it's supposed to turn out?"

CHAPTER 8: IMMEDIATE FEEDBACK

Smith, in *Insult to Intelligence: The Bureaucratic Invasion of Our Classrooms*, states that learning does not require coercion or irrelevant reward. Learning is its own reward. Feedback that tells us we have succeeded at a learning task produces a burst of fire from neurotransmitters, producing a "chemical high" that is readily observable in the spark in a child's eye as the "Aha" registers.

In contrast, each of us has personal experiences with learning when the feedback was confusing, either because it came after the fact or because it was inappropriate to what we were doing or thinking at the time. Examples abound. Many among us experience the frustration of fumbling over the spelling of a particular word; our two choices are always the same two, the same incorrect version vs. the correct. We are never sure which is which.

Contrary to popular belief, the hardest thing the brain does is forget something it has learned, as distinguished from forgetting something it never learned in the first place or which was never meaningful . . . which occurs for 80 percent of the students on the bell curve who stopped just short of mastery, just short of building a *program*. If you doubt that forgetting is difficult, talk with a Vietnam vet who still experiences flashbacks, or think back to your own reoccurring nightmares that replay a horrible experience. When we say *"I taught it but the students forgot it,"* what is really so is that *"I taught it but the students never learned it."* Feedback (and adequate time) was insufficient for the student to develop a correct *mental program*.

The importance of immediate feedback to the student, then, is obvious. **Feedback, accurate and immediate, is needed at the time the learner is building his/her *mental program*** in order to ensure that the *program* is accurate. Yet, in a classroom with thirty students and desks in rows, giving feedback is difficult and time consuming.

BUILDING IN IMMEDIATE FEEDBACK

There are numerous ways to build in immediate feedback. Some of the changes needed must occur schoolwide, some can occur classroom by classroom.

Change the Curriculum

First, re-evaluate the starting point of your curriculum content. Traditional curriculum content areas are primarily composed of factoid statements and the parts never add up to the whole. Instead, *start* with the whole, i.e., the real world and *being there* experiences and slice off a chewable piece. The real world has a great deal of built-in feedback for learners; in fact, it is the best form of immediate feedback because feedback is almost always built into the learning event itself. Such firsthand feedback from *being there* in a real world setting is instantaneous and more intrinsic—and thus more powerful—than feedback from an outside source, the teacher or the answer sheet for the workbook or reading kit.

Second, encourage your district to move away from a laundry list curriculum to a continuum of concepts, K-12—concepts such as living/non-living, interdependence, diversity, adaptation, change, revolution, evolution, beauty, war/peace, stability, and so on. Concepts which are meaty and worthy of in-depth and thoughtful pursuit. Remember, less is more.

Change the Instructional Materials

The best learning environments are those in which the materials and events themselves provide the feedback, e.g., driving a car, riding a horse, hitting a curve ball, building a model bridge, sewing a dress. These are settings which allow learners to sit in the driver's seat, able to judge for themselves whether they have mastered something or not, thus allowing them to direct their own learning.

CHAPTER 8: IMMEDIATE FEEDBACK

This is a far cry from the typical activities and materials of the traditional school. Few worksheets or dittos provide feedback of a self-correcting kind. As a consequence, children feel rudderless, confused, powerless, and either anxious or bored. Hardly the characteristics of a lifelong learner.

Change the Structure:
Increase the Number of "Teachers"

Remember the one-room, little red schoolhouse? The eight or ten or twenty children, all of different ages—grades 1-8 or even 1-12? What were the advantages? An older, more experienced student was always there to help, support, point out the obvious, and otherwise act as a teacher or mentor to the younger children; they provided immediate feedback. Compare that to thirty lower tracked students with one teacher. Where does the immediate feedback come from? How many of the students receive timely, sufficient feedback from the teacher during each activity? During an entire day? Given the arithmetic of it all, each student on average will get less than two minutes of personalized feedback a day. At the instant when they are trying to make sense out of the learning (pattern-seeking), or practicing application *(program-building)*, where can they get feedback to see if they are correct? Certainly not from fellow same-age, same-ability students who are also struggling with the same task.

If we want greater learning, we must increase the number and availability of "teachers" who have sufficient mastery to provide accurate feedback to the fledgling learner. This is easily done by eliminating tracking and creating heterogeneous classes of students representing a wide range of experiences and expertise. Multi-age grouping of students deserves consideration.

BUILDING IN IMMEDIATE FEEDBACK

Change the Structure:
Change How We Schedule and Use Time

Currently, teachers do 90 percent of the talking and students have little time for "doing." To build in immediate feedback, the ratio of doing and being talked at must be reversed.

ITI teachers are encouraged to limit their direct instruction to not more than sixteen minutes an hour. Three reasons for this guideline are:

- it demands that the teacher absolutely knows what it is he/she wants to convey to the students (a clear, concise, succinct, this-is-what's-most-important-to-know lesson)

- the remainder of the time (hour, morning) is spent circulating among the students giving them immediate feedback on the activity structured by their chosen (or assigned) inquiry (see Chapter 13 for a discussion of inquiries). This is a time for re-teaching, for further explanation, and discussion one-on-one

- it provides an opportunity for the teacher to immediately assess the effectiveness of the direct instruction and the subsequent assignment

Further, design more action-oriented inquiries—ones that ask for action by applying what is being learned to the real world.

Again, unlearning something incorrectly stored in the brain is much more difficult than learning it right the first time. It is imperative to stop a student if he/she is on the wrong track and building an incorrect *mental program*.

CHAPTER 8: IMMEDIATE FEEDBACK

ELIMINATE DELAYED FEEDBACK

If one understands the nature of *program-building*, one cannot avoid reaching the conclusion that, in most instances, it is a waste of teacher time to grade papers overnight (or at even longer intervals). The only exception is long-term, comprehensive projects which are multi-step. For students to do a page of long division problems incorrectly as a follow-up to the in-class lesson and not be told whether it is right or wrong until their next paper is graded and returned the next day is meaningless feedback for *program-building*. The student has already logged in the incorrect *program*. Further damage occurs when the student is sent home with more long division problems for homework . . . more incorrect practice, more incorrect *programs* in the brain.

So, our best advice to you is to drastically reduce grading papers overnight. Provide time during class for feedback. Make sure that the practice they do at home is cementing the correct *mental program*. For the teacher, the implications are enormously freeing. What a time saver, what a burden to unload! Imagine what terrific curriculum could be planned during the time traditionally set aside each day for grading papers with letter grades, smiley faces, etc. And, more importantly, what fun teaching could be!

GUIDELINES
FOR PROVIDING IMMEDIATE FEEDBACK

- be very selective in what you take home—busy work for students creates busy work for teachers

- structure work groups so that feedback is provided to each participant on a wide range of issues—content and process by teacher or fellow students

- utilize the two basic tenets behind the authentic assessment movement: assess what is of value (not just what's easy to assess) and make sure that the product or project utilized for assessing students is one that has worth to the student in and of itself

- help sensitize students to the feedback built into the real world; help them learn to direct self-talk toward analyzing their own work and to develop confidence in their own ability to provide themselves feedback, a necessary capability for a lifelong learner

- change your curriculum and materials; start with real life content and use real life resources and events. When firsthand assignments are given to cooperative work groups, giving individual (and group) feedback is a much easier task

- don't overlook or underestimate the power and value of peer feedback

CHAPTER NINE

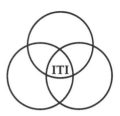

MASTERY

While putting my thoughts together on this book, I was aboard a ship sailing up the inland passage to Alaska. My first cruise was in 1976, my last in 1993. Although I had a delightful time on the more recent cruise, the change in the tone of the general workers on board was noticeable, so much so that I spoke to the "man in charge," someone who has spent at least twenty-five years of his life on ships in a variety of capacities. I asked him to explain the difference. His perception was that the young people under his supervision had never had to do a job at a high level of mastery and that if they were forced into compliance they would do it (e.g., having a sponge with them as they cleared lunch trays on the outside deck), but within a few days their old behavior returned. He then made a very telling statement, "My mother would never have allowed me to do an incomplete job."

I was reminded of my father's similar statement about growing up in San Francisco. Although the family had little money and the front stoop was made of bare, unpainted wood, his mother demanded that weekly house cleaning include scrubbing the wooden steps every Saturday morning with soap and water. In contrast, while at a shopping mall early one Saturday, I was struck by the number of young people who were already "hanging out" for the day. Perhaps mastery must begin in the home, modeled in the real world, a part of the family culture ("the way we do things here"), modeled from an early age by an adult we respect. Maybe we have accepted too readily and too completely the sloppiness in many areas of our lives because that's the way it is: the plumber who leaves a little leak behind; the mechanic who sets the timing gear by aligning two hatch marks as described in the factory specs and ignores the fact that your car then has less pick-up than before; the gardener who puts in his time but leaves the yard looking as if it was never touched; the attorney who gives you a boiler plate contract with little data specific to your situation and charges a fortune for it. The list goes on and on.

Another example comes to mind. During the month I spent in Czechoslovakia working with educators in a variety of cities, I was overwhelmed by the magnificent buildings that had been constructed 300 to 600 years ago. There they stood—tall and majestic. Alongside these incredible feats of architecture and craftsmanship were the buildings built during the communist regime—ugly, devoid of craftsmanship, already disintegrating, creating pollution, and, in some cases, not very safe to be in. Apartments, for which one waited ten to twelve years, were made of unfinished, unpainted concrete, and had bare bulbs in the hallways.

Everywhere we turn, the examples of non-mastery being the accepted norm haunt us. I believe formal training in non-mastery is received in school—and it starts early. In school, low expectations of students by teachers allow a student the option to understand or not understand; we merely give him/her the commensurate grade, an *A*, *B*, *C*, *D*, or *F*, and blame lack of learning on the students—lack of preparation, limited experiences, cranky attitudes, or less than perfect home environment. As a consequence, America's schools graduate almost one million illiterate students a year. But they graduate! They receive a piece of paper which indicates an achievement level satisfactory to society and taxpayers. They will then go on and get jobs (maybe), not understand why their employers are frustrated with their performance, and wonder why their salaries and positions are not commensurate with their aspirations—all because the *mental programs* they have acquired incorporate marginal standards because marginal was good enough in school. So much for mastery!

MEANINGFUL CURRICULUM

Gardner in his book, *Unschooled Mind*, puts it another way:

"To declare oneself against the institution of the three *R*s in the schools is like being against motherhood or the flag. Beyond question, students ought to be literate and ought to revel in their literacy. Yet the essential emptiness of this goal is dramatized by the fact that young children in the United States are becoming literate in a *literal* sense; that is, they are mastering the rules of reading and writing, even as they are learning their addition and multiplication tables. What is missing are not the decoding skills, but two other facets: the capacity to read for understanding and the desire to read at all. Much the same story can be told for the remaining literacies; it is not the mechanics of writing nor the algorithms for subtraction that are absent, but rather the knowledge about when to invoke these skills and the inclination to do so productively in one's daily life."[1]

How do we set expectations for ourselves and our students? In ITI classrooms and schools, expectations are set in three ways:

- creating meaningful curriculum worthy of children's time and interest, and allowing adequate time for practicing real world applications
- implementing the Lifelong Guidelines, particularly personal best and the LIFESKILLS
- eliminating *A* through *F* grading and the bell curve in favor of the "3 Cs" of assessment

MEANINGFUL CURRICULUM AND APPLICATION

Today, with brain research behind us, we can ask three very specific questions of the teacher:

- What *mental program* did you intend to build?
- Did your curriculum clearly provide the skills and knowledge necessary to build that *program*?
- Did you provide adequate time and real world applications?

CHAPTER 9: MASTERY

From the brain's perspective, learning things which are not immediately useable is an exceedingly hard task. If not useable, what good is it? Inability to answer this question affects where and how—and *if*—the brain stores it. Any discussion of learning and application of learning must make the distinction between rote memorization and learning which is accessible to assist children to understand and act upon their world.

IMPLEMENTING LIFELONG GUIDELINES AND LIFESKILLS

High expectations legislated by external rewards do not constitute a firm foundation for creating a lifelong learner. High expectations are a way of life, a philosophy for conducting one's personal world. We have found that the Lifelong Guidelines, and particularly personal best and LIFESKILLS, are powerful tools in the classroom for helping students internalize high expectations, and to help them begin operating from an internal locus of control and empowerment.

Another element of great value to students is large doses of exposure to the real world, especially the world of work, and the personal, social, and professional level skills required to succeed in those arenas. Upper elementary students should be assigned a mentor who will let the student shadow them for a day—a real day from the beginning to end of the shift, be it city hall, the police station, fire station. And not just once but at least three different times during the year.

ELIMINATING GRADING AND THE BELL CURVE; INITIATING ASSESSMENT USING THE "3 Cs"

The educational system and the American public have come to expect the bell curve with its *A* through *F* grading—it is a process as apple pie and Chevy-on-the-levy as any tradition can be. It expects and assumes that some students will understand, some will understand a little, and some not at all. So far so good. But the percentage of students expected to fit those categories are neither desirable nor defensible—10 percent *A*s, 80 percent *C*s, and 10 percent *F*s. Simply translated this means that 90 percent of our students are failing to master what is expected of them by their teachers because an incomplete or an inaccurate *program* results in thin air—nothing is retained (except possibly a negative bias about studying that topic again). Consequently, after thirty-five hundred hours of schooling at a cost of roughly $45,000 per student, the United States graduates 1.1 million functionally illiterate students; approximately 30 percent of the students drop out before graduation day, and still others walk the carpet for a diploma that means little to many of today's high-tech employers.

Or, take the other end of the spectrum. The University of California, Berkeley, admits only the top two percent—the best students from across the country . . . and then it proceeds to put them in classes of hundreds and grades them on the bell curve. Distressing? Absolutely. It makes one question the goal and purpose of public schooling: *Is it to sort, or to educate for competence?*

The bell curve is a dangerous tradition in all its applications: the classroom level, the institutional level, the workplace level. If what we value is learning and competence in the real world, the bell curve is nonsense, counterproductive, expensive, and damaging—to students and to society.

I believe the compelling reason for public education is to produce students who are literate and competent citizens. Literate, so they can study and understand the issues that appear on voting ballots; competent personally, socially, and economically so that they are able to contribute to society and help perpetuate our democratic way of life.

Thus, the goal of the ITI model—and the innate drive of the human mind—is mastery. Mastery, not in the sense of "mastery learning" with its 834 discrete skills of reading, but rather mastery as in competence: "capacity, sufficiency, enough to live on with comfort." That is, the learner understands the skill or concept, knows how to apply it in the real world in similar (but varying) circumstances, and has incorporated it into a *mental program*. Such mastery or competence is at the heart of positive self-concept, of a sense of empowerment and ability to direct one's life, and it is consistent with the brain's innate search for meaning.

From a student's perspective, grading causes stress, redirects the learner from intrinsic rewards to external rewards, pits student against student instead of assessing all students against a standard of competence, and creates low self-esteem or false assurance. From a teacher's perspective, the demands of the system distort what's valuable to know into what's easy to assess in order to ensure "alignment" of curriculum with assessment tools.

There is yet another, more fundamental reason why traditional evaluation and grading is brain-antagonistic—*it simply ignores how learning takes place*. As Hart states: "Learning is the acquisition of useful *programs*." Information that does not become embedded in a *mental program* is information that is unretrievable. Brain research makes it quite clear that, if meaning has not been reached, there is nothing for the brain to remember except confusion and, quite possibly, distaste for the topic or even the entire subject area ("I hate science. I've never been good at math. Spelling has always been difficult."—common reactions from adults and students alike). **Brain research does not substantiate our devotion to the spiral curriculum notion.** *The brain cannot build on bits and pieces that were meaningless at the time they were encountered.*

From a teacher's perspective, mastery/competence is built into a student's day through both curriculum planning and instructional strategies.

Before we go on, check with your own experience. Do you recall your college days? Sitting up all hours of the night studying for the essay exam for your college world civilization course. Mountains of data, little or no application of the information, no *"program"* created. By the time the blue book essays were returned, there was information in that essay exam book you had never heard of before! Even the handwriting looked strange! Surely, this must be someone else's exam book! What a waste of time, money, and effort.

Even in more active forms of assessment, doing something once or twice does not a *mental program* make. Thus, even an *A* can mean little in terms of long-term memory. And grades of less than an *A* usually mean that the learner, at the time, still harbored uncertainty or misunderstandings. Such tentativeness is a clear indication that an accurate *"mental program"* had not been put in place. Thus, a *D* or *F*, even a *B* or *C*, means that little or nothing will be remembered six weeks later.

In real life outside of the classroom, the difference between mastery and the bell curve is quite stark. In the real world, a *C* or even a *B* is wholly insufficient. Who would want to fly in an airplane that had been serviced by a mechanic who had just passed skill tests with a *C-*? Would you? Certainly not! How about exposed electrical wires left behind by your electrician? Is that okay with you? Of course not!

In reconceptualizing evaluation and grading toward a notion of assessing competence, there are two hopeful trends—the application of current brain research (a major topic of this book) and authentic assessment, often referred to as performance-based assessment. Both entail making massive changes in student learning assessment, curriculum content and structure, and attitudes—of teachers, students, and the system.

Two key ideas from the authentic assessment movement which are particularly powerful are:

- using real life settings and levels of expectation*
- assessing what's worth assessing rather than assessing what's easy to assess

In my own schooling, the class that taught me the most about mastery was Mr. Womack's eighth grade social studies class. That was the year we studied city/county government. In the early

---

*Fred Newman, one of the primary leaders of the authentic assessment movement, states "The idea of authentic achievement requires students to engage in disciplined inquiry to produce knowledge that has value in their lives beyond simply proving their competence in school."

fifties, San Jose, California, was on its way to becoming a large metropolitan area. People were moving in faster than the city could keep up with basic neighborhood services. As the neighborhoods and schools swelled, it became obvious more libraries were needed. (Television was still new.) Taking that need into consideration, Mr. Womack taught us how to make people aware of a problem and take the steps necessary to solve the problem. Today, there is a Rose Garden Branch Library because of the capability of a classroom teacher to make learning meaningful and give his students lifelong skills that access our democratic system.

In my own upbringing, I was constantly reminded of how democracy worked. My parents were always active in the community, helping to make things better. I vividly recall the countless hours of canvassing, telephone tree calling, organizing, petitioning, and so forth. Without question those activities are excellent vehicles for applying all the basic skills (reading, writing, arithmetic), as well as practicing democracy. Thus, ITI has always had a political action component. It has been an aspect of the model that I have insisted on. However, I never realized how few teachers had the experience of knowing how to use this method as a means of applying what they were learning. Few teachers were able to feel comfortable about specific steps to produce action. This dilemma was solved when Barbara Lewis wrote a book entitled, *The Kid's Guide to Social Action.* The subtitle says it all: *How to Solve the Social Problems YOU CHOOSE—and Turn Creative Thinking Into Positive Action.* It is so comprehensive that it received the Susan Kovalik & Associates Gold Medal Award in 1991 for the book that best assists students in an ITI classroom. It is a step-by-step guide showing students how to make a constructive difference. It is about application of knowledge, which is what mastery is all about.

THE 3 Cs OF ASSESSMENT

Setting Standards for Mastery: The "3 Cs" of Assessment

Three criteria determine mastery: **complete, correct**, and **comprehensive**.

Complete. This means that the work called for by the inquiry met all the requirements or specifications of the inquiry, including timeliness. As when on the job, the task is complete from beginning to end, and done within the requested time frame. (For an explanation of inquiries, see Chapter 13.)

Correct. This means that the work called for by the inquiry contained accurate information, the information used was the most recent available, and more than one source was consulted. The work was performed with the requisite job specifications (such as a plumber or electrician performing work in accordance with the Universal Code for plumbing or electrical work and the project design).

Comprehensive. This means that the work reflects thoroughness of thought and investigation, not just a one-line response, an opinion forged from a single point of view. What is important and worthwhile about the issue or problem was researched thoroughly, looked at from different points of view (not just one's own opinion or "what it said in the encyclopedia"), and the conclusion was supported with relevant data. On the job, comprehensiveness of response can be as simple (but very valued and valuable) as a secretary researching the price of office supply items from several stores before placing the order, or a doctor analyzing the problem from all vantage points, not just the "drug fix."

Although students may balk at such criteria and complain about "changing the rules of the game," the notion of completeness and correctness will not be new to them. If they have played team sports they know the importance and the consequences of doing it right the first time. However, comprehensiveness is a concept that the teacher will have to teach because it is the antithesis of "study" done out of *the* textbook (with emphasis on "the"). It may take some weeks to shift students from the viewpoint and habits attendant with such notions as: seatwork as learning, quantity is quality, piling up points equals learning.

CHAPTER 9: MASTERY

IMPLEMENTING ASSESSMENT OF MASTERY/COMPETENCE

Using the Tools at Hand

Just as learning should be brain-compatible for students, assessing student learning should be brain-compatible for teachers. In an ITI classroom, there is no need to invent or buy tests or assessment instruments beyond what the teacher has already created in the process of orchestrating learning.

- the *rationale* for the yearlong theme is also the rationale for learning the information (see Chapter 11)

- *key points* identify precisely what concepts and skills are to be learned (see Chapter 12). Key points **are** the curriculum and they provide the focus for assessment. If they have been selected and developed well, i.e., if they are truly what is essential to learn and are conceptual rather than factoid in nature, then they are clearly what's worth assessing. Thus, they are what should be assessed and what students (and teachers) should be held accountable for

- *inquiries* provide the opportunity to actively experience how to apply the concept or skill to the real world and to develop a *program* for use in the future (see Chapter 13). Inquiries are the engine of the curriculum—they give it power (from the teacher's perspective), and pizzazz (from the student's perspective). And, with the addition of the "3 Cs" of assessment, they are ready-made performance-based assessment tools

A note of caution: carelessly crafted inquiries, inquiries which reflect only linguistic or logical/mathematical intelligences, inquiries that are busywork or have no real world application (or for other reasons are just simply not brain-compatible), are useless as assessment tools.

If the above tools are well and firmly in place, assessment for mastery/competence on a wide range of skills and concepts is an extraordinarily easy task because the difficult part of authentic assessment has already been accomplished, i.e., identifying what is important to measure and finding real life, non-paper and pencil tasks to measure mastery.

Steps in Designing Assessment for Mastery/Competence.

Step 1. Select an inquiry or inquiries that you feel would allow the most realistic expression of the skill or concept to be assessed. Be sure that your choice(s) will allow students the opportunity to function using their strongest intelligence capacity.

Step 2. Analyze your inquiry(ies) to see if it, as written, will allow you to say yes or no, mastery or not, upon its completion. It may be useful here to recall the basic structure of successful measurement. Simply put, any assessment procedure must answer the basic question: **Who** will do **what, how well**, as measured by **what, when**.

- **who**—all students (not just the "good" students)
- will do/understand **what**—the key points
- **how**—by doing the inquiries
- **how well**—so the concept can be applied and generalized to the real world
- **when**—by the end of the semester (not by an arbitrary date such as Friday, quiz day)

Step 3. Decide whether the performance on the inquiry can be cooperative or individual. Before you make that decision, remind yourself to challenge the old notion of cooperation equals cheating. If the work is done substantially in the classroom, you will have an opportunity to observe the group and each individual in action.

Step 4. Beyond applying the "3 Cs" and determining that the job performed is complete, correct, and comprehensive, you must make a judgment about whether or not the student has developed a *mental program* for using the concept/skill in the future. In other words, is this a one time event from short-term memory or has the child truly developed a *program* allowing him or her to use the concept or skill under the following conditions in the future:

- the ability to solve real problems using the skills and concepts
- the ability to show, explain, or teach the idea or skill to another person who has a real need to know
- the ability to use the language of the subject in complex situations and in social interactions
- the ability to perform appropriately in unanticipated situations[2]

Such ability to use what is learned is the fundamental difference between real learning and the traditional assessment for letter grades and on a bell curve. I would also recommend that you look with some suspicion at rubrics being developed to assess portfolios and so forth. Most are just more explicit, detailed descriptions of gradations along the bell curve. Again, the point here is that the ITI classroom is in pursuit of mastery/competence as applied to life in the real world, not just in the classroom. Anything less than preparation for life is a waste of both student and teacher time and effort.

GUIDELINES
FOR IMPLEMENTING COMPETENCE ASSESSMENT

- emphasize personal best rather than "grades"; make sure that your yardstick for personal best is not an absolute standard, but one appropriate to each student. Remember, you are trying to build attitudes and skills for lifelong learning, not sort students into high, middle, and low

- if "grading" is required of you by the system, institute a "Pass/No Credit" approach based on action-based, true-to-life performances

- explain thoroughly to your administrator what you are planning to do and the brain research behind it; also explain how you will communicate your approach to parents

- explain thoroughly to parents what you are planning to do before you begin. Give them plenty of examples from the real world by way of explanation; also give them examples of assessment that they can use at home to give feedback to their child using authentic assessment standards

- demystify assessment; know that the more real life the application of knowledge and skills, the more readily students can judge for themselves if they "got it" or not and thus judge their own progress toward mastery. This is true also for parents (and for teachers and administrators!)

CHAPTER TEN

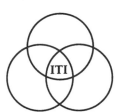

CURRICULUM: WHAT'S WORTH LEARNING?

The gray-haired and slowly-grown-wise among us have observed that the curriculum reforms of the eighties were an exercise in much ado about nothing. We struggled and struggled to pull education up by its bootstraps by rewriting curriculum in order to build in higher expectations and greater rigor and all things good. But our struggles produced little if no change in what students take with them when they leave our schools. Student outcomes in 1994 are no better than in 1984 or 1974. If anything, the crisis in education has deepened. So why should ITI focus on curriculum?

Simply put, what a teacher aims to teach greatly prescribes and circumscribes how he/she goes about it. Such a statement should not surprise us: architects the world over (even designers of Chrysler automobiles!) accept, as a basic tenet, that function follows form. How we teach is a function of what the system asks us to teach. Rewriting the same curriculum content to meet higher expectations or changing the scheduling of the high school day from departmentalized classes to core offerings produces as little change as pouring old wine into new containers or rearranging the deck chairs on the Titanic. In the end, the wine leaves a bad taste in one's mouth and most of the passengers drown.

In like manner, Integrated Thematic Instruction based upon *traditional curriculum* will not work. I repeat, will not work. It will not produce significantly improved results for students. Not because the teacher somehow failed in his/her implementation of ITI and not because of some undetected flaw in the ITI model but rather, because our centuries-old curriculum is inherently brain-antagonistic and, thus, an inappropriate tool for both teacher and learner. Therefore, while 80 percent of the ITI model is its brain research base and its implementation through the eight brain-compatible elements, the 20 percent that is about curriculum is crucial; we must work to make content meaningful to our learners. And making curriculum brain-compatible requires new tools.

WHAT IS BRAIN-COMPATIBLE CURRICULUM?

Curriculum that is brain-compatible enhances the learners' pattern-seeking and program-building capabilities, i.e., their ability to *make meaning* (part one of the learning process) and to *use* what they understand in real world situations and retain what they learn (part two of the learning process). Having read chapters 3, 5, and 8, the reader will recognize that *pattern-seeking* and *program-building* have very specific meaning here. The reader will also recognize that the need for curriculum to enhance pattern-seeking and program-building is itself a criterion for judging the adequacy of the curriculum given to teachers by their district.

Characteristics of Brain-Compatible Curriculum Tools

Curriculum that is brain-compatible meets the following criteria as explained on pages 128-130:

- It is *locally based* and invites the teacher to select a physical location, easily visitable, upon which to base instruction.
- It *provides a rationale*—a why—for teaching the content and explains what one hopes to accomplish by teaching it.
- It *clarifies* what it isn't and what it does not intend.
- *Content is stated as concepts*—giant patterns from which significant key points can be easily derived and molded to best fit a teacher's particular group of students and their prior knowledge. Because the statements are conceptual in nature rather than factoid, and thus rich in pattern-detecting

potential, *pattern-seeking is built in naturally* and easily for both teachers and students.

- *One is not left to one's own devices* to come up with what's important to know yet there is real flexibility in making the best possible fit with specific students, their prior experience and knowledge, interests, etc.
- *A picture of "so what?"* is provided. What would it look like if students learned this well and were able to use what they had learned?
- *Hooks for integrating* other content areas are built in— California history with science as well as math and language.

In contrast, and quite brain-antagonistic, the district-adopted curriculum in many districts is the table of contents of its adopted texts. The question then is to what extent does the current textbook series assist students to extract pattern/meaning from its pages? Most textbooks earn an *F* because they are sterile presentations which, among many things, greatly restrict input (thus limiting ability to perceive pattern) and offer few opportunities to practice applying what is presented in real world ways in order to build useful programs. Even the best of textbook series, with extended lessons and multiple books, etc., are an inadequate curricular tool from which to teach.

Strings of "the student will. . ." statements fare no better as curriculum tools for teachers because they are usually mere distillations from textbook outlines and other traditional listings of facts to be learned. Nor do the statements, "Do your own thing," or, "Follow your intuitions," rate well if brain-compatibility is the goal. The simple one-page description of K-6 curriculum, even if conceptually based is insufficient; it fails to provide teachers with needed background information.

What is needed is a thoughtful expression of what is important for students to know—a continuum of concepts—provided by the district and coupled with classroom-developed opportunities for students to apply what they are learning to real-life situations.

CHAPTER 10: CURRICULUM

New Tools for Creating Brain-Compatible Curriculum

In my own classroom days and later, while working in gifted education across the country, I considered both the what and how of curriculum development to be the job of the teacher. Today I know that that is neither realistic nor desirable. It isn't realistic because the task is too big to be accomplished by individual teachers snatching a few minutes here and there, working off a generalist's knowledge base. It is not desirable for students because schoolwide agreement needs to be reached about what all students are to learn as they deserve a coherent program from year to year, one without repetition of favorite topics (e.g., years of dinosaurs) and bereft of others (physical science).

Today I am convinced that it is the job of the district—and perhaps a district's most important job—to provide brain-compatible curriculum tools for teachers. This statement somewhat surprises me because my opinion of district "scope and sequences" has never been very high. As a teacher, I always considered them something less than useful, an often silly mix of the profound and the inconsequential (as if all were equally important and useful), and incredibly stifling; like so many teachers, I tended to ignore them. Today we need a new view of curriculum and curriculum development, a tool for leading and supporting teachers not for controlling them. Tools to enhance their curriculum and daily lesson planning efforts, not confound them.

So what would brain-compatible *curriculum tools* at the district level look like? Following is an example of brain-compatible curriculum, part of a K-6 Continuum of Concepts developed by the Mid-California Science Improvement Program, a seven year, $3 million effort funded by the David and Lucile Packard Foundation. Written for teachers teaching fourth grade, it gives guidance and support without strangling or insulting teachers. It is instructive without being pedantic. Its concepts can easily be crafted into significant key points for students.

Mid-California Science Improvement Program
SCIENCE CONTINUUM OF CONCEPTS
FOURTH GRADE[1] —Draft

MAIN SCIENCE IDEA: Plants and animals interact with each other and their environment in ways that allow them to meet their basic needs. Keep in mind that humans are animals.

RATIONALE: The goal here is to give students many opportunities to investigate the interaction of plants and animals and their environment so that they can construct for themselves the concepts of habitat, food chain, and the impact of weather and terrain (landforms) as a basis for understanding the many issues of ecology which they will face in the polling booth and their personal lives. What we wish to eliminate is the teaching of ecology as "preaching about" or object lessons in "good versus evil" without a firm scientific understanding of what actually occurs. We believe a scientific understanding is essential preparation for citizenship.

KEY CONCEPTS TO BE LEARNED:

- Within a habitat, the resident plants and animals interact with other plants and animals and the environment in ways that allow each to meet its basic needs of food, water, sunlight, shelter, and reproduction.

- Interactions to meet the need for food are called "food chain." Food preferences can usually be predicted based upon the physical characteristics of the plant or animal (refer to second grade curriculum) and can be categorized as carnivorous, herbivorous, and omnivorous. Food chains are significantly and often disastrously disrupted by human activities, including pollution.

- Interactions to meet the need for potable water involve the food chain, weather, terrain, and human interventions, like pollution.

- The weather (climate: temperature ranges, amount and frequency of precipitation, and amount of sunlight) and terrain (landforms and soil) significantly shape a habitat. Ability to survive in a particular climate and terrain can often be predicted based on the physical characteristics of the animal or plant (refer to second grade curriculum).

- Weather and terrain determine availability of needed shelter and food.
- The reproductive process of some plants and animals is extremely dependent upon other plants and animals; a species may completely die out without this needed plant or animal. Others rely on constants such as wind with no interaction of other species and are thus considered very hardy. Those relying on interaction of other species are highly at risk when humans intervene in the environment. Essential factors in reproduction are extremely varied and quite fascinating.
- Chemicals used in our area by business and people in their personal daily lives have polluted the environment, disrupting the food chain and reproductive cycle of many plants and animals in our area. The chemicals involved in the most pervasive pollution problems in our area are:_____.

  Where do they come from, what was their intended use(s), how did they get out of hand, how are they carried into and through the environment, what is their effect on plants and animals, including humans. How would this problem vary if the climate and terrain of our area were different?
- Humans have adapted their environment to meet their needs primarily through the use of machines. Machines make work easier. Forms of simple machines used in 1850 for transforming California were (wheel) the wagon, water-powered mills; (lever) crow bars, wagon jack; (inclined plane) gang planks, ramps of all kinds, conveyor belts, (screw) drill bits, presses, rock stampers; and (pulley) hay and meat lifters, etc. Today's version of these machines include:_____.
- Machines allow us to apply force (push or pull) objects to move them. Motion is the act of changing place or position, usually measured in distance and time. (Bring gold rush era machines to the classroom to demonstrate force and motion.)

The best approach to teaching the previously mentioned issues is through numerous "being there" experiences in varying ecosystems. Begin locally—the school grounds, a richly landscaped neighbor's yard, a nearby creek or park, Pacific Grove tide pools, Elkhorn Slough, and Point Lobos.

Remember that the purpose of starting locally is to provide real world, "being there" experiences for students, thus allowing rich input for pattern-seeking and meaning-making. This shifts the burden of teaching from "talking about" to exploration, thus making pattern-identification, transfer of learning, and program-building for long term memory more likely. When possible, sequence the study of your locations to coincide with the locations students are studying in history/social studies.

Introduce a range of observational techniques such as the 1" x 1" grid; comparisons below, on, and above the ground; pick a tree (and graph all observable residents), etc. (A good resource for framing observations is *Science Is . . .: A Source Book of Fascinating Facts, Projects, and Activities* by Susan V. Bosak.)

EXPECTED PERFORMANCE LEVELS FOR STUDENTS:

- Using the ecosystem of your area, compare and contrast the food chain needed to support the most common carnivore, herbivore, and omnivore in your area. Describe how that food chain has altered in the past twenty years and why. Select two other ecosystems found in California and do the same analysis. You may depict your findings as an essay, diorama, picture, or graph.

- Describe the major weather and terrain of your area and of two other locations in California that you choose. Make a legend for each; describe how weather and terrain determine what plants and animals live there. Describe how the landforms also influenced European migration into California—how people came, where they settled, and what they did to survive.

- In less than 150 years, from the gold rush of 1849 to 1994, humans have transformed terrain and, in many areas, altered the weather. Illustrate three machines from the mid-1800s, two from the turn of the century, and two from the 1990s which you feel have made the greatest impact on terrain and the weather. Explain why you think so. Are these machines, or their derivatives, still used today? Do we use them for the same purposes, have we changed how/when/where we use them?

*See order form at the back of this book

CHAPTER 10: CURRICULUM

The previous continuum of concepts illustrates several important features of curriculum which are brain-compatible for students and teachers. It is a good example of curriculum tools that districts should provide for their teachers.

Locally-based curriculum—Creating locally-based curriculum is the only way to deliver on education's goal of preparing children for success in life as compared to success in later schooling. While the skills and knowledge to success in later life are adequate to the task of succeeding in later schooling, the reverse is not true. Thus, I believe that I must give children the ability to understand and act upon the real world around them. That is possible only if we base our curriculum in locations which are readily visitable on a regular basis.

Provides a rationale—Teachers need to know why they teach what they teach, the why for the children and the why for them. Out of all the information that could be included in curriculum, why these things and not those? And what should the end result be? Not in terms of a multiple choice or true-false test, but in terms of mental programs that can be applied to the real world. What level of power do we expect children to possess in handling themselves and their world (and ours)?

Clarifies what the curriculum is and isn't—What is in the curriculum and what isn't; what is intended and what not? Such clarifications are needed if teachers are to leave behind the old pictures of curriculum and the old favorite units ("But I've always done pioneers"). And such statements cannot be couched in code or educationese; they must also speak clearly to parents.

Content is stated as concepts and, thus, pattern-seeking is built in naturally—This is at the heart of brain-compatible curriculum. No more factoids. They are too small to provide a sense of pattern. No more "the student will" statements which can be performed from rote memory, no more simplified content which distorts the real meaning and is so piecemeal and divorced from its real context that students see no connection to the real world.

Brain-compatible curriculum is curriculum that provides teachers tangible direction but allows him/her to sculpt and mold it to meet the particular needs of this year's crop of students. For example, the second concept in the continuum of concepts for fourth grade, (page 125), is a gold mine of patterns. Depending on the prior experiences and background knowledge of this year's students, I would develop anywhere from a dozen to three or four key points.

For inner city students with little or no *being there* experience with nature-based habitats, my first key point would be about chains, their attributes and "chain" metaphors in our language (a chain is only as strong as its weakest link, the chain of events ended in predictable outcomes, etc.). I would bring in a real chain, have students bring in chains that they see used in their world, and have students make chains. I would then have them label their chain using a sequence of events they currently experience and understand. Next, I would start a chain sequence of events that they have experienced but one for which they may not have verbalized the connections, incorporating examples from what they are studying in history/social studies.

Once the pattern called "chain" has become rich and powerful, students would be ready to apply it in situations with which they have limited experience and knowledge such as the food chain in the wilds. Again, the usefulness and power of patterns is that they help us generalize and predict.

My next key point and inquiries would be about the physical characteristics of plants and animals in order to assess whether the students had mental programs for carnivore, herbivore, and omnivore food relationships that were part of the second grade curriculum. If not, I would develop a number of key points about these kinds of animals before going back to the concept of food chain.

Considerable program-building about the food chain would need to be in place before launching into key points about how, where, and when human activities have disrupted food chains, and to what degree.

CHAPTER 10: CURRICULUM

For advantaged children who possess much firsthand experience with and knowledge of nature-based habitats, this concept might be conveyed with only one or two key points, fewer inquiries, and in much less time.

One is not left to one's own devices. I do not believe that just because curriculum is developed by a classroom teacher it is necessarily better than that written by textbook publishers. It is only if it is. And teacher-developed curriculum, like that produced by publishing companies, is only as good as its source. Starting with traditional curriculum and/or a generalist's knowledge bank is not adequate to the task. Consequently, it is my belief that the task of creating brain-compatible curriculum development tools for teachers is a job to be done at the district level.

A picture of "so what?"—Brain-compatible curriculum should provide clear descriptions of what students should be able to do in the real world if they had truly developed mental programs for using the key points. Whether you call this "authentic assessment," or a well-crafted inquiry (see Chapter 13), the curriculum should provide clear pictures of expected performances that would be accepted by teacher, administration, parents, and students as proof of mastery.

The proof of good curriculum is in what students walk away with. In fact, curriculum should be defined not as what is contained in a district scope and sequence or even what the teacher taught but rather as what students can do when they leave the classroom.

Hooks for integrating—Powerful concepts are seldom limited to the field that generates them. Most are useful in other areas, many have infiltrated our language and show up in everyday speech such as the chain metaphor. Curriculum becomes a useful tool for teachers when it has hooks for snagging pieces of real life and bridging old, artificial barriers between traditional subject matter areas.

WHY CURRICULUM?

THE BOTTOM LINE: WHY CURRICULUM?

A discussion of curriculum is not complete without reiterating why . . . why is curriculum important? As a teacher, curriculum is not a discussion of abstractions or a handing down of the traditional. Curriculum is at the heart of why we do what we do as teachers and what we leave as our legacy to the next generation. The purpose of ITI is to create contributing members of a democratic society by providing the opportunities and the practice that results in learning the personal and social skills for solving problems, in recognizing the need for participation by everyone in decisions that affect everyone, and in accepting responsibility for taking action, personally and as a member of society.*

A WARNING TO ALL:

Lest history repeat itself, we must take note of the fact that it is not only the curriculum that must be transformed. Designing brain-compatible curriculum is a complete waste of time if the classroom environment and instructional strategies are not brain-compatible. In other words, 80 percent of the power of the ITI model comes from its brain-compatible base which must be in place before curriculum can play its proper role in the classroom.

To underscore this critical point, we developed the ITI Rubric which provides a roadmap for your journey into ITI. Level 1 of the rubric is described as the entry level into a brain-compatible environment. Level 2 is the entry level into brain-compatible curriculum. Further, the reader is admonished not to apply Level 2, curriculum, until Level 1, brain-compatible environment, is firmly in place.

---

* I heartily recommend that you read *Renewing America's Schools: A Guide for School-Based Action* by Carl D. Glickman, the 1994 Kovalik Gold Medal winner for best ITI teacher resource.

CHAPTER 10: CURRICULUM

THE ITI RUBRIC

The ITI rubric is designed to serve two purposes. First and foremost, it paints clear pictures of what ITI looks like, sounds like, and feels like in the classroom and schoolwide, from both teacher and student perspectives, throughout the journey toward full implementation. The rubric is developmental and without time frames and, thus, points toward priorities and goals for implementing ITI from beginning efforts to full and powerful implementation for students.

Second, it is a tool for assessing progress toward full implementation the ITI model, individually and collectively. Areas examined are curriculum, instructional strategies, expected results, and indicators by which to assess expected results. The descriptors of expected results are not written to describe pie in the sky; they are consistent with results now achieved in ITI classrooms.

Please note that the stages are cumulative rather than shopping list in nature, i.e., *all* criteria of stages one and two must be true before one begins to implement/apply later stages. This underscores the message that 80 percent of the power of the ITI model comes from its brain-compatible base and only 20% from its integrated theme and curriculum. Thus, jumping ahead to implementing more minutes per day of ITI curriculum before Stages 1 and 2 are firmly in place is unwise because attempts to move forward without a solid brain-compatible base produce little real improvement for students.

When using the rubric, be aware that some stages apply to the entire day, others only to that time of the day, week, or month that the teacher is implementing his/her brain-compatible curriculum. Also, because Stages 4 and 5 apply schoolwide, they are useful for assessing the underpinnings necessary to effect significant systemic restructuring as well as progress in a single classroom.

We hope you find the rubric useful. As you travel its highways and byways, be assured that there are thousands of fellow teachers across the country, Canada, and Slovakia journeying with you.

ITI RUBRIC STAGE 0

STAGE 0 — Traditional means and ends

CURRICULUM	INSTRUCTIONAL STRAT	EXPECTATIONS	INDICATORS
Subject areas and specific skills are taught in isolation.	The classroom is textbook and lecture driven.	Students are teacher-dependent.	Standardized tests and other paper and pencil tests graded on the bell curve are the primary means of assessment.
Curriculum is textbook driven and teacher centered.	Students sit in rows; there is little collaboration; students are unfocused and mental fibrillation is apparent.	Students do not understand the interrelationships among concepts common to various subject areas.	
Social development and interaction is based on external rewards and consequences.	Environments are sterile and/or cluttered with competing colors/patterns and old materials.	Students do not see connections between school and real life.	

133

ITI RUBRIC STAGE 1

STAGE 1 — Entry level for making the learning environment brain-compatible

CURRICULUM	INSTRUCTIONAL STRATEGIES	EXPECTATIONS	INDICATORS
The elements of absence of threat are taught as an important and on-going part of the curriculum: Lifelong Guidelines, including the LIFESKILLS, the triune brain, problem-solving and product-producing using the seven intelligences, and collaboration.	The teacher's classroom leadership and management is based upon modeling the Lifelong Guidelines and LIFESKILLS. "Discipline" is based upon helping students develop personal skills and behaviors needed to successfully practice the Lifelong Guidelines rather than upon a system of externally imposed rewards and punishments.	Absence of threat has been established in the classroom. Students are beginning to take responsibility for their own behavior through the use of LIFESKILLS.	Post-lesson processing about academic or collaborative experiences occurs daily. Decline in classroom and school-wide discipline problems.
	The calmness of the teacher's voice contributes to a settled classroom environment.	An atmosphere of mutual respect and genuine caring is obvious among and between students and adults. Students do not put each other down; their behaviors with each other support absence of threat.	Differences in student engagement when real life experiences are provided are obvious to teacher and parents.
	The classroom is healthful (clean, well lighted, and pleasant smelling), aesthetically pleasing (calming colors and music, living plants, well laid out for multiple uses), and uncluttered yet reflects what is being learned.	Students demonstrate collaborative skills, e.g., active listening, taking turns, and respect for other's opinions.	Teacher includes student input when selecting work for the student's portfolio folder.
	Written procedures and agendas provide consistency and security for students.	Students focus their attention on learning as soon as they enter the classroom.	
Time frames for activities and areas of study are no longer rigid and students are given adequate time to complete their work.	Students sit in clusters with easy access to work tools; collaborative learning is a frequently used learning strategy. Teacher is developing a variety of instructional strategies to supplement direct instruction.	Lack of self-directedness and responsibility for learning has been replaced by a student focus on school as a safe and pleasant place to learn and grow; there is a growing sense of calm and openness.	
	Teacher includes real life experiences—being there, immersion, and hands-on experiences—to supplement classroom instruction; resource people are invited to the classroom.	Parents understand the purpose and research behind brain-compatible education and are supportive of the teacher's efforts.	
	Limited choices are introduced through student selection of supplies, time allocations, mediums used for completing projects, etc.	Parents notice evidence of LIFESKILLS at home.	
	Teacher meets frequently with a professional or peer coach who supports the implementation of a brain-compatible learning environment for students.	Teacher confidence and enjoyment in teaching increases.	

ITI RUBRIC STAGE 2

STAGE 2 — Entry level for making curriculum brain-compatible

The beginning steps in making curriculum brain-compatible assume that significant progress has been made implementing Stage 1, making the learning environment brain-compatible.

Whereas rubric Stage 1 is applied to the classroom 100 percent of the time, rubric Stage 2 is applied only to that portion of the day, week, or year for which teachers have developed brain-compatible curriculum using the ITI model. The time frames and content that teachers may select to begin implementation of their brain-compatible curriculum vary widely. Typically teachers begin where they feel they will be most successful and stretch from there. Whatever the starting point, however modest or bold, the rubric at this stage applies only during the time when a teacher is implementing his/her brain-compatible curriculum.

CURRICULUM	INSTRUCTIONAL STRATEGIES	EXPECTATIONS	INDICATORS
Teacher provides for real-life experiences by basing the integrated curriculum upon a physical location, event, or situation that students can and do frequently experience through "being there." Science is either the core for or a prominent part of the curriculum integration.	Immersion and hands-on-of-the-real-thing are the primary input used to supplement and extend being there experiences.	Students participate actively, initiating ideas, responding to teacher's questions, staying on task with minimal guidance from the teacher.	Post-lesson processing about academic and social experiences.
Teacher has identified the concepts and skills which will be taught to mastery and application. Key points focus on critical concepts rather than isolated facts.	Instructional strategies are varied and provide the most effective methods for the particular content at hand: direct instruction, ITI discovery process; collaboration, personal study time; mindmapping; organizing materials; cross-age/multi-age interaction, etc.	Students see the connections between the classroom and real life.	Use of selected inquiries to assess mastery of key point, e.g., projects, presentations, and some traditional tests.
Inquiries for each key point provide students choices, multiple opportunities for real world application, and allow for multiple ways of problem-solving and product-producing.	Resources to support the theme are multiple, varied, and rich. Resource people and experts are regular visitors to the classroom and off-campus learning sites.	Mental fibrillation has been replaced by a sense of calm, relaxed alertness, confidence in success in learning, and purposefulness.	Teacher and student select work for the student's portfolio folder.
	Choices are regularly provided through inquiries and other means.	School as a place to learn and exercise one's personal best is the accepted norm.	Assessment of mastery is based upon the 3 C's of Assessment.
The curriculum includes most of the elements which appear as a natural part or extension of the being there focus, e.g., science, math, technology, history/social studies, fine arts, as well as reading, writing, and oral expression. Integration of content is natural, not contrived.	Adequate time is allowed to let students complete their work.	Absentee rates are dropping, library checkout rates are increasing.	
	There are sufficient inquiries for students to complete to ensure mastery and development of mental programs for using the knowledge/skills of the key points.	Students engage in problem-solving in a collaborative manner at least once a day.	
Content is age-appropriate.	Collaboration is effectively used and enhances learning for academic and social growth.		

135

ITI RUBRIC STAGE 3

STAGE 3 —

Stage 3 assumes that a brain-compatible learning environment has been established and is consistently nurtured and maintained (Stage 1) and that the tools for developing brain-compatible curriculum are consistently and effectively used (Stage 2). Stage 3 represents a refinement of those tools and a consistent implementation of brain-compatible curriculum for students, i.e., at least 25 percent of the time during the school year. If either Stages 1 or 2 is not fully in place at this time, do not attempt to apply this rubric stage regardless of the amount of teacher-developed curriculum being implemented. It is the quality, not the quantity, of teacher-developed curriculum that is key. The power of the ITI model lies with its brain-compatible underpinnings.

CURRICULUM	INSTRUCTIONAL STRATEGIES	EXPECTATIONS	INDICATORS
A yearlong theme, prominently displayed on the wall for both students and teacher, serves as the framework for content development. On average, more than 25 percent of instruction during the school year is based upon brain-compatible curriculum developed for this theme.	Immersion and hands-on-of-the-real-thing are the primary input used to supplement and extend being there experiences.	Students demonstrate LIFESKILLS throughout the day (in and out of the classroom); students are self-directed.	Celebrations of learning and social/political action are key assessment tools for each component; they are designed to allow students to demonstrate mastery and application of the key points in the curriculum.
Curriculum content, as expressed in the key points, enhances pattern-seeking, making it easy for students to perceive and understand the most important ideas and concepts in the curriculum; inquiries are designed to help students make connections to the real world and to develop mental programs for long-term memory.	All instructional time during the theme and for a growing portion of time during traditional instruction is based upon the progression of "being there > concept > language > application to the real world" rather than the traditional "language > concept . . . application."	Students as well as the teacher use the 3 C's of Assessment as a means of assessing learning.

Students exercise more shared leadership while doing collaborative activities and actively seek connections to and applications in the real world. | |
| Most of the time, the curriculum includes almost all of the elements which appear as a natural part or extension of the being there focus, e.g., science, math, technology, history/social studies, fine arts, as well as reading, writing, and oral expression, including second language acquisition. | Collaboration is used daily whenever it will enhance pattern-seeking and program building.

Time is allocated in accordance with the nature of the tasks and student and teacher need for adequate time; such time allocations are made in recognition of the need to develop mental programs for using knowledge and skills in real world contexts. | Student absentee rates drop to less than 3 percent; visits to the school nurse due to emotional upset-based problems drop significantly. Library circulation rates increase by 50 percent.

Parents report student levels of interest in school and learning as being higher than ever before. Parents' support levels are higher than ever before; volunteerism has doubled. | Selections, for the portfolio folder, of work completed as part of the theme is selected primarily by the student. |
| The content of the theme is consistently used as a high interest area for applying the skills/knowledge currently being taught in at least one basic skill area (e.g., math, reading, writing).

Curriculum for collaborative assignments is specifically designed for group work. | Peers and cross-age tutors substantially increase teaching and practice time for students in areas of individual need. | | |

ITI RUBRIC STAGE 4

STAGE 4

Stage 4 assumes that a brain-compatible learning environment has been established (Stage 1) and that the tools for developing brain-compatible curriculum as described in Stages 2 and 3 are fully in place. Stage 4 represents a further refinement and extension of those tools and a consistent implementation of brain-compatible curriculum for students, i.e., at least 50 percent of the time during the school year. If Stages 1, 2, and 3 are not fully in place, do not attempt to apply this rubric stage regardless of the amount of time teacher-developed curriculum is being implemented. Again, the power of the ITI model lies with its brain-compatible underpinnings.

CURRICULUM	INSTRUCTIONAL STRATEGIES	EXPECTATIONS	INDICATORS
Curriculum is based predominantly on visitable locations which provide being there experiences and connections with the real world.	Learning experiences are predominantly based on real life, immersion, and hands-on of the real thing; the teacher regularly utilizes explorations and discovery processes to make learning real for students.	All students master the key points in all content and basic skill areas.	Except for district-required assessments, grading on the bell curve has been replaced with assessment of mastery and program-building demonstrated by culminating performances chosen by the teacher (using selected inquiries and the 3 C's of assessment).
The yearlong theme includes a rationale statement and conceptual idea which provide an unforgettable pattern-shaper. On average, more than 50 percent of instruction during the school year is based upon brain-compatible curriculum developed for this yearlong theme.	All instructional time during the theme and for a growing portion of time during traditional instruction is based upon the progression of "being there > concept > language > application to the real world" rather than the traditional "language > concept . . . application."	Students demonstrate responsibility for their learning and act in a self-directed, self-initiating manner throughout the day; they have internalized the Lifelong Guidelines, including LIFESKILLS, and use them as the basis for interacting with others off campus as well as in the classroom and school.	Students' yearlong research projects reflect high interest and understanding.
The content of the theme is used daily as meaningful content for teaching *at least one* area of basic skills (e.g., math, reading, writing, oral expression, second and primary language acquisition) and is used for applying *all* the basic skills.	Basic skills taught within the theme are taught as a means to an end, not as an end in themselves. Thus, while the teacher utilizes specific techniques for teaching the basic skills on a daily basis, such as Early Effective Teaching, the primary focus of students is on meaningful content which the basic skills help the student unlock.	Students use what they learn in school to creatively solve real-life problems.	Guest resource people acknowledge the high degree of student understanding.
	The teacher takes advantage of the power of "incidental learning" (as defined by Frank Smith) to build mental programs applying the basic skills.	Student absentee rates drop to less than 1.5 percent; visits to the school nurse are for serious physical illness, none for emotional upset.	The class newspaper or magazine, published at least twice a year, reflects writing skills at least one year above grade level.
	Choices, to allow for individual students' ways of learning, interests, and needs, are consistently provided for.	Library circulation rates are double those before the implementation of brain-compatible/ITI learning.	Students, having learned to assess their own learning, participate in parent-teacher conferences, describing how selections of their work demonstrate their progress (academic, personal, and social) and their goals for learning during the next component/quarter.
	Students use technology as a natural extension of their senses to explore and learn.	Students who have experienced a consistent brain-compatible program for three years or more perform at grade level. The average for the classroom is at least one grade level above national norms.	

© Susan Kovalik & Associates, 1994

137

ITI RUBRIC STAGE 5

STAGE 5

Like Stages 3 and 4, Stage 5 assumes that a brain-compatible learning environment has been established (Stage 1), and is being maintained, and that the tools for developing brain-compatible curriculum are in place and are highly refined as described in Stages 3 and 4. Stage 5 represents an extension of those tools and a consistent implementation of brain-compatible curriculum for students 100 percent of the time during the school year. If either Stage 1 or 2 is not fully in place and consistently nurtured and maintained or Stages 3 and 4 are not in place, do not attempt to apply this rubric stage. Again, the power of the ITI model lies with its brain-compatible underpinnings.

CURRICULUM	INSTRUCTIONAL STRAT.	EXPECTATIONS	INDICATORS
The yearlong theme serves as the framework for content development and implementation for all basic skills and content 95 percent of the day/year. Key points and inquiries effectively enhance pattern-seeking and program-building.	All instructional strategies identified in Levels 1 through 4 are in place 95 percent of the day/year.	Self-responsibility for and self-initiated engagement in learning are valued schoolwide and clearly evident. Students display a love of learning and keen curiosity; they are mastering the skills and attitudes for lifelong learning.	Parent-teacher conferences have become student-parent-teacher conferences that, in the upper grades, are led by the student.
	Students have the same teacher two or more years (either due to multi-aging or the teacher moving with the students).		
The curriculum of the district, upon which there is both school- and district-wide agreement, provides each teacher with pattern-enhancing tools for curriculum planning.	Teacher utilizes the power of incidental learning during both planned instructional strategies and the unplanned teachable moments.	Students direct their own learning by assisting in the development of inquiries, refinement of key points. They can identify and know how to pursue lifelong interests and career options, and in focusing their efforts, they can apply what they know to real world situations.	Students initiate and engage in a wide range of community volunteer tasks, social and political action projects, and other means of contributing to society.
Brain-compatible curriculum is implemented schoolwide, providing consistency for students as they move through the school.	Technology in the classroom allows teacher and students full access to databases and communications systems throughout the country. Being there experiences are fully extended to locations/situations around the world as age-appropriate to the students.	Students have learned the personal and social skills for solving problems. They recognize the need for everyone's participation when making decisions that affect all.	

Acknowledgments:

Developed by Susan Kovalik & Associates with the indispensable assistance of the coaches and mentors of the Mid-California Science Improvement Program (MCSIP) and Jeanne Herrick, Alisal Elementary District, Coordinator of Bilingual Education and Restructuring, all of whom built upon the pioneering work of Vickie Hogan (ITI Coach), Jackie Munoz (Restructuring Coordinator) from Frank Paul School, Alisal Elementary School District and Dr. Victoria Bernhardt, Education for the Future, a project of Pacific Telesis.

Our thanks to these pioneers whose vision and perseverance have given birth to a new generation of tools for self- and program assessment.

CHAPTER ELEVEN

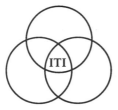

DEVELOPING CURRICULUM: CREATING A YEARLONG THEME

The primary goal when developing curriculum is to enhance pattern-seeking and program building. In the ITI model, pattern-seeking is enhanced through the use of a year-long theme, as explained in this chapter, and through key points (see Chapter 12). Program-building occurs through inquiries (see Chapter 13).

The yearlong theme is a context within which both student and teacher can use, store, and retrieve information. This and the following two chapters provide a step-by-step description of how to develop curriculum to implement the ITI model.

The three stages in creating curriculum for the class-room are:

Stage 1   **Creating a yearlong theme with monthly components and weekly topics**

Stage 2   **Identifying key points which all students are to learn (Chapter 12)**

Stage 3   **Developing inquiries and activities which allow students to understand and apply the concepts/skills of the key points (Chapter 13)**

CHAPTER 11: CREATING A THEME

The yearlong theme is a cognitive structure which facilitates pattern identification and recognition of interrelationships among ideas, theories, events, and objects. It serves several important functions:

- for students, it is a powerful tool, enhancing their capacity to more effectively process, store, and retrieve what is learned, to anticipate what comes next, and to generalize to other situations

- for the teacher, it serves as an organizer for curriculum building and material gathering throughout the year, providing a thread that connects one month to the next as well as relating everything to the organizing concept for the entire year

- for both teacher and students, it establishes the game plan for the year, month, week, and day

A yearlong theme has three organizing structures:

1. the *theme*, consisting of the organizing concepts, rationale, and kid-grabbing title
2. monthly *components*
3. weekly *topics*

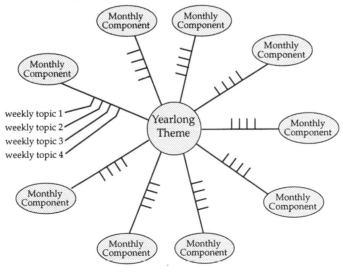

ITI CONSTRUCTION TERMINOLOGY

Creating a yearlong theme is not a linear, sequential thinking task nor is it a process of arranging a set number of given pieces. You will find yourself working on several steps simultaneously, circling back, and changing direction many times. There are, however, two prerequisites: 1) you must have scouted your school's environment for physical locations which provide the best *"being there"* experiences for teaching your curriculum content and 2) you must have reached some general agreements with yourself and fellow teachers regarding *what* your students are to learn at your grade level or levels.

Construction Terminology for Building an ITI Theme

YEAR THEME: A yearlong organizational structure consisting of the organizing concept (theme), with its kid-grabbing title, plus the rationale for the theme, monthly components, and weekly topics.

COMPONENTS: The physical locations and human issues (situations, events, happenings, contributions) experienceable by students (approximately one month in duration)

TOPICS: Aspects of the location or human issues to be studied (approximately one week)

KEY POINTS: Essential concepts, skills, knowledge, attitudes/values *all* students are to learn (expressed as a *pattern*)

INQUIRIES: Applications of the knowledge, skills, values/attitudes of the key point(s) being taught/learned (opportunities for developing *mental programs*)

THEME TITLE: A kid-grabbing vehicle that will lead teacher and students to a study of *here and now* curriculum

---

CHAPTER 11: CREATING A THEME

The steps in creating a yearlong theme are:

Step A: Determine your starting point for integrating

Step B: Rethink WHAT students are to learn; finalize your decisions as a school staff

Step C: Select the physical locations which will provide *being there* experiences for students and the human issues which best exemplify, or most powerfully convey, what you want students to learn (key points)

Step D: Identify your organizing concepts and rationale

Step E: Select monthly components and weekly topics

Step F: Dream a theme title that fires up the students (and teacher) with enthusiasm and imagination and provides a cognitive hook for the organizing concept and entire year's content and skills

STEP A: DETERMINE YOUR STARTING POINT FOR INTEGRATION

Full integration of all basic skills and content areas is a three to five year task. Do not try to do everything the first year. My advice to you is to focus on the experienceable world—science, particularly for primary students, and, for upper primary students, science and social studies.

Next, determine which of the basic skills you want to have students apply, such as oral language and writing or math. Lastly, decide when and what block of time you will devote to ITI during the coming year. I recommend that you select a 1 1/2- to 2–hour block to start.

STEP B: RETHINK WHAT TO LEARN

STEP B: RETHINK WHAT STUDENTS ARE TO LEARN

The content and structure of the curriculum is critical in creating a brain-compatible learning environment. You must be clear about what you want students to learn and be able to do. "Less is more," conceptual vs. factoid, and *here and now* are essential guidelines.

This is not an easy step because the weight of tradition drags heavily at our feet. The pictures evoked by the content of the traditional curriculum in no way resemble what students see out the windows of their classrooms. If the purpose of schooling is to help students understand their world, and I believe it is, then we must make drastic changes in our curriculum content.

If your district does not have a scope and sequence for the subject area you wish to include in your theme, or if it is so old and out of date that no one pays any attention to it, then you move immediately to base your content on the physical locations you have chosen.

If, however, your district does have a scope and sequence that it expects its teachers to take seriously, then you must work within its structure. Begin by analyzing it with several concepts in mind:

- "less is more." Like textbooks, scope and sequences typically have so much content at each grade level that it is impossible for teachers to cover it all; then, each teacher's selection of what to address results in a hit-and-miss, haphazard curriculum for students from year-to-year. In this situation, sit down with your colleagues and agree upon a few major topics students are to learn at each grade level or levels; the emphasis, then, can be mastery of those topics, not "covering" the material

- avoid the infamous spiral. There is so much repetition from year-to-year that it is possible for students to study the same areas three or four years running—and still not "get it" because of the pace and superficiality that accompany "covering" the material

- age-appropriateness. So much of our curriculum K-6 is age-inappropriate and a waste of time for students and teachers

Again, this issue of what is to be learned is absolutely vital to the success of your curriculum; yet, it is often out of the control of the teacher. However, your window of opportunity lies in the fact that textbooks and district curricula are typically overly stuffed. The culling process will allow you room to sculpt curriculum which lends itself to *here and now, being there* experiences and, thus, to helping students understand their world.

STEP C: SELECT PHYSICAL LOCATIONS AND HUMAN ISSUES

The most powerful *here and now* physical locations are those beyond the schoolyard. Whether your primary focus involves human issues or a science slant, the school and its immediate environs (10-20 minute walk, bike, or bus ride) usually provides the real world application needed to support your curriculum.

All events occur in time and space, including human issues. Context is half of the story and a powerful shaper of thoughts and actions. Select those human issues—situations, events, happenings, contributions—that are both central to what you want students to know and that can be powerfully framed by your available physical locations. Remember, there is no one "right way" to orchestrate curriculum; choose that which seems most effective and powerful for your students and you today, given what is happening within your classroom, the school, the community, the nation, and the world. Human events and issues, and their teachable moments, resemble a bat on the wing; they flit with speed and ever-shifting directions throughout our lives.

STEP D: IDENTIFY YOUR CONCEPT (THEME)
AND RATIONALE

This step in theme building requires holistic thinking, a look at the forest, not just the trees. Given the nature of the brain as a pattern-seeking device, this is the most important step. It is the step that builds power into your curriculum, ensuring that it "hangs together" and is worthy of the time and effort that both you and your students will invest in it.

Organizing Concept (Theme)

The organizing concept of the theme is the universally recognized big idea that is worthy of students' attention. It is something that you believe is critical for students to understand and be able to do, a notion that is big enough and conceptually powerful enough that it can hold and organize a welter of ideas and thoughts, not to mention examples and facts by the barrel.

Webster's Dictionary, defines concept as "a general notion . . . the formation in the mind of an image or idea . . . a recurring, unifying subject or idea, motif." This definition is useful for it points at two powerful qualities of the theme: first, given the brain is a pattern-seeking device, the theme is a general notion—big enough to reveal an important aspect of the real world, natural science or human action. Second, the concept is an idea which reoccurs in the world and marries other thoughts, ideas, and skills.

Examples of big ideas include systems, evolution, revolution, form and function, homeostasis, living/non-living, balance, beauty, change, courage, cycles, dependence, independence, interdependence, democracy, diversity, equality, equity, freedom, happiness, honesty, honor, cooperation, leadership, stability, necessity, justice, labor, law, liberty, imagination, celebration, life/death, time, responsibility, progress, power, truth, revolution, youth/aging, scarcity/abundance.

CHAPTER 11: CREATING A THEME

As the previous examples illustrate, concepts are generalized, reoccurring, and unifying ideas. They are not the details of curriculum. They are notions that, once understood, allow us to generalize in order to problem-solve the problems of today and tomorrow.

Theme as cognitive structure. How often have we heard an old song on the radio that snapped us out of the present and sent our minds zooming back through the years to a particular person, event, or location. And each time we hear that song, it evokes the same images—vivid in detail, unwavering in their clarity—impressed upon our brain through all 19 senses. Don't we wish that we could create such powerful "hooks" to pull up curriculum content from our classrooms! Well, we can. And the hook is the concept of the theme, the reoccurring idea or, more accurately, the omnipresent idea.

Why a yearlong theme? Many teachers have used month-long units before. Why change? Answer: To increase meaningfulness and ability to apply learnings in the real world. A yearlong theme is designed to allow students to acquire depth of knowledge. If information is to be meaningful and have flow it must have continuity and depth. A unifying focus with a purposeful plan is essential to capture the students' attention and propel them into life-long learning.

Concepts for a theme should be notions that children intuitively understand and that, therefore, work immediately to organize and integrate what children are learning. This brings up an important distinction between themes that work for ITI and many "themes" from subject matter content which may not work. The difference is point of origin. To work, themes must be concepts that students already understand and are enthusiastic about—starting points for the year. In contrast, some "themes" or "big ideas" such as scale, structure, and stability in science are ones which many students have little or no understanding of; they thus have little power to organize future content. **What is unknown at the beginning of the**

year serves as a poor cognitive organizer for students. By that we mean that if you have to teach the organizer, its attributes can't serve as a powerful cognitive tree upon which today's, next week's, and future learning can hang. For a theme to work, the knowledge of the concept and its attributes must already be fully and richly internalized. *The stuff of themes must come from students' experience and be solidly in place before you attempt to build upon it.*

"Themes" or "big ideas" which are foreign to children's prior experience are what students are *to end up with;* they are appropriate as end goals for teachers but do not work as an ITI theme for students. While they constitute *your* outcome goals, they **should not be the beginning** curriculum development organizers *for students.* In other words, a major ITI rule for curriculum development is that one should begin where the students are; give them lots of *being there* experiences from which they can distill the themes as "natural knowledge," not memorized stuff. New content should be provided to students in such ways that it can be integrated into students' existing worlds and the existing neural networks of their brains.

Theme as curriculum builder and materials organizer. If there is to be power in your curriculum, it must come from tapping the energies and curiosities of your students, freeing them of artificial fragmentations, and unleashing the awesome power of the brain when operating consistent with its design.

Once your theme flows outward to the monthly components and weekly topics, it begins to take on a life of its own. And, if you have taken care to make it reflective of the complexity of real life, you will begin to "see" your theme in day-to-day events, even the seemingly mundane. Just as the spoon collector visiting Europe easily identifies establishments selling spoons when you and I are completely oblivious to them, the existence of your theme will sensitize you and your students to perceive books, current events, billboards, newspaper articles, and happenings of all kinds, which are related to your theme. They will spring out at you as you walk by a bookstore or supermarket, drive down the highway, or chat with a friend on the telephone.

With a new compass heading, it then becomes possible to throw away the familiar, to pass up the "cutesy" and fun "hands-on" stuff (including holidays and dinosaurs!) if it doesn't directly contribute to your ITI theme. Instead, explore new ways to utilize the input of the real world. You will eventually hit upon a new set of criteria for judging curriculum content and teaching/learning materials. Be forewarned, at first it may not be comfortable. But, when your theme is "right," you'll know it. Suddenly, instead of resisting or eluding you, it will snuggle into your classroom, a perfect fit, a part of you. The results will be electrifying for your students; their feedback to you will be immediate.

The Rationale for Your Theme

The rationale is your explanation to yourself of why the organizing concept (theme) is so important to your students. For example, in the theme, "What Makes It Tick?," the organizing concept is "function and systems." The rationale, why these two concepts are vital to students, is the importance of understanding the impact of technology on everyday life. How do everyday things work? what are they connected to? how does this specific knowledge help us understand the larger world?, etc.

Do remember that the steps in creating a theme are not linear and sequential. You will repeatedly come back to your rationale and use it as a touchstone to assess your work. Ask yourself the questions: What's worth knowing? What is most important for me to teach my students?"

**STEP E: SELECTING MONTHLY COMPONENTS
           AND WEEKLY TOPICS**

The source of monthly* components and weekly* topics is, obviously, the organizing concept of the theme. They are then driven by the physical locations and the human issues you select as offering the

---

* Please note that "weekly" and "monthly" are only approximations.

best *being there* opportunities for students. The "rest of the story," so to speak, is filled in by your content decisions as a result of Step A.

Thinking It Through . . .
Tips on Developing Components and Topics

The thinking process for selecting monthly components and weekly topics is illustrated below.

Step one. Brainstorm! Brainstorm as many ideas as you can from your organizing concept (theme), your physical locations and human issues, and your sense of what you want students to learn and be able to do by the end of the year. Stretch yourself! This is the creative, playful part of curriculum development. The sky is not the limit, only your imagination is.

Step two. Research! Good curriculum simply cannot be written off the top of one's head. Gather together a wide variety of resource material. Start with an encyclopedia to give yourself a quick overview but don't stop with summary material; discover the world of trade books and primary sources. Develop a close working relationship with your local librarian. Show her your theme; ask her to make recommendations to you. Be sure your knowledge base is solid enough to be able to select the appropriate components and topics and, later, the most important key points.

Step three. Sit down with the following list of *pattern shapers.* Use them first to expand your brainstorming. Next, use them to help you to group and organize your brainstormed ideas.

Step four. Use the *pattern shapers* to help you make final decisions about what you will and will not include in your theme's monthly components and weekly topics. As you do so, keep in mind that the "cover the material" tradition will get in your way. Remember that you are selecting a few important content areas to be done well—to the level of full understanding and application, to the level of competence and therefore long-term memory.

CHAPTER 11: CREATING A THEME

This list of pattern shapers is only a beginning. The mind is, after all, a sophisticated pattern-seeking device; there are many pattern shapers in the real world from which to choose.

Pattern Shapers

1. a location from which a perspective is taken—e.g, ecologist, lumbermill owner, logger, spotted owl
2. a person or theory from which a perspective is taken
3. habitats
4. systems—e.g., transportation, communication, law, school
5. time chronology or event sequences (start from *here and now)*
6. familiar patterns—e.g., vegetables, flowers, underground animals, rocks, soil, grasses, weeds
7. backyard to universe—e.g., neighborhood, city, nation
8. structures—e.g., bridges, houses, coliseums, airports
9. famous, exciting explorations
10. classifications—e.g., mammals, reptiles, European, African
11. varied uses—e.g., recreation, trade, transportation
12. seriation—e.g., small to large, rough to smooth
13. famous people or groups of people
14. a happening (large or small) or major event
15. geography/region
16. comparisons, e.g., now/then, predator/prey
17. a wondering or question
18. a concept or a big idea—research/development, change
19. other . . .

STEP E: SELECTING COMPONENTS/TOPICS

How to Use *Pattern Shapers* When Selecting Monthly Components

When selecting monthly components for your theme, determine which *pattern shaper* is most consistent with the conceptual nature of the organizing concept (theme). That single *pattern shaper* will then be used to identify each and every monthly component so that there is continuity and flow from the central organizer for the year to each month. Keep in mind that the brain is a pattern-seeking device so do not switch horses in the middle of the stream. Once the child has the *pattern shaper* in mind, he/she can anticipate the next month's study and understand the relationship between what has already been learned and "where we're going next." The result is a cognitive structure which will hold the entire year's learnings.

The obviousness of the *pattern shaper* which connects the theme to the monthly components and the monthly components to each other is important. For example, for the yearlong theme, "The World From Where I Stand," in the following illustration, possible pattern shapers could have been #3, habitats; #7, backyard to universe; or #15, geography/region. For primary grades, the author chose *pattern shaper* #7, backyard to universe. The decision was made primarily on the *being there* locations available to the students.

For the upper grade theme illustrated on the next page, "What Makes It Tick?," possible pattern shapers were #4, systems; #5, time chronology or event sequence; or #17, a wondering. The *pattern shaper* #5, time chronology or event sequence was chosen because it was more concrete and memorable than systems or a wondering. The location of each monthly component was readily accessible to the students.

In each of the two themes previously discussed, the nature of the locations selected for frequent visitation strongly influences the teacher's choice of *pattern-shaper*. With the six themes on pages 152-157 built upon the Colorado River, anticipated science and history/social studies content also influence the teacher.

The following are possible yearlong themes using the Colorado River as a physical location. Which to choose? It depends upon the content areas one chooses to emphasize, the experiences and interests of students (and the teacher), and which locations students can readily visit. Critique each using the criteria for a yearlong theme.

Critique them using the criteria for a yearlong theme.

CONCEPT: Cause/Effect, Basic Needs, Balance, _____ , _____

PATTERN SHAPER: Perspective (through the eyes of:)

RATIONALE: Our actions are formed by our needs

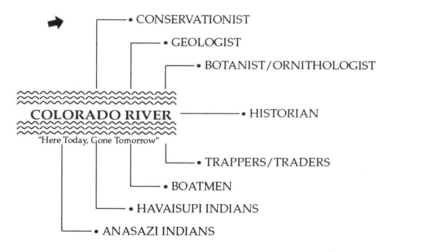

©1992 Susan Kovalik & Associates

Perspective Theme

Comments: Each of the above perspectives, with the exception of the extinct Anasazi tribe, have modern day counterparts as well as famous (and not so famous) personalities from years back. The perspective of the Anasazi would probably best be approached through interviewing people from a current group of Native Americans.

What pattern shaper would you use to develop the weekly topics for "Conservationist"? For "Historian"? For "Trappers/Traders"? For "Boatmen"?

STEP E: SELECTING COMPONENTS/TOPICS

CONCEPT: Stability_____ , _____ , _____
ORGANIZER: Varied Uses
RATIONALE: Water is necessary to sustain life

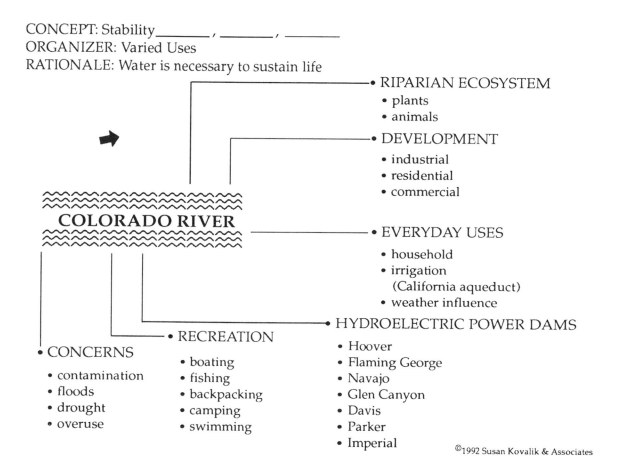

• RIPARIAN ECOSYSTEM
  • plants
  • animals

• DEVELOPMENT
  • industrial
  • residential
  • commercial

COLORADO RIVER

• EVERYDAY USES
  • household
  • irrigation
    (California aqueduct)
  • weather influence

• HYDROELECTRIC POWER DAMS

• RECREATION

• CONCERNS
  • contamination
  • floods
  • drought
  • overuse

  • boating
  • fishing
  • backpacking
  • camping
  • swimming

  • Hoover
  • Flaming George
  • Navajo
  • Glen Canyon
  • Davis
  • Parker
  • Imperial

©1992 Susan Kovalik & Associates

Varied Uses Theme

Comments: The pattern shaper for the year theme is varied uses. Identify the pattern shaper for each of the monthly components used to develop weekly topics.

CONCEPT: Cultural Diversity _____, _____ , _____
ORGANIZER: Familiar patterns
RATIONALE: The Colorado is but one of many rivers that have shaped our country

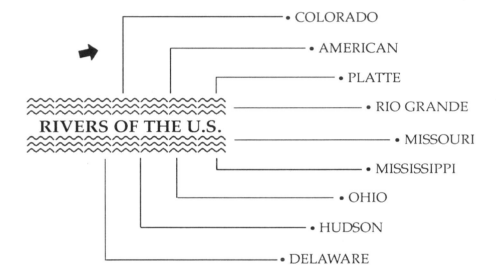

• COLORADO
• AMERICAN
• PLATTE
• RIO GRANDE
RIVERS OF THE U.S.
• MISSOURI
• MISSISSIPPI
• OHIO
• HUDSON
• DELAWARE

Familiar Patterns Theme

Comments: The pattern shaper for this theme, familiar pattern, uses the collection of attributes of settlement by rivers as a way to enable students to generalize and predict much of the history of the westward expansion rather than approach each wave as something unexplored and unknown, something to be learned from scratch.

STEP E: SELECTING COMPONENTS/TOPICS

CONCEPT: Ecology_____ , _____ , _____

ORGANIZER: Geography

RATIONALE: Communities form along the tributaries continuously altering the river

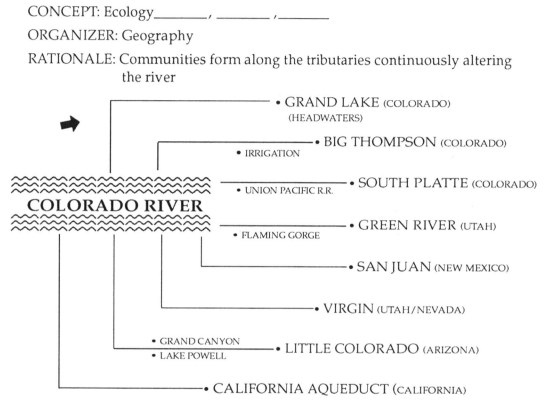

©1992 Susan Kovalik & Associates

Geography Theme

Comments: How can the mighty Colorado turn into a mere trickle? What pattern shapers would you use to develop the weekly topics for each of the monthly components?

CONCEPT: Survival _____ , _____ , _____

ORGANIZER: Native People

RATIONALE: Times change, people come and go—basic needs remain
the same

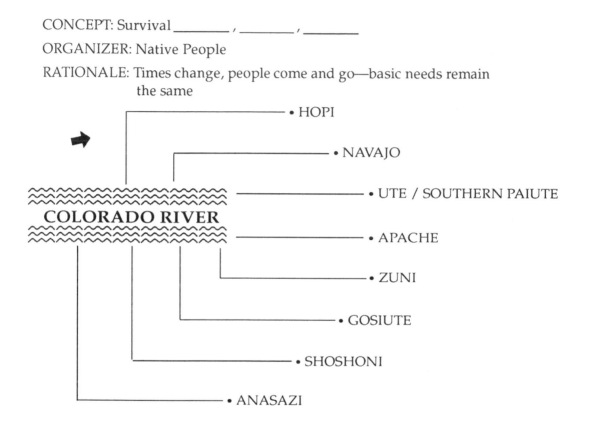

• HOPI

• NAVAJO

• UTE / SOUTHERN PAIUTE

COLORADO RIVER

• APACHE

• ZUNI

• GOSIUTE

• SHOSHONI

• ANASAZI

Survival Theme

Comments: Although this theme suggests a strong historical bent, it
would probably best be studied by including perspectives of current day Native Americans rather than a Hollywood version of the
past.

STEP E: SELECTING COMPONENTS/TOPICS

CONCEPT: Exploring the unknown _____ , _____ , _____

ORGANIZER: Explorers

RATIONALE: Adventurers are always seeking new ways to understand and use the river

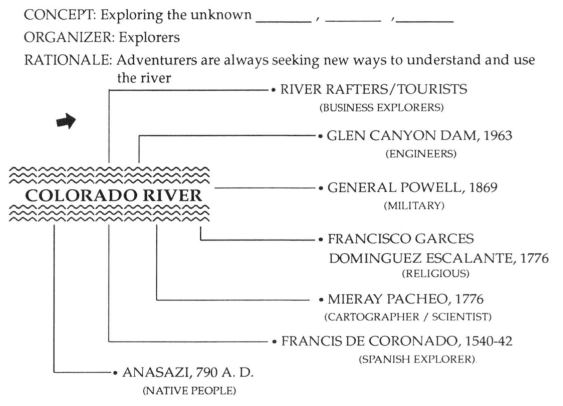

• RIVER RAFTERS/TOURISTS
(BUSINESS EXPLORERS)

• GLEN CANYON DAM, 1963
(ENGINEERS)

COLORADO RIVER

• GENERAL POWELL, 1869
(MILITARY)

• FRANCISCO GARCES
DOMINGUEZ ESCALANTE, 1776
(RELIGIOUS)

• MIERAY PACHEO, 1776
(CARTOGRAPHER / SCIENTIST)

• FRANCIS DE CORONADO, 1540-42
(SPANISH EXPLORER).

• ANASAZI, 790 A. D.
(NATIVE PEOPLE)

Risk Taking

Comments: There are many more pattern shapers than those 18 listed on page 150. Conceptually, all nouns and verbs are pattern shapers in that they are a collection of attributes. Those known to children serve as pattern shapers for their learning.

CHAPTER 11: CREATING A THEME

How to Use Pattern Shapers When Selecting Weekly Topics

When developing weekly topics, use the pattern shaper that will allow you to hit information most critical to the concept and key points of the component and theme. This is not a time to stick to your favorite perennials, those topics you've always done because the kids have always liked them so. Time is limited; traditional and cutsey must make way for difficult decisions about what's most important for students to know. Be tough with yourself. Look afresh at what's worth knowing. Our students face challenging, if not daunting, times ahead. We owe it to them to provide the best possible curriculum content.

For example, in "The World from Where I Stand," the following pattern shapers could be used to develop the first monthly component of "Backyard": #3, habitats; #4, systems; #6, familiar patterns; or #10, classifications. All sound promising. Choose the one strongest for students based on your ability to orchestrate *being there* experiences.

Similarly, for the third month's component, "Golden Gate Park," one could select any one of the following pattern shapers: #1, a location from which a perspective is taken; #6, familiar patterns; #8, structures. Any of the three would lead to powerful topics thereby enhancing and expanding students' understanding of their world.

Remember, your goal here is to amplify students' pattern-detecting capabilities—first to make meaning and then to organize, store, and retrieve what they learn.

To check your understanding of how to use pattern shapers to identify and choose weekly topics, take a moment to complete the planning for "What Makes It Tick?" Sketch your ideas on the mindmap. There are no right or wrong answers. Just give yourself and opportunity to brainstorm. Next, cull through your ideas, selecting those with the most appealing attributes from a child's point of view.

STEP F: DREAM A THEME TITLE

STEP F: DREAM A THEME TITLE

The theme title is simply a "kid-grabbing" name for the organizing concept for your yearlong theme—a catchy word or phrase that represents the organizing concept behind the theme and that hooks into students' imagination and their prior experience. Be sure you settle on something that fires your enthusiasm as well as that of the students. You cannot model being an active learner if the theme doesn't speak to you, if it does not elicit your genuine enthusiasm.

The theme title must speak to the students the first day of school, not years later when they finally can "get it" or even at the end of the year after you've spent the year teaching about it. It must be a notion which students—through ample experience or intuition—**already understand and are motivated by**. Understanding the organizing concept for the theme should not depend on prior experience—many of our students are not so fortunate as to have enriched backgrounds. The themes must already be a part of their experience and understanding and be at the center of a surge of curiosity and interest. It can be playful or imaginative but not distort understanding of important concepts to be studied during the monthly components.

So, What's New? For those of you who have been teaching for a while, this discussion of components and topics may sound a bit familiar. The pre-brain research discussions of thematic curriculum talked about "units" and "interdisciplinary" study. So, what's the difference here?

The two major differences are: 1) the theme is yearlong and there is a clear connection between the theme and each of the components and from component to component; the entire school year is one conceptual whole; and, 2) the environment and all aspects of curriculum and instruction are specially designed to be brain-compatible.

CHAPTER 11: CREATING A THEME

CRITERIA FOR EVALUATING YOUR THEME

If your experience in putting together your first theme is at all typical, you will not be satisfied or feel that things "click" for you until draft number eight or twelve! Curriculum is both highly personal and very intellectually challenging. You will know you are on the right track when your theme, monthly components, and weekly topics meet the following criteria:

- you're excited about it! and so are your students

- it has substance and application to the student's real world

- it can be implemented primarily using *being there* experiences; other resources are also readily available

- the conceptual idea underlying the theme and related content is meaningful (from the students' point of view)

- the rationale behind the theme is truly compelling for you and for the students

- the content is age-appropriate

- it is worthy of the teacher's time spent creating and implementing it and of the students' time studying it

- there are readily available materials plus easily frequented physical locations

- the theme is a clear pattern; there is "flow" from the theme outward to each component and back to the central organizing concept as well as from component to component

CRITERIA FOR EVALUATING A THEME

INSIDE THE MIND OF A TEACHER

The following pages are a "stream of consciousness" visit inside a teacher's head as he/she thinks through developing a yearlong theme, its monthly components, and weekly topics. This internal dialogue will familiarize you with various tools and thought processes for developing curriculum. It's a paddle trip you might enjoy. More than anything else, it conveys the "no-boundaries" approach to curriculum development for ITI. Go with the real world!

"What Makes It Tick?"
(Or how everyday technology influences your life)
A possible theme for grades 4 - 6

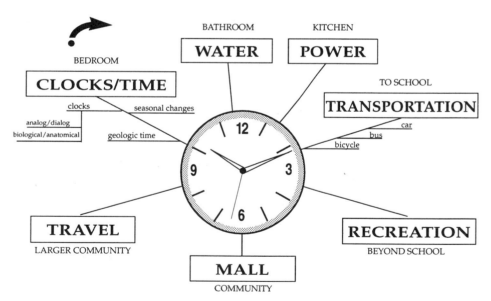

WHAT MAKES IT TICK?

© 1992 Susan Kovalik & Associates

CHAPTER 11: CREATING A THEME

This yearlong theme follows you through everyday activities starting when you awaken in the morning and continuing until you've experienced the variety of activities that your house and community have to offer. From the standpoint of meaningfulness, it allows each student to develop lifelong capacities for taking care of their personal environments. Highly firsthand, it allows for a great variety of real life opportunities for the students all along the way. Within each component the teacher can decide how deeply to explore the topic.

The following stream of consciousness monologue illustrates early stages of brainstorming for step #1 of "Thinking It Through...Tips on Developing Components and Topics."

The flow in this theme is achieved by using *pattern shaper #5,* the chronology of events we encounter each day—from getting up in the morning to shopping at the mall at the end of the day to going on a trip.

Component 1—Clocks/Time. The alarm rings, you hit the snooze button and turn over for five more minutes. Our day starts with time. Real time.

Hmmm, some possibilities for exploring time: the earth's rotation, the seasonal changes, daylight savings time, the calendar, the atomic clock, international date line. All of these topics can be a prelude to how clocks work in our homes.

Possible pattern shapers—*varied styles and uses, historical time line, geography*

- *clocks of the past*—history of the different ways man attempted to record the passing of time, e.g., putting seeds into gourds, Chinese water clock, sundials, hourglass
- *geologic time*—ways in which we define the age/eras of planet Earth

- *famous clocks*—Big Ben, Black Forest cuckoo clocks, etc.
- *kinds of clocks*—mechanical, weight-driven, spring-driven
    -electric clocks—battery-powered or line-powered
    -pendulum clocks—weights and measures
    -digital clocks—microchips, quartz
- *creation of watches*, mainsprings, gears
- *thermostat timers* (on your home's heater or spa)
- *biological clocks* of all plants and animals, including humans

As you can see, the possibilities are endless. It is also obvious that, with the vast amount of content which could be included, each component might be longer than a month—five weeks, six weeks, or even more. Therefore, one must choose carefully from among the brainstormed items. What is essential for students to know? What resources are available in your community to support these topics?

And now, your body clock is telling you it's time to go to the bathroom! Onward to the next component. . . .

Component 2—The Bathroom. The big idea in the bathroom is where does the clean water come from and where does the dirty water go? Many issues here!

Possible pattern shapers:, *varied uses, systems, structures*

Ideas to pursue:

- *water*—rain, springs, lakes, snow, glaciers, ice caps
- *water storage*—dams, percolation ponds, tanks, wells, springs
- *water delivery systems*—pipes from the source to the house, bottled water, trucked water
- *water exit systems*—septic tanks, sewer systems, water treatment plants, purification systems

CHAPTER 11: CREATING A THEME

Understanding the scarcity and preciousness of water could be tied into:

- *amount*—of water needed per person per day to take care of basic needs in the U.S.A., in the former U.S.S.R., in Africa, in South America
- *drought*—luxurious uses of water, e.g., golf courses, hosing down driveways and walkways, dishwashers, washing machines, swimming pools, spas
- *necessary uses of water*—irrigation/agricultural food processing, personal needs
- *salt water*—desalinization facilities

Ahhhh, the smell of bacon, pancakes, and hot chocolate beckons you to the kitchen and ultimately to the uses of electrical power.

Component 3—Electrical Power. How did the electricity get into the house? Where did it come from and where does it go when we are not using it? A home depends on electricity for light, heat, and the power to run dozens of small appliances. Which should we focus on?

Possible pattern shapers for this component could include: *classification, sources, varied uses, perspectives, famous people*

Topics of investigation could include:

- source of electrical power, where does it originate?
- how is it "sent" through lines to a house?
- how is it dispersed throughout the house?
- what is a fuse?
- what is a circuit? How many do you need in a house? (each work group can create a model of a four-bedroom, two-bath house and determine its electrical needs)
- how is the quantity of electricity used in the house recorded (in order to prepare your electrical bill)?
- what is the difference between direct and alternating current?

From your electric toothbrush to your hot coffee and toast, cold milk from the refrigerator, your heater to your air conditioner, your washer to your dryer, almost every helper you know and love is dependent on electricity.

Let's see, time to let the fingers go a'walking. I'll consult the yellow pages to find the resource people who can come and share with my students (anyone from the electric company to the appliance repairman can assist in providing students with real world, first-hand experience). Each student can choose the one appliance about which he/she wants to become the class expert; then each of them should explain it to the rest of the class. Even more exciting is the invention of a new appliance to take care of an unmet need.

While we are in the kitchen, there is "kitchen chemistry" to explore and understand: food preservation, food spoilage, cooking, baking, cleaning (vinegar, baking soda, lemon juice). If we are really making connections, perhaps this is the time to investigate eating, digestion, and stomach chemicals.

While in the kitchen we grab our lunch as we head out the door for school. On to the next component. . . .

Component 4—Getting to School. The bike, the bus, the car (walking is a preferred way ecologically but, from the standpoint of "What Makes It Tick?", this next component will be about transportation the American way—a nation on wheels or something about 18-wheelers . . . "convoy," that's it!)

Ah, I can't resist; I simply must use the song, "The Wheels on the Bus Go Round and Round"!

Possible pattern shapers for this component can include: *chronology—past, present, future; varied uses; famous people.* This is the perfect component to kickoff using the ITI discovery process (see appendix B). The point in using this strategy is to let the students discover what is needed and how to problem-solve those needs.

CHAPTER 11: CREATING A THEME

The discovery challenge for my students: design and build, from materials you can scavenge, a vehicle that will hold two people, has a steering mechanism, and will stop when you need it to!

By starting this component with the actual designing and creating of a vehicle, I can have the students problem-solve the issues that all car designers have faced at some time. This will also be a great place to introduce the science concept of work and the idea of horsepower.

Back to our stream-of-consciousness: delving into the historical past of car-making will now take on meaning because it will be connected to the experience the students have had with their own vehicles. Possible items of study, through *an historical perspective,* include

- first there was a steam engine, with wheels, steering, and a braking system
- the electric car came next (today we have golf carts and "around towns")
- the gasoline engine followed (and the rest is history)
- the pioneers of the American auto industry: Ransom Olds, Henry Ford, William Durant, the Dodge Brothers
- how cars are built—the assembly line, simple machines doing important jobs in creating complex machines
- the issues behind creating an entire national economy based on planned obsolescence

This is a place for many resource people: a design engineer, a brake specialist (Midas Mufflers, Amoco), an auto mechanic, the farmer who repairs all his own mechanical equipment, an inventor.

Possible political action questions to explore:

- Can we afford to have one in every seven workers in America tied to the auto industry?
- Can we continue to make our environments unlivable due to the combustion engine and its by-products?

- Can we continue to be dependent on oil from outside the U.S.?
- What alternatives must be found to confront the problems stated above?

Component 5—Alternative Forms of Transportation. Possible pattern shapers: *research and development* (e.g. light rail, subways, buses, trains, rapid transit, bicycles), or *systems, structure, varied uses for an item, geography/region, comparisons, a wondering/question.*

At this point I think I'll have students select the area of alternative transportation they would most be interested in learning more about. I'll then establish work groups where students would find all the pros and cons of their chosen form of transportation.

Hmmmm, I'll have the students begin their research on the development of each type of alternative, the hows and whys and wherefores. There should be drawings, 3-D models, resource people visiting, letters written to various agencies; and each group would design the ideal system for their city based upon their research and problem-solving of actual problems we have in the area now (land use, finances, etc.). I'll have them make recommendations to the class, the school, and the city council.

A key element in the designing of any system of transportation is planning. Creating rules and regulations for the construction of any structure and its environmental impact is vital to the health of the community.

So, via our new mode of transportation, let's go to the mall!

Component 6—Let's Go to the Mall! Pattern shapers: *habitats, systems, structures, comparisons*

The major issues included in the study of malls are: land use, sanitation, garbage pickup and disposal, parking, architectural design, recirculating air, electricity, food preparation, people movement (elevator, escalators, room to walk), ambiance: fountain, artwork, living atriums, entrepreneurship—landowner issues and taxes.

At this time of the year the students are ready to become "experts" in a specific area within this range of fields. This is the time to create a simulation:

Building a Mall in Hometown, U.S.A.

- the first part will involve the city/county planning commission, the landowners, the developers/architects
- the second part belongs to the contractors: surveyors, soil testers, land clearance and grading
- third, the builders of such things as the foundations, heating, cooling, plumbing, electrical systems; the framers, masons, carpenters (rough and finish), painters, etc. and then, of course, the inspectors to see that all work is done to building codes
- the entrepreneurs: variety of shops including food stops (designers to create stores that are attractive and functional)

At each of these stages students can select the role they find most interesting. Their responsibility is to find as much information as they can to assist them in creating a fully functioning mall. (This simulation could take more than one month!) A scale model of the mall illustrating a variety of construction stages could be made available as a mobile display to share with other classes, to be on display at the school or city library or wherever the impact of student work is appreciated.

Component #7—Travel. Trains, planes, boats, exploring the world outside our immediate area

This end of the year adventure is an opportunity to use all the LIFESKILLS and academic skills that have been developed throughout the year. By expecting the students to be actively involved in the planning and execution of this event you are providing competencies that will last a lifetime.

As is true for all travel, I'll need some degree of planning. The steps my class will have to go through are not unlike a traveller's:

- organizing the event
- fund raising
- scheduling the activities
- securing chaperones
- permission slips
- double checking on appointments
- weather alternative
- overnight responsibilities

A yearlong theme isn't constraining; always expect students to add to the curriculum at every level. Be open to the teachable moment. The theme is a guide to understanding at a conceptual level and a powerful context for teaching skills.

CHAPTER TWELVE

DEVELOPING CURRICULUM: IDENTIFYING KEY POINTS

Once the yearlong theme, monthly components, and weekly topics are established, the next step is to determine what is most essential for students to learn—the *essential concepts, skills, and significant information* within the content area(s) of your ITI theme that you want all students to master by the end of the year. The elements of this essential core of knowledge and skills are your "key points" which are clear, concise statements of the content every student is to *learn and be able to apply.*

The primary purpose of key points is to enhance students' ability to detect pattern, i.e., to readily identify the collection of attributes that is essential for understanding the concept, skill, or significant idea. Secondly, key points provide a clear focus for the teacher for instructional planning and orchestration of learning.

WHAT IS ESSENTIAL?

The development of key points forces us to answer a most critical question: What is essential to know and be able to do? What must the citizen of the 21st century know and be able to do in order to survive and to participate in/contribute to a democratic, high-tech society?

CHAPTER 12: IDENTIFYING KEY POINTS

In answering this question, tradition hinders rather than helps us. Traditions to overcome are:

- "covering" vs. learning to the level of application
- surface-level information which produces a "so what" yawn or which constitutes little more than an introduction to vocabulary and terms
- information which stops short of having relevance to the learner's world now (not in high school or in old age)
- important sounding but age-inappropriate content, e.g., particles of matter and atoms at third grade or solar system at second grade (which typically amount to little more than a hands-on arts and crafts project)
- "telling" about content rather than creating the *being there* and *immersion* environments in which students can fully engage all of their senses in the process of making meaning

Neither can this question be answered from a generalist's current bank of information. Instead, we must become in-depth learners and stretch to pull out conceptual understandings that will survive over time, e.g., concepts such as cause/effect, interdependence, community, responsibility, taxation, systems, etc. Remember, you are in search of content that will assist students to understand their world—now and as far into the future as possible.

This is a very different perspective than that taken by E.D. Hirsch, et al, authors of *The Dictionary of Cultural Literacy*. I would argue that a well-educated, successful-in-the-world citizen *ends up* with much of the knowledge Hirsch recommends; however, such knowledge consists of factoids which cling to a strong base made of larger, more powerful patterns of understandings needed to survive and thrive in the 21st century. I argue that the central goal and focus of the classroom teacher ought to be the larger understandings, not the factoids, of "cultural literacy" or the bits and pieces of our traditional curriculum.

THINKING STEPS

A fresh, and brain-compatible, approach to curriculum building is needed. Key points must be stated and framed in ways that create a road map for the teacher—a road map which marks the beginning of the journey toward learning and sets the course of classroom work for the teacher and the students.

If your district has provided you with brain-compatible curriculum tools—a continuum of concepts—the task of developing key points will be much easier; you can skip steps 1, 3, and 4 of the following chart. If the available tools are traditional, study Chapter 10 and follow the recommended thinking steps.

Recommended thinking steps for developing key points are:

1. brainstorm what you believe are the essential concepts for students to know

2. visit the physical locations you've selected as providing the best *being there* experiences for the content of your theme

3. look through your district's scope and sequence

4. hit your library and begin serious research to gain perspective on what is essential from expert points of view

5. test potential key points against the "childhood why and wherefores"

6. become a learner again; frequent your city/county library weekly and interview experts to give yourself a rich, in-depth background in the essential concepts of the curriculum

7. begin to identify what *immersion* and hands-on of real world things you will be able to provide in addition to the *being there* experiences of the physical location

8. recycle back through steps 1–6 (not necessarily in orderly sequence)

CHAPTER 12: IDENTIFYING KEY POINTS

THINKING STEPS FOR DEVELOPING KEY POINTS

1. *Brainstorming* Brainstorming, based on what we currently know, is useful in two ways. First, it helps us to uncover what we know (and don't know) about an area and gives us an inkling of how much research we must do to prepare ourselves to teach our content areas.

Second, brainstorming helps us test the depth of understanding we hold. A long list of factoid information with few conceptual statements alerts us to the need to explore the "whys" behind the area of study and to search for real world applications for students. Before we can expect to teach students, we ourselves must have answered the question: "Why is this information important, what is meaningful to my life today and in the foreseeable future?"

If at all possible, get together with an ITI buddy—one at your grade level if possible but, if not, someone who understands your search for more conceptual rather than fact-oriented key points. Use him/her as a sounding board. "What is essential?" is the most important question you can ask yourself; the quality of its answer will determine the power of your key points.

2. *Visit Your Selected Physical Locations* Observe the location through the eyes of your students—what would they perceive at these locations given their developmental levels and prior experiences? Interview people who work and live there and those who often frequent the location. Don't try to force fit the site to reflect your school's scope and sequence. First, view the location and what's most important about it from the point of view of real life. Then let the curriculum filter in.

3. *Look Through Your District's Scope and Sequence* If your district's scope and sequences are old, and few teachers actually use them, or, if they are aligned with previous textbooks, it might be best to ignore them. If, however, they have been recently done, are age-appropriate, and there are high expectations that they be implemented, look through them carefully.

If they are highly detailed, treat them as a portion of your brainstorming. Be forewarned, however, that highly detailed scope and sequences tend to be highly factoid and may need to be "chunked up" or taken up a notch in generalization to get to truly useful and powerful key points.

4. *Hit Your Library* The world around us is so rich, knowledge explodes so exponentially, and our memories from our early schooling are so inadequate, we simply must accept that **research is essential.** Elementary grade content doesn't mean simplified notions taught from elementary or rudimentary understandings.

Use the mindmap of your yearlong theme to communicate with your public and school librarians. Give them a copy, along with the dates you will need resources to plan each component. My experience has been that librarians are thrilled to be presented with a research request whose materials will be studied with care.

Key points, developed after the teacher has secured a knowledge base about the subject area, are statements of what students should know when the topic is completed—the essential core of knowledge students will have at the end of the component or topic studied. *Key points are concise, straightforward statements which capture concepts, skills, and significant information which the teacher considers most important for students to know and be able to do.*

5. *Testing Potential Key Points Against "Childhood's Why and Wherefores"* Before beginning with step five, compare the results of your brainstorming, location visits, district curriculum review, and research. Are some significant notions or concepts beginning to emerge? Or are you still awash in a sea of unrelated facts?

To help sift out more conceptual aspects from the sea of facts, it is helpful to take a student point of view of the material. Do the potential key points provide a truly in-depth exploration of the concept or skill? Will they fully answer the onslaught of "why" questions of the young? In other words, from a child's perspective, have you captured the essence of the point and made it truly fascinating and relevant? Have you remembered his/her developmental capacities?

There is much we can learn about learning by listening to a young child go about the business of extracting meaning from his/her world, particularly during the "why?" stage when a child's active and intense pursuit of learning is most transparent. The intensity of a two-year-old's whys, their intention to master in both breadth and depth, is phenomenal. While Eskimos have twenty-one words for snow, two-year-olds have twenty-one meanings for "why," chief among which are:

- **why do** you do what you're doing? (why is this important to you and, thus, perhaps to me?)

- what's the **purpose** of this? (why and when would you use/do it?)

- **how/why**? (how do you do this and when is it important to do it?)

- **cause**? (what made this happen?)

- **reason**? (why did you do this/why did it happen?)

- **reason for which**? (what's the rationale used for this choice/decision?)

- **so what**? (what does this mean to me, why should I learn this?)

This battery of meanings (and sometimes to the parent of a persistent two-year-old it definitely feels like "battery"!) illustrates the range of exploration a worthwhile key point should be able to sustain. This range of whys is summed up in *Webster's Dictionary* under the phrase **"why and wherefores,"** meaning **"the whole reason."** Thus, the term "childhood's why and wherefores" can be thought of as a summary of the "whys" which your key point should be able to bear. Children want to know EVERYTHING as it applies to their lives. Little escapes their attention, and whatever catches their attention catches their interest and keen and persistent questioning.

Key points that can be answered yes or no, or responded to in a single sentence, are very likely too simplistic, too factoid, too self-evident, not worthy of full-scale why exploration.

6. *Become a learner again.* Living in an age of rapid change and an era that we so blithely characterize as the "Age of Information," the future for which we hope to prepare our students is rewritten almost monthly. Accordingly, we can no longer expect traditional curriculums or textbooks to provide us with the current, in-depth information needed to give our students what they need and deserve. We, as they, must become active learners, participating in the making of our future, not just being a passive coattail rider. As professionals, we must set aside a minimum of 20 minutes per day to read, 5 minutes for professional literature and 15 minutes for content (science, history, etc.). Make it a habit to stop by your public library at least once a week. Let the magic of learning recapture your heart and mind.

7. *The Search for Being There and Immersion Sources.* Having researched your topic (through trade and reference books, school educational materials such as district curriculum, CD-Rom discs, computer network sources, etc.), and gathered together your knowledge of the real world through visiting your selected locations, you are now ready to cull through the "stuff" and get down to what really counts.

8. *Revisit steps 1–7, hopping about as needed.*

The thinking processes needed to identify effective key points are neither linear nor sequential. Jump around from one step to another. You cannot complete the job by using one framework at a time.

CHARACTERISTICS OF GOOD KEY POINTS

Key points which are powerful for teacher planning and useful for enhancing student learning are key points which

- clearly and concisely describe what is essential to know and to be able to apply or use
- enhance students' ability to detect pattern and thus make meaning of what they are studying
- provide clear direction for long- and short-term curricular and instructional planning
- are meaty enough to warrant the time that will be spent on them (by both teacher and student)
- say something important enough to warrant 11 to 16 minutes of direct instruction or an hour plus of the discovery process
- apply to the real world and the student's world (now and in the future as foreseen by the learner)
- are age-appropriate
- can be studied using "being there" sources
- are more conceptual than factoid
- are specific enough to guide both teacher and students in their planning and working
- are specific enough to serve as assessment tools for both short- and long-term purposes

EXAMPLES OF KEY POINTS

Key points are not tricky to write but they require some thinking, analysis, and decision-making. Use common sense! Just remember that their purpose is to enhance pattern-seeking for students and to provide focus for your long- and short-term curricular and instructional planning, including daily lesson planning.

Powerful key points lead toward conceptual understanding rather than mere listing of factual data. Key points can be simple or detailed depending on your topic and your students, but each is as conceptual as possible. The following examples illustrate key points for a portion of a weekly topic that includes the study of owls. The examples range in effectiveness as explained.

Not good

The ears of the owl are located in openings on either side of its head. Their hearing is very keen. Most owls have large eyes which, unlike most birds, are directed forward and are fixed. Owls can see well in almost total darkness.

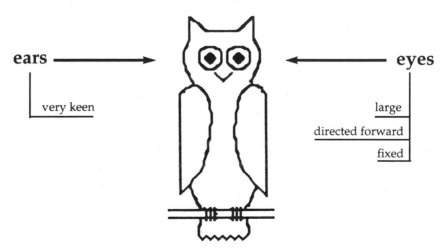

Comment: The "not good" key point is not conceptual, just a welter of facts which don't add up to anything of significance; it has little power for generalization. It is typical of knowledge level statements so common in the traditional curriculum.

Good Key Point for Primary Grades

Owls are predators with keen senses to allow them to hunt at night. Although the ears of an owl are on the sides of its head, sounds are directed into its ears by the facial disc feathers around its eyes. Their eyes can see in almost total darkness.

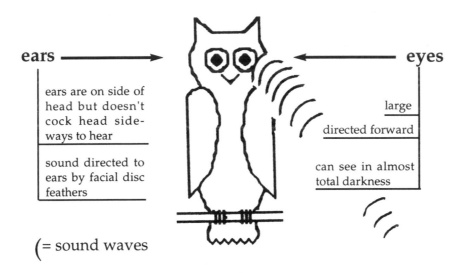

ears ——————————➤

ears are on side of head but doesn't cock head sideways to hear

sound directed to ears by facial disc feathers

(= sound waves

eyes

large

directed forward

can see in almost total darkness

Comment: The level of conceptualization of this key point is appropriate for primary grades where the focus is still on discovering the world, exploring what is, and then using knowledge of one particular animal or thing as a basis for generalizing to others, i.e., starting with specifics and then generalizing. This key point hints at a conceptual idea that could be grasped by students with considerable prior experience but does not require such understanding in order for students to observe and compare.

EXAMPLES OF KEY POINTS

Good Key Points for Intermediate Grades

The following key points are part of a weekly topic about predators, the concept for which is: each predator has developed unique physiological characteristics to enable it to detect and capture its prey. Nocturnal hunters, such as the owl, have especially keen sight and hearing.

Key Point 1: Eyes. Unlike most birds (but typical of most birds of prey), the owl's eyes are forward-looking. They are huge in proportion to their head and body and are uniquely adapted for night and day hunting. The pupils can expand to let in enough light to see in almost total darkness. For example, in an area as large as four baseball fields, a single candle placed anywhere in the area is sufficient for an owl to see a mouse 200 to 300 feet away. Also, the eyes of the owl are fixed, thus requiring the owl to turn its head to visually follow its prey. Turning the head with the movement of the prey ensures that the sound from the prey will be directed very precisely to the ears, the owl's primary tracking system.

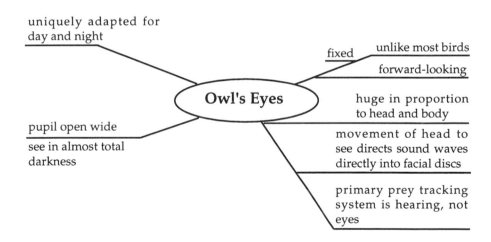

Key Point 2: Ears. Although the owls' ears are on the sides of their head, they do not cock their head sideways to hear like most birds do, but rather stare straight at the object they are listening to. The facial disc feathers around the eyes of owls and the moveable skin flap of the ears work like a parabolic microphone dish, picking up sounds and directing them into their ears.

Key Point 3: Ears. One ear of the owl is higher than the other. This allows them to pinpoint with complete accuracy the location of their prey below them—both by depth and by distance away. Owls use a process called triangulation to pinpoint the exact location of its prey. After taking three "readings" through its ears, the owl knows the location, speed, and direction of the prey and where it will be when the owl arrives to snatch it.

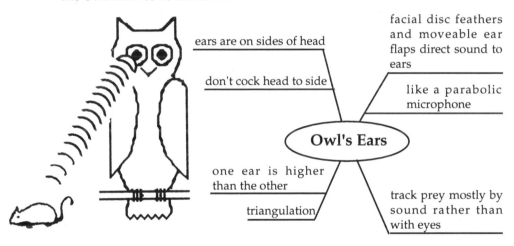

ears are on sides of head

facial disc feathers and moveable ear flaps direct sound to ears

don't cock head to side

like a parabolic microphone

Owl's Ears

one ear is higher than the other

triangulation

track prey mostly by sound rather than with eyes

Comment. These key points for primary and intermediate grades provide a conceptual base which creates a cognitive structure or hooks with which children can grasp, retain, and use information. They meet the criteria for a good key point.

The above owl inquiries for grades 4–6 are examples of "chunky" or lengthy key points. "Chunky-style" key points are needed when the individual elements are fairly self-evident once pointed out OR the individual elements *by themselves* would feel fairly factoid, leading nowhere, eliciting little meaning. Keep in mind that the age of the learner makes a significant difference in the scope of a key point.

USING KEY POINTS

Clearly, not all key points are lengthy; some can be easily and concisely expressed in a single, short sentence: "Soil is not just 'dirt'—it is made from broken rocks, decaying plants, decaying animals, and animal waste (fertilizer)." Or, "$E=MC^2$. Rule of thumb: Let the content dictate how best to represent a key point."

The primary consideration in stating key points is that each statement represents content which warrants 11 to 16 minutes of direct instruction or one hour plus of a discovery process. This limit of 11 to 16 minutes for teacher presentation time helps eliminate "the lecture" and student passivity in the classroom.

For further examples of key points and examples of weekly topics and monthly components see appendices D and E.

USING KEY POINTS

Keep in mind that key points have a dual audience. *For the students*, they are a guide to daily work and long-term adventure. There is no vagueness as to purpose for the lesson, day, week. The perennial questions, "What are we going to do, teacher?" or, "Why are we doing this, teacher?" are answered before they are asked.

For the teacher, they are a guide for short- and long-term curriculum planning and for daily lesson planning.

When the teacher believes that the *discovery process** would be the most powerful instructional approach, key points focus the teacher's material-gathering and planning efforts and they help frame clear questions for the students to pursue. For example, the *discovery process* with the topic of owls would utilize outside resources to bring in live owls, present a few necessary facts (hunts at night, very few enemies) and then allow the students to discover the various concepts about the predator/prey relationship by observing and asking questions.

---

* See appendix B

CHAPTER 12: IDENTIFYING KEY POINTS

When the teacher thinks that *direct instruction* would be the most appropriate instructional format, key points provide the goal and content for the teacher's presentation. The teacher then presents the information in such a way that students can mindmap the material and begin to see connections to their world.

In addition to their instructional uses, key points also lay the foundation for authentic assessment. Because they are the statements of what's important to know and be able to do, they are also statements of what should be assessed through an authentic assessment process.

IMPORTANCE OF MULTIPLE RESOURCES

Obviously, the depth of information needed to write key points, such as the example key points about owls, is not available in school textbooks. Textbooks are but generic guides. Textbook publishers admit their books are intended to be general guides, not comprehensive *programs*. Textbooks used as the only resource severely limit the knowledge base for all—students and teachers. It is important to free ourselves of our dependency on textbooks, using them only if they support what we have orchestrated for the students. Imagine how much money is spent on textbooks, books which provide little breadth and depth, and often aren't even used. Imagine the *real* resources you could purchase with that money!

Only the teacher is in a position to evaluate the full range of resources for his/her students. The teacher, through planning and sleuthing, can amass a great variety of materials, including current writings, resource books, magazines, pamphlets, and, whenever possible, resource people. Each group of students is unique; the materials must be made to fit their needs, interests, and ways of learning. In some cases the textbook provides a sequence for the unfolding of events—but always, it is the teacher who creates a rich learning environment.

Therefore, when implementing the ITI model, it is essential for teachers to provide a variety of resources for the students to use during each monthly component. The public library offers the most comprehensive collection of materials at a wide number of reading levels. The librarian at the public library could be your closest ally in implementing your theme. Don't be shy. Ask your librarian. Provide him/her with a copy of your key points about two to three weeks before the start of your next component. Be sure to specify the range of reading levels in your classroom (and make sure you stretch the top level). You will likely receive anywhere from forty to sixty resource books per component.

A librarian can also provide other types of resources for teachers to use when writing their curriculum. Some of the resources available from the public library are: lists of all the local, state, and federal governmental agencies and their addresses; lists of all the state and federal senators and representatives; contact information for all the local, state, and national groups concerned with the environment and conservation of natural resources; addresses for the chancellors of foreign embassies with diplomatic relations with the United States; and, at times, journal articles which have to do with any aspect of the monthly component. Needless to say, the professional dedication of the librarian and his/her expertise makes it easier for teachers to implement the ITI model.

Resources we recommend:

Books:

AT&T Toll Free 800 Directory
55 Corporate Drive, Room 24C36
Bridgewater, NJ 08807
800/555-1212

Conservation Directory
NWF
1400 Sixteenth St. N.W.
Washington D.C. 20036-2266
202/797-6800

The Corporate Address Book
by Michael Levine
A Perigree Book (Putnam Publishers Group)
200 Madison Ave.
New York, NY 10016

Corporate Giving Yellow Pages 1993
Taft Group
12300 Twinbrook Parkway, Suite 450
Rockville, MD 20852

Educator's Guide to Free Materials
Educators Progress Service
214 Center St.
Randolph, WI 53956

Encyclopedia of Associations
Burek, Koek, Novallo, Editors
Gale Research, Inc.
Detroit, MI 48226

The Kid's Address Book
by Michael Levine
A Perigree Book (Putnam Publishers Group)
200 Madison Ave.
New York, NY 10016

Libraries Unlimited
Department 92
P.O. Box 6633
Englewood, CO 80155-6633
> Designed for the library media specialist, a very broad selection of reference and informational material.

National FAX Directory
Gale Research
835 Penobscot Building
Detroit, MI 48226-4094
800/877-GALE

National Trade & Professional Associations of the U.S.
Columbia Books, Inc., Publishers
1350 New York Ave. N. W., Suite 207
Washington, D.C. 20005

Science for Children
National Academy Press
2101 Connecticut Ave. N. W.
Washington, D. C. 20418

The Timetables of History
by Bernard Grun
A Touchstone Book (Simon & Schuster)
1230 Avenue of the Americas
New York, NY 10020

The Timetables of Inventions and Discoveries
by Kevin Desmond
M. Evans & Company, Inc.
216 E. 49th St.
New York, NY 10017

The Timetables of Science
by Alexander Hellemans and Bryan Bunch
Simon & Schuster
1230 Avenue of the Americas
New York, NY 10020

To Help People Help Other People:
A Complete Fund Raising Guide
Non-Profit Organization Handbook
Patricia/Daniel Goby
Prentice Hall 1979

Resource Companies:

Cornucopia Pull
2515 East Thomas, Suite 16
Phoenix, AZ 85016

Fund-Raising Management
224 Seventh St.
Garden City, NY 11530
800/229-6700
516/746-6700

Multi-Cultural and Minority Source Materials Company
16 Park Lane
Newton Centre, MA 02159-1731

If we are to create an enriched classroom where students have access to a varied and thorough range of resource materials, we would expect teachers to collect between twenty-five and a hundred books, magazines, and other materials from libraries, swap meets, friends, etc., to support their particular topic of study. Further, writing weekly letters to various people and organizations identified in these resources strengthens students' communications skills and helps them realize the unlimited resources available for the asking.

The issue is meaningfulness! Critical and higher level decision-making are moot if students don't have the opportunity to look at issues through multiple resources—from all vantage points, i.e., from the eyes of different authors with differing points of view!

CHAPTER THIRTEEN

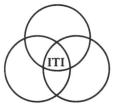

DEVELOPING CURRICULUM: CREATING INQUIRIES

Inquiries are the footbridge between the "what" and "how" of curriculum—what is to be learned (key points) and how students will go about learning and applying the information and skills. *Webster's* definition for "inquiry" is useful here: "the act or an instance of seeking truth, information, or knowledge about something; examination into facts or principles; research, investigation" (*Webster's Third International Dictionary, Unabridged*).

The primary purpose of inquiries is to enable students to develop mental programs for applying, in real world situations, the concepts, skills, and significant information of the key points (see discussion of program-building on pages 70 to 76). They make learning active and memorable. For that reason, they are the heart and soul of your curriculum building efforts. They are the point at which words become realities and the talked about becomes one's own experience, e.g., "talking about science" melts into "doing science." Inquiries frame the real life opportunities which allow students to apply their learnings and, in doing so, build *programs*.

Inquiries are also the point in curriculum development at which you begin to involve students in directing and assuming responsibility for their own learning, the point at which you invite students to join you in the driver's seat, to learn to take an active role in shaping the content and processes of their day-to-day learning; unlike the development of textbooks and workbooks. The development of inquiries is neither a one-way street, nor a specialist-only activity.

This is the third step in developing curriculum for Integrated Thematic Instruction. This chapter on inquiries includes:

- **refining the essential content to be learned**
- **writing inquiries**
- **example inquiries**
- **getting a little help from the kids!**
- **criteria for evaluating inquiries**
- **how to use inquiries**
- **evaluating student work on inquiries**

REFINING THE ESSENTIAL CONTENT TO BE LEARNED

The process of writing inquiries is an extension of the thinking processes begun with identifying key points. That is, as you continue your exploration of what firsthand experiences/resources you can provide, you will want to: continue refining your statements of what is essential for students to know and be able to do; revisit your library (this time with a more focused perspective); continue testing potential key points against the childhood why and wherefores and begin to anticipate instructional strategy issues.

The most important consideration when developing inquiries is to stay within the realm of here and now with *being there* experiences which children can absorb through all 19 senses. Avoid lessons which involve "over there" accounts and events which happened in the past (prior to students' immediate experiences of self, family, grandparents, etc.) because none are "experienceable" and do not result in the same degree of dendritic growth.

WRITING INQUIRIES

Writing inquiries puts the action into the students' day. Be creative. Be daring. Remember that *mental program-building* requires application to the real world and lots of practice. Go for the gusto! Go for the real life, the *being there* experiences, the tangible product. And, last but not least, each inquiry should be perceived as a meaningful event (from the students' perspectives, of course), worthy of time and energy, and, if possible, it should be something that students can use at home or in class during further learning.

When writing inquiries, follow the "ABC" guidelines:

1. **A**lways start the sentence with a process verb (see the following chart). This makes it an imperative statement, a directive for action rather than a stimulus for a convergent answer.

2. **B**e specific about what the inquiry asks the students to do. Avoid words like "all," "some," or "as many as you can." If the instructions are clear, you will be spared each child coming to you for clarification of what he/she is supposed to do.

3. **S**ee ("C") the outcome or finished product the students are asked to create. Have you stated exactly what you are expecting them to end up with? Is it feasible with the resources and time available? Don't underestimate!!! Are there choices within the inquiries that entice and challenge every child in your class to get excited about learning? Have you allowed for the seven intelligences?

The following Inquiry Builder Chart provides an array of process verbs, from Bloom's Taxonomy of Cognitive Objectives, with which to construct inquiries for your students. They are categorized according to five of the seven intelligences: logical/mathematical, linguistic, spatial, bodily-kinesthetic, and musical. Accommodation of the interpersonal and intrapersonal intelligences is easily done by providing either a group or a more individual assignment context to inquiries based on any of the other five intelligences.

INQUIRY BUILDER CHART

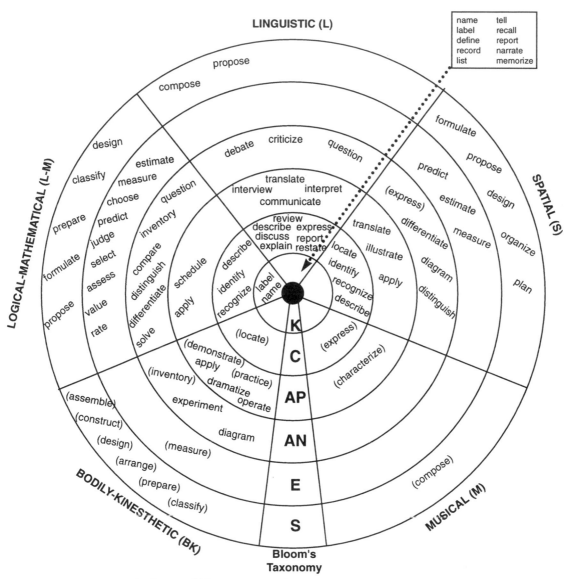

name tell
label recall
define report
record narrate
list memorize

LINGUISTIC (L)

SPATIAL (S)

LOGICAL-MATHEMATICAL (L-M)

BODILY-KINESTHETIC (BK)

MUSICAL (M)

Bloom's Taxonomy

( ) indicates verbs that would be appropriate for this intelligence if specifically designed to be so

INQUIRY BUILDER CHART LEGEND

Concentric circles marked with the letters K, C, AP, AN, E, S contain process verbs associated with Bloom's Taxonomy of Cognitive Objectives.

Pie chart wedges contain the process verbs of Bloom's Taxonomy for five of Gardner's seven intelligences: logical/mathematical, linguistic, spatial, musical, and bodily-kinesthetic.

While Bloom's Taxonomy directs the learner to various areas or kinds of applications of concept or skill, the seven intelligences help frame inquiries which call for different problem-solving approaches. This gives students many and varied opportunities to expand their repertoire of successful problem-solving approaches. Strive for balance as you select verbs with which to write your inquiries. A balance of the seven intelligences and the taxonomy levels will ensure the widest possible choice for students. **An empowering curriculum assists learners to expand their range and power of problem-solving capabilities—our goal ought to be the creation of 21st century Renaissance minds.**

To refresh your memory, Bloom's levels are:

knowledge—the student recalls or recognizes information

comprehension—the student understands the information

application—the student solves a problem using the information and appropriate generalizations

analysis—the student separates information into component parts

evaluation—the student judges the information according to set standards

synthesis—the student solves a problem by putting information together which requires original, creative thinking

CHAPTER 13: DEVELOPING INQUIRIES

A Primary Grade Version of Bloom's Taxonomy

KNOWLEDGE—The student recalls or recognizes information:

name, tell what____looks like (describe), tell when, tell who, make a list, match, find (locate), memorize, tell how many

COMPREHENSION—The student understands the information and can present it in a different form:

tell what___means (define), explain, tell the main idea, tell in order (sequence), tell why, show (illustrate), tell how__, felt, give a definition of

APPLICATION—The student solves a problem using the information and appropriate generalizations:

change, use___in a new way, show how to (demonstrate), act out (dramatize), draw or paint a picture that shows (illustrates), give an example, tell the purpose of, tell how___is used in this example

ANALYSIS—Student separates information into component parts:

put into groups (categorize), tell how___and___are alike/different; tell why you think___did___(infer); tell why you think___felt ___(infer); tell what is true/not true, real/make believe; tell what___learned from___

EVALUATION—The student judges the information according to set standards:

tell why____is better/worse/more fair, etc.; tell why you agree or disagree with____; tell which you chose for 1st, 2nd, 3rd place (rate); compare; decide; tell what will happen (predict); summarize; prove; judge

SYNTHESIS—The student solves a problem by putting information together that requires original, creative thinking:

tell or write a new story about (create); make up a new; build or construct; put together___make; tell something else___could do; tell how to make___better; combine; invent; plan; develop; pretend; tell what you think will happen next (predict)

EXAMPLES OF INQUIRIES

These example inquiries were designed to accompany the example key points illustrated in Chapter 12. They follow up on lessons using live and stuffed owls. Also, because owls are found throughout the United States, the probability of students hearing them or finding their pellets is very high.

Students were provided with opportunities to observe how the owl's head moves toward sounds in order for the facial disc feathers to guide the sound.

Owls' Hearing

Some example inquiries might look like those below which were designed for grades 4-6. The initials following each inquiry are, first, which of the seven intelligences are addressed, and, second, which kinds of questioning are evoked according to Bloom's Taxonomy and whether the inquiry is for an individual (I) or group (G).

1. Prepare a skit for the class illustrating the triangulation method used by owls to pinpoint by sound the exact location of their prey. Assign the following roles to members of your work group: left ear, right ear, beak (and observer), squeaky mouse. Station the left and right ears 8' to 10' apart (with eyes closed and toilet paper tube over the designated ear) and the beak in the middle. Dramatize the skit for the class. *Needed materials: two toilet paper tubes and one squeaky mouse.*—LM and BK—application (G)

2. Draw a diagram, actual size, of an owl's brain; indicate the size of the brain dedicated to vision and hearing.—S and BK—analysis (I, G)

3. Compare the facial discs of an owl to a parabolic microphone. Describe at least five similarities and differences. Record your description in your journal.—LM—analysis (I, G)

4. Measure how far an owl can hear its prey; place an "X" (using masking tape) on a window of your classroom and measure out toward the playground. Place an "X" on an object that is the correct distance (if none exists, place an object there for the class to see).—BK/LM—evaluation (I, G)

5. Predict how big our brains would need to be if we kept our current brain power but enlarged the brain's vision and hearing processing centers to be in proportion to that of an owl. Compute the total volume or weight of this new brain. Explain how you estimated your answer.—LM and S—evaluation (I, G)

6. Using clay, make a model of the transformations of a human head that would be needed to improve our hearing to be more like an owl's.—BK—synthesis (I, G)

7. Compose lyrics for a song (choose a melody or use a rap rhythm) chronicling an owl's hunting expedition using its hearing. Perform the song for the class. Include at least three verses and a refrain.—M/BK— synthesis (I, G)

Inquiries for the Primary Grades

In flavor and purpose, inquiries at the primary grades function the same as for grades 4-6 with some necessary adaptations to take into account the basic work tools available (or not available) to the younger learner.

Necessary adaptations include the following:

- Make sure the inquiries are age-appropriate. Of the example inquiries, #2, #3, and #5 would be inappropriate for primary students. However, #1, #4, and #7 would make good whole-class inquiries in follow-up to direct instruction or initial discovery process. (For #7, delete the step of composing the song unless expert help is available.)

- Control the range of choices offered at any one time. Primary students typically cannot handle a wide range of choices because they have neither the reading and writing skills to interpret and respond to the inquiry nor the social/work skills to work unassisted. The younger the student, the more restricted the range of choices needs to be. For example, at K-1, the teacher usually chooses the inquiry for the class but gives the students choices as to medium of response, e.g., choices offered with inquiry #6 could be clay, finger-paints, crayons/markers, pencil sketch, etc. At second grade, the teacher might offer students two inquiries to choose from. By the third grade, the range of choices should continue to expand.

- Make sure that the inquiries are based on and provide *being there* experiences, not just hands-on of representational items

- Make sure the statements (key points and inquiries) are conceptually accurate. Don't distort the facts and concepts in an attempt to "water them down" for "kid consumption." If the truth is too complicated, leave it for a later year

CHAPTER 13: DEVELOPING INQUIRIES

GETTING A LITTLE HELP FROM THE KIDS!

Does this sound like an incredible amount of work? Initially, yes. But once your awareness of students' capacities and how to meet them expands and you have developed a *pattern* and *mental program* for writing inquiries, you will find that your mind will automatically be searching out activities to support your theme. Also, students as young as third grade are very adept at writing inquiries according to Bloom's Taxonomy once they are familiar with the six questioning levels. They love to do so, filling their inquiries with imagination, great creativity, and surprising challenge. Their inquiries are often even better than what the teacher comes up with; carefully selected and mixed with those developed by the teacher, they constitute a significant contribution to the teacher's task of developing curriculum. Developing inquiries is also a good thinking exercise because one can't pose a good question or frame a worthwhile learning task without a good understanding of the key point and its application in the real world.

CRITERIA FOR EVALUATING INQUIRIES

When developing inquiries, there are several criteria to keep in mind. Good inquiries:

- offer firsthand applications in a real world context and encourage students to ask questions and seek answers
- are clearly related to the key point(s)—they apply and expand the key points and show real world connections
- provide ample opportunities to apply the concepts, skills, and significant information of the key points in varying real world situations to ensure that all students develop mental programs
- provide genuine choice for students
- promote development of all seven intelligences
- are worthy of the time to be spent

HOW TO USE INQUIRIES

Inquiries serve two important functions. First, they are the part of written curriculum which ensures that children learn how to apply what they learn to real world situations and develop mental programs for such use that will be retained in long term memory. Second, they are the bridge between curriculum development and the planning of instructional strategies and the orchestration of learning in the classroom

As a resource in planning instructional strategies, they are the building blocks for lesson design and the selection of instructional strategies. For example, a specially designed inquiry can become the structure for a discovery process, or an inquiry can become the activity that follows direct instruction so that the teacher can check for understanding, or inquiries can provide choice for a collaborative learning group or for individual choice. Or, when specially crafted, an inquiry can become the means of authentically assessing mastery of a key point.

EVALUATING STUDENT WORK ON INQUIRIES

If we truly believe that the information we put forth to students has value for them, then anything less than mastery is a failure on our part. Given the model's focus on competence, mastery, and application, the following criteria for assessing student work on ITI inquiries and other work in the classroom are recommended:

1. **COMPLETE:** Was the assignment completed as stated? Is it ready to be handed in? Does the presentation of the paper or project meet the specifications described in the inquiry? Does it reflect real world standards for work performed in the workplace while remaining age-appropriate? Does it reflect pride in workmanship and personal best?

2. **CORRECT:** Is the information correct? Has an effort been made to use a variety of resources including those with the most recent copyright date?

3. **COMPREHENSIVE (covered the topic or concept):** Has the student addressed the topic as thoroughly as possible? Are all sides of an issue covered or just one? Is there a resource to back up the information? Does he/she demonstrate an understanding of the content, e.g., he/she can explain it to another?

If student work does not meet these three standards, it should be returned to the students to be redone until it meets the standards. **No work should be accepted from a student unless it meets these standards.** For example, students should be held to mastery on spelling, punctuation, and other language and writing mechanics in order to ensure that they develop accurate *mental programs* for using language. This might mean that a student completes fewer inquiries but what work he/she does accomplish will result in information that has application. The goal of an ITI teacher is: Do less, but do it well (to the level of application and *mental program* building vs. doing/covering a lot with little real learning occurring).

If letter grades must be used on the report card (and they should be used only as a last resort when mandated by the system), they should be based upon mastery of the learning accomplished. All students who master the key points should receive an *A*. Learning is its own reward; if the content is meaningful and meets the CUE criteria, students will push onward past the *A* to lifelong learning.

For a full discussion of mastery, see Chapter 9.

CHAPTER FOURTEEN

INTEGRATING BASIC SKILLS

A major fallacy about the Integrated Thematic Instruction model is that it is fine for the content areas, such as science and social studies, but that it doesn't teach those skills which are necessary to become a literate citizen, i.e., reading, writing, and mathematics. **This is an inaccurate perception**.

First, ITI does lend itself powerfully to the content areas. Social studies and science are excellent sources for meaningful themes. It is easier to build interest around a yearlong study of "The Mississippi River" or "I Adoregan" (I Adore Oregon) than, say, "Punctuation." Second, while the possibility does exist that skills might be neglected, such neglect is not inherent in the ITI structure but is a result of failure in the implementation of the model. Examples of poor or misdirected teaching can be found everywhere, even in the ITI model. When it occurs, it is due to a lack of full understanding of the model and of how the brain learns. Knowledge of the skills inherent in reading, writing, speaking, and mathematics, and skill in teaching them, are prerequisites for successful implementation of this and any model of teaching.

The following eighteen pages are taken directly from the ITI book, *Classroom of the 21st Century* by Robert Ellingsen. This book is a companion to a video of the same title (published by Susan Kovalik & Associates—see order form at the back of this book). Together, they document Robert's classroom application of the ITI model as a framework for integrating all basic skills and content areas.

CHAPTER 14: INTEGRATING SKILLS

THE CLASSROOM OF THE 21ST CENTURY

Skills are taught in the brain-compatible classroom, but only within the context of the content of the integrated theme. The difference is that skills do not drive the curriculum. Instead, they are placed within a meaningful framework. For example, learning the sound "a" in isolation has no meaning without the larger context of a word. The word "heel" only has meaning within the larger context of a sentence because the "heel" of a shoe is different from the "heel" who broke last night's date. Likewise, learning how to compute the area of rectangles has no meaning without the context of a useful application such as "How many cans of this color paint do we need for this part of the room?" Without the context of the theme, the mastery of the skill becomes meaningless. The question invariably will be asked, "Why?" and "Because I told you so" is not a satisfactory answer.

Skills only have meaning within the larger context of their usefulness. When they are useful, they are learned. Children do not learn to speak because adults want them to; children learn to speak because it is useful. This is true of adults as well; we know it from our own experience. I took five years of Spanish while attending public schools, but it wasn't until I moved to an ethnically diverse area that I had a need to know Spanish. Suddenly it became useful; there was a reason to learn a second language. Reason and purpose accelerate learning.

So how does one make something like computing the area of rectangles useful within a theme? I teach the skill within a meaningful framework. Each year my class performs a Shakespearean play. As part of our preparation, the class designs and paints stage flats of scenery for our performance. Each of the five flats are 4' by 8' and the students need to construct scale drawings of their set design. Students find the area formula a useful tool as they construct their own three-dimensional, miniature sets. Frank Smith states that "learning is incidental."[1] Learning takes place within the course of everyday, real activities. It is within the context of this real activity—building a stage set—that students learn the geometric concept of area.

Although skills are taught in the Integrated Thematic Instruction classroom, they do not drive the curriculum. Content drives the curriculum and skills are taught as they relate to the content, as their usefulness becomes apparent. Before public education took hold in this country, many young boys were apprenticed to skilled laborers in a variety of fields. This is the perfect example of the power of relevant context for learning skills. As they learned a trade, boys learned all the skills associated with that trade, and there was never a doubt as to "Why?"

READING

You learn by doing. A child does not learn to speak by learning about speaking; a child learns to speak by speaking. So, first and foremost, when teaching reading, let students read. And since usefulness is a prime motivator, what the students read must relate to the topic being explored in some meaningful way. Sara Zimet notes that conventional "reading texts emphasize skill, and reading is taught for the sake of the skill itself [whereas] we need to shift our emphasis from 'reading to learn to read' to 'reading about something meaningful while learning to read.' By emphasizing the process to the exclusion of meaningful ideas, we sacrifice the raison d'etre for learning to read."[2]

Children's fantasies and realities are so much more exciting than the boring words and scenes of most basal reading texts. For this reason my method has been to use children's novels to teach reading. As I plan my year theme, I brainstorm possibilities for the reading component. During the PATHFINDERS component of my theme, the novel I selected was *My Side of the Mountain* by Jean George. It is the story of a boy who ventures into the wilderness and learns to survive without the trappings of modern life—a perfect fit with our study of Lewis and Clark and the other pathfinders of history.

CHAPTER 14: INTEGRATING SKILLS

All students should have equal access to rich, significant literature. Oftentimes educators separate their poor readers from their good readers. And where are these poor readers placed? Into a basal text that is even more simplistic and contrived than the one from which they were pulled, thereby compounding their difficulty in searching for meaning. **ALL students should have an enriched curriculum.**

All students of all abilities in my classroom read *My Side of the Mountain*, some with ease, some with difficulty, but all with fascination and enjoyment. Each day a selection is assigned. Students make the free choice of whether to read silently, with a partner, or orally in a group. The only requirement is that they meet with the teacher at least once a week for an oral reading check. When students are entrusted with the power to make their own choices, they tend to self-select the appropriate placement given their ability. My poorer readers chose to meet with me daily. But when they came to reading group, they were joined by other students making the choice to read orally, a heterogeneous group full of good reading models. Why do we put poor readers only with poor readers? Who will model correct reading behaviors for them?

Heterogeneous reading groups, in addition to being academically sound, have the extra benefit of building self-esteem. There is no "dumb group." It builds the sense that "we're all in this together" and encourages understanding and acceptance of individual differences.

Granted, there are students who can legitimately benefit from extra help. I do think moving to a more enriched curriculum will eliminate the need for some prescriptive services, but not all. What about those students? They do need extra help but that help should be **offered within the bounds of the curriculum and tied closely to the theme** of their classroom experience. And the single most meaningful place for a child is with the classroom teacher. Pull-out programs should be avoided at all cost. I propose, instead, a **pull-in program** where specialists work with students within a self-contained, safe, supportive classroom. Logistics can be a problem to overcome but we need to do what is best for kids, not what is most convenient for the bureaucracy.

Comprehension

The best way to learn to read is to read. But there is more to reading than correctly decoding words. The Spanish alphabet is phonetically regular and I have learned my sounds well. I can go into many classrooms, pick up a Spanish reader and pronounce word after word with only the slightest Anglo accent. But am I reading? Correctly calling words with no understanding is not reading, and phonics, while a helpful tool, is only that—a tool for correct decoding. Phonics does not concern itself with understanding. How is comprehension addressed in the ITI classroom? Not with worksheets.

I propose to involve students more actively in the comprehension process. Once more I find Bloom's Taxonomy to be an amazing aid in this respect—simple to use, but powerful. Daily, after reading period, the class comes together for a discussion of the day's selection. A copy of Bloom's Taxonomy is placed on the overhead and the class uses this to discuss the story. This copy is the only comprehension worksheet the students receive during the year. At first, the teacher may use it to ask questions, but, with practice, students become quite adept at generating the questions and at knowing the level at which they are being asked to think. This is metacognition at its best—knowing how to learn and knowing when you are doing it.

To obtain a written record, once a week the activity is written. Learning teams brainstorm questions, present them to the class, and choose a specified number to answer. Students then write the questions and answers neatly, in complete sentences, and with correct spelling and capitalization—a much more active approach than the passive lines and circles of most commercially produced worksheets. How, you might ask, do students complete a neat and grammatically correct paper? First, they are held accountable for it. Expectations are everything. Second, in the absence of worksheets, students have many more opportunities for real writing; the worksheet doesn't do the writing for them. And finally, no one is left without support. Students have their cooperative learning team to assist them and the teacher, as part of the learning team, is constantly circling the room, encouraging and giving **immediate feedback**.

CHAPTER 14: INTEGRATING SKILLS

Reading Skills

Another component of reading is the skills, represented by those omnipresent workbooks. First, realize that skills are there to support reading. If the skill does not directly aid a student in the decoding and comprehending of a passage, then its viability needs to be seriously questioned. I have clear and painful memories of trying to teach students how to identify accent marks in words with a program that even went so far as to differentiate between primary and secondary accents. The irony, of course, is that the students could already read the words. Nevertheless, they failed in that all-important skill: the fine distinctions in stress. The question remains: "Was the skill useful?" And a further question continues to haunt us: "How many of these workbook skills, which consume such a large part of a student's learning time, are necessary to produce successful and lifelong readers?" Teaching skills is not teaching reading; reading teaches reading—the practice of extracting meaning from print. Skills can be a useful aid, but only within a larger context, and only when they are useful. They are not an end in themselves.

When content truly drives the skills component of curriculum, skills are taught when they make the most sense. For example, using the index is taught when students begin their research projects and find using an index a helpful way to locate information; time lines are taught as students study historical events; and outlining is taught as students write research papers. Workbooks, which present skills in an arbitrary fashion, are unnecessary.

Parts of speech. We all teach them. Apparently students never learn them—why else do we ALL teach them? My class is introduced to parts of speech during our GEOGRAPHY component. As students study our state, they find one location for each letter of the alphabet, plot it on a grid, compute miles and kilometers from our own location, and use that location in an ABC book. This provides ample opportunity for work in a wide variety of skills: alphabetical order, map skills, and mathematical computations. Students then write their own ABC books, using a pattern established in the *Oregon ABC Book:* "Adrian Albright, the adorable actress, anticipates acclaim in Ashland's amphitheater."[3] Children identify proper nouns for people and places, adjectives to describe the nouns, verbs to state the action, and adverbs to describe the verbs. And all this is done within the context of their own writing, about locations they have studied in their home state. This is the teachable moment, that point in time when students are most in tune with the learning. Why? Because it is useful, it is creative, and it is emotional—there is a healthy dose of fun as students stretch their imaginations.

As I developed the skill component of the reading program, I found that the skills are repeated in a cycle. Of the thirty skills taught in the intermediate level of the Houghton-Mifflin reading series, twenty-one are taught at two grade levels, and an amazing *seventeen* are taught at all three grade levels. Why, then, must students be placed in ability groups, forever labeled, with no chance for reprieve, when all levels are working on the same skills?

In the ITI classroom, skills are introduced in the large group, students work on the skill only until they have mastered it, and students continue working on that skill until it is mastered. There is no low group, middle group, or high group. Instead there is a guide word group, a syllabification group, etc. Within these temporary, flexible groups are students with a wide range of achievement levels, all in need of practice with the same skill. Once again, the "we're all in this together" attitude is developed. Artificial demarcations convenient to the authorities are torn down and students work in heterogeneous settings.

CHAPTER 14: INTEGRATING SKILLS

Vocabulary

Vocabulary development is an ongoing process. In a meaningful classroom environment it happens continuously at an informal level, just as children originally learn the spoken language. "All children except the most severely deprived or handicapped acquire a vocabulary of over 10,000 words during the first four or five years of their lives. At the age of four they are adding to their vocabulary at the rate of twenty new words a day. By seven this rate may have increased to nearly thirty words. . . . By late adolescence the average vocabulary is at least 50,000 words."[4] How is this done? Not by worksheets, not by looking words up in the dictionary, not by formal instruction. It is done because the brain is the organ for learning; it will learn what is useful. The 50,000 words children pick up by adolescence are words they find to be useful.

The key to formal vocabulary instruction is to make it useful and meaningful to the student. The obvious method in an ITI classroom is to closely tie vocabulary instruction to the theme.

Current events are an integral part of the brain-compatible classroom because the brain-compatible classroom focuses on the real world. Knowledge of current events is essential for the politically active populace of a democracy. The brain-compatible classroom is the classroom that prepares students to take on this role as active citizens.

OREGON TODAY is the name given to our current events strand. Each morning one student is responsible for sharing an article related to the theme. That article then becomes part of our classroom collection folder where all articles are filed and classified. Once a week an article is chosen to be the class' reading selection for the day. Learning teams read, mindmap, and discuss the article. They are also responsible for choosing the one word that interests them most. Learning teams share their word with the class and the class then has five new vocabulary words, one word per learning team. These words are entered into the students' personal dictionaries and onto our OREGON TODAY vocabulary chart for continual reinforcement. Whenever a student finds that word in any other reading, a star is added to the chart. A very simple approach but, tied to the theme, it becomes meaningful. And the probability that the word is learned and stored increases.

WRITING

A pattern is forming: children learn to speak by speaking and to read by reading. Little wonder, then, that children learn to write by writing. That is not to say that merely writing, with no skill instruction, will produce literate citizens. But we do know that heavy doses of skill instruction, separated from the meaningful context of real writing, do not work. The literate student must write every day. And that writing must have purpose and an audience.

The journal approach to daily writing is an exceptional example of real writing assignments. Students keep a notebook full of their own musing: dreams, concerns, and questions, a daily record of their lives. This is real writing in its truest sense because it is student-centered and student-directed. There are no contrived topics or arbitrary limits on length. Writing is useful because it becomes a vehicle by which children connect with the outside world, taking what is within and giving it form and substance.

I have had much success with this method, yet I know not all teachers have. When I've compared notes with my colleagues for whom it hasn't worked, I find one noticeable difference: I write back to the author—not just a few sprinklings of "great" or "good point," but writing of significant length and meaning. If a child writes to me about his/her pets, I write about my pets. If a child writes about favorite foods, I write about mine. The journal becomes a dialogue between us; it establishes rapport. Finally, it provides a meaningful context within which to place skill instruction.

I recommend several different approaches to writing. Journals are but one component of the writing program, writing folders are another. Journals are daily jottings. The writing folder is for long-term story development. Work with writing folders occurs during a portion of the day called WRITERS' WORKSHOP, a time when students learn the writing process: pre-writing, rough draft, revision, editing, and publishing. Children use the skills developed during writers' workshop to develop their own creative writing. Works in progress are filed in the writing folder until that time the student determines the piece is ready for publication. Occasionally specific assignments are given if they fit the theme, but more often students are engaged in constructing stories from their own imaginations. Many states have ongoing summer institutes where teachers learn the writing process. The key is that the teacher also becomes a writer and models for the class his own ongoing work. My students assisted me in writing my story "Reggie at the Bat." The students, in a sense, become apprenticed to the teacher as author.

Writing Skills

The daily journal and the writing folder provide the structure for direct instruction of skills. They are the blueprint. Once they are in place, the skills, which are the building materials, can be used to construct literacy. But where would they be placed with no blueprint as a guide? Teaching skills such as capitalization and noun/verb agreement, apart from any meaningful writing, is like giving the carpenter the 2' x 4's and asking him to build a house without a plan. The product would be a haphazard, rickety construction, destined to come tumbling down and ill-fitting the needs of its inhabitants.

Once the framework of real writing is in place, skill instruction can proceed. A variety of methods can be used. Basal English series offer pages of practice, and there is nothing wrong with their occasional use as need dictates. But why go through the book cover to cover? Why let the textbook publisher dictate the curriculum when it is the classroom teacher who is the educational expert? It is the teacher who, having student writing in hand, can diagnose and prescribe skill instruction appropriate to the needs of each particular group of writers.

If, in their writing, students are writing conversations, and writing them incorrectly, then that is the teachable moment—the appropriate time to teach the correct use of quotation marks. If certain words are consistently misspelled, then they become a part of that student's spelling list. If letters are continually formed illegibly, then handwriting instruction is called for.

The theme itself may provide opportune times for addressing particular skills. During our Shakespeare unit, the class play is *A Midsummer Night's Dream*. This is the perfect opportunity to introduce apostrophes. The play's title becomes a meaningful "hook" on which to attach the skill instruction.

To ensure that skill instruction proceeds at a systematic pace I have a daily editing practice modeled after the DAILY ORAL LANGUAGE series (D.O.L.). Admittedly, the name is a bit misleading. A more accurate title might be DAILY WRITTEN LANGUAGE, as the editing task is with paper and pencil. The program's title stems from the fact that once the written editing assignment is complete, it is processed orally.

A short selection, full of errors, is placed on the board most mornings when students enter the classroom. They know from the posted daily agenda that their first task is to edit this selection. Once again, cooperation is encouraged. Later in the morning the class meets together and orally processes the passage, finally recopying a fully corrected final version. This happens over time until the majority of the class has mastered the skill and can independently write a perfect copy the first time. New writing skills are then introduced, taken from common errors occurring in journals and writing folders. Those students who still have not mastered the original skill continue to meet with me during Writers' Workshop.

MATH

For five years I had avoided integrating mathematics. I was tied to the text, my own math anxiety holding me back. Finally, I had no choice if I wanted a fully integrated classroom—math was the only subject still on the outside. What I found, to my amazement, was that math is the simplest of all skill areas to integrate. All that is needed is statistics, real life numbers to work with. How lucky! Statistics are everywhere!

Cobblestone magazine is a history magazine for young people. In September, 1980, the entire issue was devoted to Lewis and Clark. This, in effect, became our "basal text" for the week, the base of study for all subjects, including math. It is a rich source of statistics about the Lewis and Clark expedition. Those below are only a small sampling of the statistics available, providing many opportunities for real world "story problems." But, given the full immersion of the students into reliving the Lewis and Clark expedition, they become more than mere "story problems"; they become real life applications.

Available Statistics:

- Lewis and Clark started their journey up the Missouri River on May 14, 1804

- The entire central basin of North America was purchased from the French for four cents an acre, or a total of $15,000,000

- A Scotsman named Alexander Mackenzie had published an account of the same region in 1793

- The Great Falls were a series of five large waterfalls that stretched over 15 miles on the Missouri River

- From beginning to end, the walk over the Rocky Mountains took three-and-a-half months

- On their return trip, Lewis and Clark separated for six weeks to explore different regions

- Lewis and Clark returned to St. Louis on September 23, 1806

MATH

Problems to Be Solved Based on the Available Statistics:

- How many years ago did Lewis and Clark begin exploring the Louisiana Purchase?

- How many acres of land did Thomas Jefferson purchase from France?

- Approximately how many miles were between each of the Great Falls of the Missouri River?

- Assuming that all months are thirty days long, how many days did it take Lewis and Clark to cross the Rocky Mountains?

- Using your previous answer, how many weeks did it take Lewis and Clark to cross the Rocky Mountains?

- How many days were Lewis and Clark separated during their trip?

- 30 days have September, April, June, and November. All the rest have 31, excepting February, which has 28. Knowing this, what was the total number of days of the Lewis and Clark expedition?

This last problem is the most difficult of all. Very few of my fourth graders answered it correctly at first. But I've never seen such excitement, motivation, and problem-solving strategies as when students attempt it.

Problems such as these form the core of THEME MATH, a term I use with students to distinguish it from other components of the math program. Theme math uses **real world** problems closely tied to the content. Students attack these problems with more motivation than the artificial problems of basal series. The interest is built in; the students have some curiosity to find out more about whom and what they have been studying.

The amount of thinking involved is awesome when compared to a basal text. Students need to identify the problem, find the data necessary to solve the problem, identify the operation needed to solve the problem, and then finally compute the answer. What's more, the statistics are not conveniently listed for them as they are for you here. Students search for them within the context of the historical narrative.

THEME MATH is a prime motivator for students in learning mathematical skills. Suddenly there is a reason for memorizing those basic facts, to KNOW—to **really know** everything about the Lewis and Clark expedition. In addition, theme math is an excellent method for building conceptual understanding of the four operations. Students develop a sense of what addition looks like, how it "feels" and sounds in comparison with the other operations. *And all the while they are working in the realm of the real world, with real numbers*—**APPLICATION!**

It is essential that the teacher understand the purpose of THEME MATH. It is to build *conceptual understanding*, not to drill on memorization of facts and computations. Students who do not have their multiplication facts memorized are still capable of understanding the concept of multiplication. *Memorization of facts should not be a prerequisite to opportunities for applying concepts.* If anything, building the concepts should come first, giving the student the meaningful framework before the individual skill bits are put into place.

Math Skills

Mathematical computation is still an essential life skill. THEME MATH does not replace that. But it does enhance computation by giving it meaning and purpose. Computation is still addressed. In fact, within this meaningful context of the theme, computation is learned much more readily.

DAILY ORAL MATH (D.O.M.) is one way to reinforce math skills. Similar to daily oral language (the daily drill in written language), it is a short and sweet math review. Alternating with D.O.L., it may consist of four problems reviewing the four operations, or it may be other math skills more closely aligned with the day's thematic activities. Skills such as a review of the formula for computing area during our Shakespearean set design, or using a scale of miles to compute distance during our GEOGRAPHY component can be reinforced during D.O.M. The daily agenda points out that this is one of the first tasks to be completed. Later in the day, student volunteers solve the problems for the class, modeling correct form and computation.

A DAY IN THE LIFE OF

So how does it all come together? How does the teacher orchestrate all the various elements of a brain-compatible classroom? The ITI model is truly unique in that it draws from a wide variety of excellent approaches and sources and synthesizes them into a unique whole. Language experience is an excellent approach to teaching reading, but what about math? The university sponsored writing projects teach writing in a brain-compatible way, but what about social studies? Math Their Way is an experiential and hands-on approach to mathematics instruction, but what about science? The ITI approach seeks to break down these artificial walls between curricular areas, take the best from each, and infuse brain-compatible instruction into all subjects for a truly integrated whole. And it does so with a profound respect for the professional expertise of the classroom teacher.

Flexibility is the key word in planning a fully integrated day, week, month, or year. School schedules are arbitrary demarcations of time and **are highly brain-antagonistic**. Lessons should not be forced into the artificial constraints of a set time period; **the content should determine the schedule.** The self-contained classroom offers the greatest opportunity for fully integrating subject areas.

I hesitate to share specifics of a daily schedule because the model will find a unique implementation in every classroom. **The power of the model lies in its adaptability to individual teaching styles.** Nevertheless, offering a picture of a typical day in the life of a brain-compatible classroom may provide teachers with a starting point. Schedules are merely those starting points, flexible frameworks to be altered as content dictates. My 9:00 a.m. starting time and a 3:30 p.m. closing time made it possible for me to think of the instructional day as being divided into four blocks: two morning periods and two afternoon periods.

I recommend you begin the day with the theme. It provides students with a focal point for the day's activities. In a classroom not yet fully integrated, this would mean beginning the day with the content area on which the theme is based, e.g., a classroom whose theme is "Entomology" would begin the day with science. The benefit of the fully integrated classroom is that all subjects relate to the theme and the day may begin with whatever subject area makes the most sense within the context of the day's topic. What the teacher organizes is a blend of common elements which maintain a sense of stability and comfort for students, intermixed with a daily flow of ever-changing events and topics—a miniature slice of real life.

Generally, I begin my day* with a language arts block. When students enter the classroom, they are greeted by me personally, a daily agenda detailing exactly what will occur that day, and background music playing softly to enhance thinking. The rule is quiet study as students begin their tasks: DAILY ORAL LANGUAGE and/or DAILY ORAL MATH to review skills, then on to silent and/or oral reading of the day's selection, followed by independent work with ongoing INQUIRY projects. At some point I bring the class together for stretching, aerobics, and relaxation—important techniques which help focus students' bodies and minds on the topic for the day. This is followed by a discussion of the day's reading based on Bloom's Taxonomy and a large group discussion and correction of the skills review. Finally, during OREGON TODAY, the current events article for the day is shared.

---

* This structure for organizing the day was developed by Robert Ellingsen, over a five year period. It is offered here as a beginning point, not a model. Structure for the day should ensure that the basic skills are included on a daily basis but should also flow with the content and encourage full integration.

A DAY IN THE LIFE OF

The second morning block is reserved for science and social studies. This is when students receive and work with the key points of instruction. Lecture, reading, discussion, films, experiments, and inquiries all receive equal emphasis as conceptual understanding of the major thematic components is built. Each day sees a different focus. Perhaps a lecture and reading on the key points early in the week, moving toward more interactive pursuits by the end of the week, with possible closure of the week, topic, or entire component by Friday.

The first afternoon block is reserved for mathematics. This is equally divided between THEME MATH for concept building and MATH GROUPS for computation practice. Oftentimes the week begins and ends with THEME MATH to provide a frame within which the rest of math instruction is placed.

The final afternoon block returns to language arts. A skill is introduced or reinforced with the large group. This is followed by a large group WRITERS' WORKSHOP where works in progress are shared and elements of good writing are discussed. Students then move on to independent writing time, engaging in real writing activities such as JOURNAL, letters, and creative writing of their own choice. During this independent time the teacher is free to confer with individuals and/or conduct SKILLSHOPS, the small, temporary, and flexible skill groups.

What about other subject areas such as art, music, and computers? They all find a place in the schedule as appropriate. Sketching and watercolor techniques are taught when the day's reading concerns that subject, e.g., Sam's sketching of his falcon. Students work with clay after reading and discussing a newspaper article about a local sculptor and his Lewis and Clark statues. Pioneer songs and instruments are used in preparation for the class' Oregon Trail adventure. Computers are used during the writing process as students edit and publish their work. Computers are also used when software exists that enhances understanding of the topic, such as the Oregon Trail or Pathfinders simulation games. Everything fits. It's just a new fit. In the traditional classroom, content is made to fit the schedule; in the ITI classroom, **the schedule is made to fit the content.**

CHAPTER 14: INTEGRATING SKILLS

A self-contained, heterogeneous classroom is a superior design for the ITI classroom. There are fewer interruptions to fragment the day, the sense of belonging is more fully developed, and students aren't segregated according to ability. Because the mathematical problems are selected mostly with an eye to their meaningfulness, assignments and group collaboration guidelines are set up to ensure that all students, of varying degrees of ability, experience success. Problems are solved within the learning team and calculators are allowed.

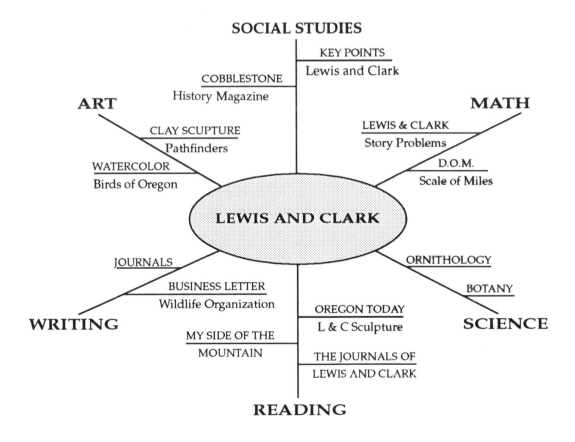

ORCHESTRATING A CONCEPT-IN-A-DAY: LONG DIVISION*

It is estimated that it takes two years and three months for students to learn long division. The division facts are introduced in the third grade, the algorithm is introduced in the fourth grade, again in the fifth and sixth grades. From year to year, the same instructional pattern, even into the basic math courses in junior and senior high—the teacher does a problem on the board, the class does a number of "practice" problems at their desks, and then students are responsible for completing ten to twenty problems for homework.

While attending a week-long Susan Kovalik Model Teaching Program, Martha Kaufeldt was challenged to address this problem by orchestrating the learning environment and curriculum in such a way that it would be possible to INTRODUCE and have the students achieve MASTERY of the CONCEPT AND COMPUTATION OF LONG DIVISION **IN A SINGLE DAY!**

Martha's work pioneered the notion of teaching a major concept in a single day. Since her Long Division Day six years ago, thousands of students across the country have been able to master division in a single day using this model.

---

*The description of Division Day beginning on the next page is a summary of Martha's experience as described in her book *I Can Divide and Conquer: A Concept in a Day!*, a teachers' handbook for implementing Division Day in their own classroom. The book is a companion to the videotape of the same name (published by Susan Kovalik & Associates—see the order form at the back of this book).

CHAPTER 14: INTEGRATING SKILLS

For the first three months of school, my thirty-three fourth and fifth grade students worked on sharpening their accuracy in addition, subtraction, and multiplication. Division facts were memorized by rote. Seventeen other fifth and sixth grade students in our school were recommended by their teachers as students who had mastered the skills of multiplication but had failed to master division.

The day before Division Day all fifty students met. I led them verbally through some relaxation techniques and also asked them to see their own success in learning long division. They all took a pretest in division and were given encouraging words about what would happen the next day.

OVERVIEW OF THE DAY'S ACTIVITIES

Theme for the day: I CAN DIVIDE AND CONQUER!

Elements used to program positive performance:

- Students saw their success

- Each student received a "goodie" box with pencil, slate, and name tag

- Students were divided into groups of five. Group building activities included adopting a famous mathematician who would serve as the group mascot for the day

- Incentives were given at every other station

- Mini-stickers were given to anyone who ASKED FOR HELP

- Lunch was provided by parents. Pizza was divided into different numbers of slices

- Each student earned an "I CAN DIVIDE AND CONQUER" badge and a certificate at the end of the day

- Warm, loving, enthusiastic adult leaders were always available

CONCEPT-IN-A-DAY

FORMAT AT EACH STATION (TELL, SHOW, SOLVE, CHECK)

- Read problem aloud—(every student)

- Discuss what the problem is asking or describing. Have students restate in own words

- Point out (ask students to identify) DIVIDEND and DIVISOR

- Ask students to close eyes while you help them visualize the problem. Use a soothing voice while using lots of descriptive words. Ask students to see themselves in the picture, doing the sorting or dividing

- Draw students' attention to manipulatives they will be using, e.g., beads, beans, etc. Point out that they are substitutes for the real thing

Show. Work out the problem with the manipulatives. If possible, students should have their own sets. Otherwise, work it out cooperatively. Repeat it one or two times if necessary. Identify quotient and remainders, if any. Have a special place for the "remainder" to be placed.

Solve.

- Demonstrate how a problem is written as a number sentence

- Identify terms

- Begin a step-by-step approach to the algorithm. Divide, multiply, subtract, bring down. Frequently relate computation to what had been done with manipulatives

- Have students work out problem on graph paper for accuracy

- Ask each to turn to partner and ask them to explain the problem in "MATH SPEAK"

Check.

- Demonstrate how to check by multiplying and adding remainder

- If there is time, make variations of the problem and ask students to solve

- Write a comment in each student passport if you feel student has mastered that problem

- If the student needs more help, continue working, or ask the student to come back at free-choice time, or direct student to a roving helper

- Repeat center to next group. Give incentive rewards to students in second center

METHODS OF ORCHESTRATING LEARNING

- Used the Library Media Center with assistance from the Media Specialist

- Twenty-six different learning stations were designed that had concrete examples to illustrate concepts.

- Students were given choices for elective stations

- Two management standards for the day: No Put-Downs and Active Listening

- Snack station was set up by parents with graham crackers and juice

- Students worked through recesses and took breaks as needed

- Students worked in groups of five

- Fifteen adults had been recruited and trained to help: parents, aides, student teachers, community volunteers

- Mini-grant money had been applied for and some parents made donations

CONCEPT-IN-A-DAY

Maximize Input to the Brain

Each segment of the day was designed to maximize input to the brain.

Visual. The problem was presented on the bulletin board and in the student handbook. Students used manipulatives to SEE the arrangement of the problem.

Auditory. Every station leader verbalized each problem. Students explained the problem using Math Speak. A hand-jive was developed for the mathematical process.

Tactile. Twenty-six different sets of manipulatives were available to use—common classroom items as well as shells, buttons, small cars, and dominoes.

Kinesthetic. Division P.E., Division Drama, Division Art, Division Music, and a series of hand motions (a "hand jive") were developed to remember the math patterns (divide, multiply, subtract, bring down).

Patterns for the Day

- format at each station
  - –Tell
  - –Show
  - –Solve
  - –Check
- direct instruction limited to eleven to sixteen minutes per hour
- forty-five minutes of group work at each station
- relaxation periods throughout day

Choices

Students chose art, music or drama stations, flexible environment breaks when needed, and they could ask for more help on a one-to-one basis.

At the end of the SEVEN-HOUR DAY (yes, they came early and stayed late!), students received a certificate and a badge.

The post-test was given the following day; some students improved as much as 150 percent. Post-tests given three months later showed continued improvement and retention. Students have shared with me that they felt this was one of the most important days in their lives!

"Thank you, Susan, for planting the seed."

A CONCEPT in a DAY!

MARTHA MILLER KAUFELDT

THREE LEVELS OF MATH

"ANCHOR" MATH

THREE LEVELS OF MATH LANGUAGE*

Leslie Hart, creator of the term "brain-compatible" and author of *Human Brain and Human Learning,* has a new book, *Anchor Math: An Informal Book for All Who Teach Elementary Math and Want to Greatly Increase Student Achievement.*

His new work clearly provides teachers with opportunities to teach math in a useful way, a way that creates *"mental programs"* for conceptualization and computation. According to Hart, it may be helpful, or at least intriguing, to think of math languages in three clusters.

First, we have "practical" math, which helps us deal with the mostly concrete world of here and now, including all of our daily transactions, ordering, physical work, current data, etc. Examples: spent $144.75 for clothes, poured 12 cubic yards of concrete, produced 12,000 widgets, have 322 patients in the hospital.

Second, we have "projective" math, dealing with what should, or could, or might happen. You plan out a trip; or work out estimates for a new business; or figure out how fast a rocket will likely be traveling within four minutes after launch; or how many cases of measles could occur within the next two years.

Third, we have "investigative" math, where we are interested in trends and relationships, limits, interactions, and, in general, digging out significant concepts by using mathematical techniques. We might analyze election results to see the role played by racial concerns or gain some insight into an intricate chemical reaction. Included would be "game" math, essentially playing with numbers or mathematical elements for no immediate, "real" purpose.

Pages 203 through 207 are excerpted from *Anchor Math: An Informal Book for All Who Teach Elementary Math and Want to Greatly Increase Student Achievement* written by Leslie Hart and published by Books for Educators (see order form at the back of this book).

CHAPTER 14: INTEGRATING SKILLS

Our purpose, or need, would determine which kind of math we do. Outside of classrooms, nobody does math without some purpose in mind. (That should make us think about some things we do in classrooms.)

THE CONCEPT OF "n-NESS"

Let us assume that a particular student is able to

– Name the digit . . . "five"
– Write the digit
– Count off objects to match the digit

It still may be true that the student does not have the sense of that number, a sense that we can call "five-ness." *This sense of number* constitutes one of the main foundational elements of grasping math and being able to do or interpret math with ease and confidence. Some people like to say that the student "feels" the number—which is all right if you like that expression.

Another way to put it is to say that the student has acquired a sense of "shape" for that number and a direct approach, not a "counting" approach.

For instance, if the student hears "five" and then counts one-two-three-four-five, that is a slow and cumbersome way, as compared with directly feeling "five-ness."

This sense of "n-ness" can readily be encouraged and developed by the teacher . . . and, as we shall see, it can be applied not only to the digits but to many numbers as they are "anchored." (The term "anchor" will be explained soon.)

Suppose we ask a 10-year-old student: "What is the difference between numbers 23 and 24?" One student may reply, "24 is one more than 23." That is correct but not the reply we are seeking.

Another student says, "Oh, they are very different! 23 is a stiff, awkward number while 24 is wonderful—it can be the hours in a day, or two dozen, or 4 x 6, or 3 x 8. . . . I can do all sorts of things with it." We can exult, "Ah, this student has really learned the "anchor" math way; this student *feels* the number." Numbers have shapes and characters and personalities, much as do people. Math becomes much more interesting and easier to do when "the numbers come alive!"

INTRODUCING "FLEXING"

We can use the problems of scanty three-ness to illustrate a simple technique for exploring numbers and patterns to which I'll attach the name "flexing." If you don't care for that term for this activity, use another or create your own. The idea is simple: *push the number, or pattern, or quantity around* in all the ways you can think of.

To flex 3, for example, you pose the question to students: how many ways can you arrange 3 markers? (The markers can be plastic chips, coins, beans, bottle caps or pebbles, or marks on paper or chalkboard. It's a good idea to vary the markers so that the patterns become attached to the number, not to the markers.)

On this page are some of the arrangements possible for 3. For higher numbers, the variations increase.

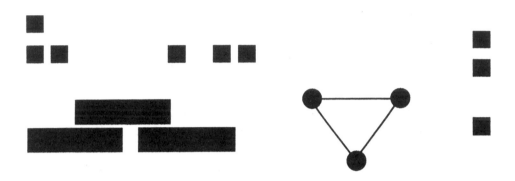

Flex . . . and find patterns.

Flexing has several purposes that enhance math learning. To begin with, of course, experience with three-ness can be greatly expanded. Of major general importance is encouraging students to *explore* on their own and as a member of a little team and at times and in ways hinted at or prompted by the teacher. Most of the time there should be no rules—anything goes. (For example, the counters can be stacked up; who said no?) At other times restraints can be imposed for the moment: the markers must be put in one dimension (or two or three), or must stay within a 2-inch square or other figure given (or must touch), and so on.

Such exploration contrasts with sitting meekly in place and doing only what one is told. Youngsters have a strong, genetic drive to *explore*—as we can plainly see by watching any normal toddler. Allowed to explore, learners find math far more interesting, even absorbing. But we can go beyond that benefit, major as it is. In the conventional math schoolroom, numbers push children around. Many become a little gun-shy as they find the numbers given to them to deal with often overpower or intimidate them. In addition, they probably tremble before the "right answer," which must be obtained on penalty of some kind of disapproval or low mark. What a difference when we begin early on to show students that *they* can push numbers! And that, in many instances in math, there is no simple, right, carved-in-stone answer, or at least none that can be found without substantial investigation. When we set students free and "empower" them, they become almost different people. Further, they begin building understanding—from experience—of when a simple calculated answer will do and when it will not. That usually makes them much better at calculating when it is required because they acquire a feeling of confidence that lets their brains work at their best. (Their brains don't "downshift," to use a Proster Theory term.)

One more benefit may be discerned. Flexing gives room for a *creative* approach, as strict calculating does not. So, some students, who might otherwise be considered on the "dumb" side, suddenly show unexpected ability. This can help teachers abstain from judgments about students which are too quick and easy—and perhaps from making unneeded judgments at all.

Get into the act yourself. Can you suggest any flexes of 3 not shown here? Here's a sample of a hint: overlap.

There is a good, solid answer available, however, on why we all need to learn arithmetic: so that we can *measure*. That's what this math is for—measuring. We need to measure how much things cost, how much they weigh, how far away or big something is, how long a trip takes, how many watts a light bulb draws, where on the dial a favorite radio station will come in, our body temperature and much, much more.

REAL WRITING EXPERIENCES

The skill of expressing oneself in written form in a variety of circumstances is very important. Often the writing experiences we are given are either creative writing or essays. In between these extremes are at least fifty real experiences that we may use in our lifetime.

CHAPTER 14: INTEGRATING SKILLS

I recommend that each student has a writing binder with examples of how to write, address, and respond to a variety of situations. The timing of a specific writing assignment can be coordinated with your theme. This binder can be added to year by year so that a worthwhile reference will always be at your students' fingertips.

In the writing binder, all drafts should be included, placed prior to the perfect copy. These edited pages are good reminders of WHY something is done as well as permitting students to peer edit.

Letters to:

> a relative
> a friend
> a pen pal
> an editor of a paper
> an association
> a service club
> congratulations

Letters of:

> sympathy
> recommendation
> farewell
> complaint
> resignation
> protest
> regret
> apology

Speech:

> a sales pitch
> a sermon
> a state of the nation
>   address
> an inauguration
> a judge's decision
> nomination
> campaign

Newspaper article for:

> front page story
> editorial
> advertisement
> obituary
> movie review
> sports story
> advice column

REAL WRITING EXPERIENCES

How-to manuals:

> operate a specific piece of
> equipment (bicycle,
> skateboard, Nintendo,
> VCR)
> survival (wilderness, on
> the subway, when visit-
> ing a foreign country)
> airline safety instructions

Writing for an audience:

> monologue
> dialogue
> poetry
> eulogy
> interview
> (ten questions to ask a
> famous person)
> recipe
> menu
> dictionary
> encyclopedia entry

Writing for social/political
action to:

> president of the U.S.
> senator, representative
> governor
> state assemblyman or
> senator
> mayor
> city council
> school board

Special issues such as:

> declaration of war
> declaration of
> independence
> civil rights
> peace

Advertisement for:

> school lunch program
> yearbook
> a magazine
> a newspaper
> television
> books or movies

Invitation to:

> a party (be specific as
> to type)
> dinner
> a weekend outing
> a conference (boy scout,
> girl scout, 4-H, etc.)
> join an organization

CHAPTER 14: INTEGRATING SKILLS

RESEARCH SKILLS

Research is the ability, over a period of time, to gather, analyze, organize, and eventually synthesize information about a topic. In the ITI program, we invite students of all ages to have a yearlong collection binder filled with data relative to a topic of their choosing from within the yearlong theme and to become an expert on that topic. If you consider that each month has at least four topics, you will see that possibilities abound.

In the theme, "What Makes It Tick?", there are topics ranging from clocks and their history, to cars, motors, advertising, and various forms of travel.

By the end of the second week, each student selects a topic. (Two students may choose the same.)

To help facilitate information gathering, ask parents to send their old magazines and newspapers to class. Provide at least forty-five minutes a week to have students seek and READ information. In addition, have at least twenty different addresses where students can write for information. (Start with the yellow pages of your phone book and then use the *Encyclopedia of Associations* at your public library.)

As information is collected, the students read, highlight important points, create a mindmap of three new facts learned from each article, and then begin to organize the information into categories. By the end of the year, students can find a resource person to come to class and eventually they can present the highlights of their research. They now have considerable expertise on a given topic (and maybe a lifelong interest). Their research binders should have a table of contents, an index, letters sent and received, pictures (of projects, locations, people visited), audio or video interviews, and a summation of what was learned about the topic through this yearlong experience. This project often spawns hobbies and paves the way for lifelong interests.

CHAPTER FIFTEEN

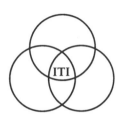

TRANSITIONS

The degree of change needed in our public educational system is truly enormous. It is unlikely that a school can make the jump in one leap. On the other hand, a clear picture of the landing site is needed before the first step is taken. We hope that this book has supplied some of the needed brush strokes to reveal a landscape for the future.

Our sense of reality and our past experiences suggest that the size of the leaps as well as the beginning point and time lines will vary from school to school. But first, a word about change and transition.

While the change needed in schooling is huge, the need for personal transition within is even greater. And, as William Bridges has pointed out in his book *Managing Transitions: Making the Most of Change*, "it isn't the changes that do you in, it's the transitions."[1] Change, he says, is situational: a new teaming structure, multi-aged classrooms, expanding one's expertise in long neglected subject areas, converting from textbook to integration curriculum based on physical locations, a new principal or school board.

On the other hand, *transition* is "the psychological process people go through to come to terms with the new situation."[2] Transitions require that we change our personal *programs* for lesson planning and classroom management, that we toss out old lesson plans and assignments, that we be willing to start from zero and be very inexpert about something that we felt quite comfortable about before and for which we received praise and recognition.

CHAPTER 15: TRANSITIONS

Bridges cautions us that change cannot and will not work unless transition occurs. And transition, he says, is internal.[3] To understand how profound this comment is, think back to your school's last big change effort that fell flat on its face. The school plan was totally and completely revamped after an extensive needs assessment and faculty and student involvement. The good ideas got written on the page, complete with detailed calendar and who was to do what. Yet, six months later . . . nothing. No behaviors changed, no new actions were taken. Things remained as before. Why? Because transition—internal shifts—did not occur.

Bridges maintains that transition is very different than change. The starting point for transition is not the outcome to be implemented but rather the ending that you must make in order to leave the old situation, actions, and attitudes behind. Thus, while situational change hinges on the new thing, psychological transition depends on letting go[4]—letting go of old beliefs, the old realities, and the old identities you had before the change took place. For example, letting go of established program structures with their familiar and comfortable boundaries and our established place as "expert" within them and our reputations as the teacher who does ___ the best. Says Bridges, "nothing so undermines organizational change as the failure to think through who will have to let go of what when change occurs."[5] Thus, transition starts with an ending. The transition must begin with letting go of the way we *were*.

Letting go need not be funereal. Many of the things we must set aside served us well and were successful for their time and use—celebrate them, thank them for the service, and then step forward with a sense of adventure and high hopes, not with regret.

Because there is much to let go of about the old model of education, it is unlikely that the transition will happen in one year, or even two; three to five years is more likely. While the ITI rubric describes the professional changes, the transitions that accompany them are a personal journey.

Bon Voyage,

Susan Kovalik

APPENDIX A

CELEBRATION OF LEARNING

Celebrations of learning give our students a chance to share their knowledge in ways that solidify long-term memory. They are orchestrated revisits of key points that allow students to show off their newly acquired skills and expertise; such application of knowledge and skill enhances *mental program-building*. Celebrations also provide opportunities to lead parents to a better understanding of the positive impact of Integrated Thematic Instruction and to let them observe collaborative learning in action.

Celebrations are an important vehicle for gaining valuable support for your program. You might think about inviting grandparents, community members, and the guest speakers you've had; also, don't forget about school custodians and administrators—our environmental and financial supporters! Everyone will be quickly caught up in the excitement of the students. By popular demand, they'll often ask for more than three celebrations per school year.

THE MAKING OF A CELEBRATION

Celebrations can take a variety of forms, allowing you to highlight your curriculum in a way that best suits the nature of a particular monthly component. As you plan your three celebrations consider the following ideas developed by our associate, Lynette Baumann.

1. Performance Celebrations

A play or other dramatization is an ideal way to close a segment of study. If the number of acting parts seems limited, think about allowing the lead roles to be played by more than one student, or switching players after each scene so experiences can be shared. Another suggestion is to form narrator teams. This keeps the audience attentive because of variety and added volume. An additional bonus derived from team narrations is that a student with reading difficulties can be supported by strong readers who model fluency and reinforce vocabulary.

Finally, don't miss the opportunity prior to a performance for students to introduce key vocabulary or background information. An overhead projector works particularly well for this.

2. "Earn Your Diploma" or "Find the Hidden Treasure" Celebration

Having worked diligently to complete some very detailed projects, designed information boards that display many of the key points from the theme, and mastered skills, students are now ready to share. However, if you are not sure parents and guests will understand the full depth of what students have accomplished, consider an An "Earn Your Diploma" or "Treasure Hunt" night. Such a structure will insure that your guests are focused and actively involved in seeking information.

As a class, prepare a "quiz," or a "treasure hunt"—a list of activities or questions to which answers or discoveries will be found in the projects, experiments, or information boards the students have prepared. The students understand they will guide or lead their parents and guests toward finding the CORRECT information. No one should score less than 100 percent. Once completed, each student evaluates the activity and awards a "diploma," or gives "buried treasure" to each participant. This type of celebration not only keeps the parents well directed but the students, too. It also serves as an ideal reinforcement of concepts learned, especially if students have to become well versed in other students' projects. It is a good idea for students to rehearse this celebration by inviting another classroom to go through the process prior to the evening event with parents and guests.

3. Station Celebration

With station celebrations, small groups of students are responsible for teaching or demonstrating certain key points while guests rotate through the stations. This is an ideal way to exhibit the different aspects of the curriculum you have covered within your theme. For example, one group could demonstrate math skills while another shows social studies concepts or performs a science experiment. Another might demonstrate how to make a mindmap or read a short story. Regardless of the nature of the stations, audience participation is always a winner and it encourages the parents and guests to be attentive.

We combined this celebration with a short performance and, when we gathered together for our play, Rudyard Kipling's *How The Whale Got His Throat*, one student introduced some key vocabulary words we had learned and another showed the migratory paths of humpback whales while telling about the whale we had adopted.

As a finale, we invited the audience to sing "The Whale Song," a ballad we had rewritten so that the lyrics reinforced the whale we had studied. Once again, the overhead projector came in handy. When it was all over, we served whale cookies and "sea swill"—yellow lemonade with blue food coloring to make green lemonade. (How scientific!)

The children love being involved in brainstorming for the type of celebration that seems appropriate for the content and skills they have been learning. We have yet to find a community that doesn't change its attitude about what goes on in school once they have attended a celebration of learning.

BASIC INGREDIENTS FOR A SUCCESSFUL CELEBRATION

- **Schedule it in the evening** when parents and guests can easily attend and you can spread out and use the media center and hallways

- **Begin planning for this event early**, ideally at least a month in advance. This allows you adequate time to orchestrate a meaningful evening and to generate anticipation in both parents and students

- **Be sure all students have a significant role.** This is their night to shine and your night to show the power of your ITI curriculum, instruction strategies, and the power of "brain-compatible" learning

- **Have a rehearsal**. Invite another class in for a dry run. Be sure everyone knows what is expected of them (performers and audience)

- **Prepare an easy-to-follow agenda.** Let your guests know what is expected of them as well

- **Make invitations clear.** Parents and other adults are welcome but, depending upon the nature of your celebration event, you may not want to include younger siblings. If so, state that clearly on the invitation and explain why. Make the starting time easy to remember and catchy—7:07 or 7:11 aren't likely to be forgotten

- **Have extra help available.** Let someone else be in charge of taking pictures or pouring refreshments, especially if you have younger students

- **Invite the custodians.** Make them your honored guests. They will love the special attention and be more likely to be helpful in the future, rather than complain about the extra work your enriched environment may create for them

APPENDIX B

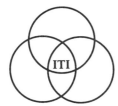

THE DISCOVERY PROCESS

The Discovery Process takes full advantage of a child's natural curiosity. It is an opportunity to present students with an object, specimen or problem and let them discover both the questions and answers. This process is exciting and allows the work groups to orchestrate their learning. It is used most effectively when the Lifelong Guidelines and the LIFESKILLS are in place.

The steps in the Discovery Process are:

1. setting standards and expectations
2. lead-up time
3. small group follow-up
4. the teachable moment
5. assessing student learning
6. outreach

STEP 1—STANDARDS AND EXPECTATIONS

- Identify the necessary procedures in regard to the specimens (live or otherwise) students will be working with

- Discuss use of tools or other special equipment they will be using

- Review what teamwork looks like and sounds like

These three steps are equivalent to your direct instruction and should be accomplished in fifteen minutes or less.

APPENDIX B: DISCOVERY

It is critical that the teacher is an enthusiastic conductor of this event. Yes, handle the snake, touch the shark, open the owl pellet, reach for the worms, and watch the live owl with fascination.

A T-chart is a very effective tool for students to organize their thoughts. On one side they list what they know and, on the other side, what they want to know. There are two parts to setting standards and expectations: confirming the ongoing standards and expectations which the teacher expects each and every day (Lifelong Guidelines), and establishing those standards and expectations specific to the nature of the event and content of a particular discovery process.

STEP 2—LEAD UP TIME

Following direct instruction, students need time to assimilate what they heard, saw, and experienced. This needs to be done both individually and as a group—time to discuss their mindmaps, sharing something from their personal experience, asking themselves, "Where does this fit into my knowledge/experience base?" This is the time for communicating, a time during which students must actively and purposefully manipulate information in order to extract as much meaning from it as possible so that information is accurately stored in the brain. What determines a child's permanent input is not just what the teacher said but the internal dialogue that occurs in answer to the question "how does this affect me and my thinking/knowing?"

During this settling in and getting comfortable period, students might be sketching a specimen, comparing pictures with the real thing, hypothesizing about what they are going to "discover," or relating their personal experiences having to do with the lesson. This time spent prior to the activity is their motivational lead-up for what they are about to do. For many students, this is the time to overcome fears and apprehensions about the unknown, e.g. a scary-looking owl. Not everyone is ready to jump in when the teacher says, "Go." Even if only ten minutes in duration, lead-up time is invaluable.

During lead-up time, decisions must be made regarding responsibility for group tasks. For example, "I'll be the recorder." "John draws well; he can sketch the parts." "Who wants to label?"

Sometimes it is appropriate for the teacher to select who will do specific jobs. This guarantees that students have an opportunity to practice various roles exercising leadership and responsibility. An efficient way of identifying who does what can be accomplished by assigning every student in the group a number . . . 1, 2, 3, 4, 5. Then, all the teacher has to do is say, "For today, number 1 is the recorder, number 3 is the organizer, and number 5 is the facilitator," and so on. Another way is to post on the agenda each morning the job assignments identifying at least five specific jobs that can be rotated:

- facilitator—person who retrieves materials needed and helps keep the group on task and using the LIFESKILLS
- recorder—person who records events, procedures, conclusions
- reader—person who reads the instructions or information out loud
- quieter—person who notices when the teacher signals for active listening
- organizer—person who makes sure the work area is organized and clean

Equal opportunity to experience responsibility and leadership is a lifelong skill and the cornerstone of an ITI classroom. Giving job responsibilities does not, however, mean that only one or two students "do" the activity, work with the firsthand materials, etc. Everyone is a learner, all must participate in the activity. The assigned group jobs are in addition to the job of learning.

STEP 3—SMALL GROUP FOLLOW-UP:
"LEARNING IS COLLABORATIVE

Can you remember how important it seemed when a teacher gave you personal feedback of an instructive, positive nature? Remember how good it felt and how pleased you were that he/she noticed?

We would like to interact with students more frequently but usually feel constrained by time. Usually students who receive most of our time are those with behavior problems or special needs. A way around this dilemma is to limit time allotted for direct instruction, suggest students ask each other for help, and then take the time to purposefully circulate during the groupwork activity.

"Purposefully circulate" means that you will especially target groups and individuals to provide **reassurance, redirection, or revival!** This is the teacher's time to observe, listen, and analyze student responses and to give immediate feedback that assists the group's level of understanding and application. This is also a perfect opportunity to acknowledge the use of LIFESKILLS. This step will continue to reinforce the efforts to work together in mutual support of learning.

STEP 4—TEACHABLE MOMENT:
"THE BRAIN IS ALWAYS LEARNING"

The teachable moment is when the student's curiosity is sparked and the teacher can enhance learning by drawing on his/her knowledge base. It is an opportunity for the teacher to model being an active and competent learner. Taking advantage of teachable moments depends upon a broad knowledge base and the willingness to diverge or extend the learning when appropriate.

In this Age of Information we live in, we are both frustrated and excited by the bombardment of knowledge all around us. In order "to find time" to increase your knowledge base, take twenty minutes a day (ten in the morning and ten in the afternoon or evening) to read subject content, professional journals, magazines, newsletters, audio cassettes, and any other materials that will enable you to collect information of a broad nature. When you are an ITI teacher, your theme will help you assimilate information and hold it organizationally in your mind. Teachers must be active learners at the understanding/applying level, not just the "talking about" level. Remembering how good it feels to learn—reliving the feeling every day with each new learning we accomplish—enables us to recognize when learning is actually taking place in the classroom and to capture the teachable moment.

STEP 5—ASSESSMENTS

> CONTENT: "The consequences of worthwhile learning are obvious"
> EMOTIONAL: "Learning always involves feelings"

The current "authentic assessment" movement is a pleasant breath of spring across the educational landscape. Brushing aside irrelevant displays of reproducing knowledge out of the context of its use in the real world (such as contrived, trivial, standardized assessments), Grant Wiggins, Fred Newmann, and other authentic assessment leaders would have us measure ability to use knowledge—producing knowledge rather than reproducing it, i.e., "authentic expressions of knowledge."

As children progress toward authentic expressions of knowledge, says Newmann, "they must hone their skills through guided practice in producing original conversation and writing, through repairing and building of physical objects, through artistic and musical performance." He adds, "A second defining feature of authentic academic achievement is its reliance upon a particular type of cognitive work which can be summarized as *disciplined inquiry*. Disciplined inquiry, in turn, seems to consist of three features: use of a prior knowledge base; in-depth understanding rather than superficial awareness; and production of knowledge in an integrated rather than fragmented form."

The point to be made here is that very seldom do we see a direct connection between standardized test scores and application of information. Personally we have all received grades of A or B in academic subjects that we have no memory of nor ability to actually use. Our short-term memory got us through the test but the "learning" was never really there. The questions we should ask about learning situations are: "What was the quality of the teaching and the learning? How was the lesson presented in terms of application and meaningfulness? Were the dynamics of the lesson vital enough to create long-term memory? Were connections made between today's learning and yesterday's and tomorrow's?"

Clearly, the catch-22 for the public schools of America is that authentic assessment is possible only when students have been given meaningful, authentic content which can then be assessed on the basis of usability!

In ITI we speak of mastery/competence in terms of performance while doing inquiries which are based on the teacher's careful selection of key points. There is a large gap between knowing and knowing how to do; in truth, it is not the knowledge and skills, but the *application* of knowledge and skills that determines what we can do; it is not facts but the application of information on a continual basis in our classrooms that reflects authentic learning of knowledge and skill. Thus, the responsibility for assessing student outcomes should rest with teachers—a far more responsible approach than depending on someone else's contrived questions and test forms.

In the ITI model, *content assessment* can be done in a variety of ways. For example, the group can mindmap their findings, interview various members in the class for understanding, create a 3-D project that reflects what they know, tape a video presentation for future reference, put on a performance that details their knowledge, write business letters that exercise their skill development, read from a variety of materials to practice their reading skills, determine where they want to go next on their learning adventure, schedule a visit from a resource person and prepare pertinent questions to ask, present a schoolwide assembly to inform others as to what was discovered, add to their expert file to enhance their personal area of interest, plot their own path toward ever more complex knowing. Worthwhile assessment is not complicated, but it demands that curriculum has been well thought through and developed with meaningfulness in mind.

The importance of the authentic assessment movement is that it encourages people to measure what is important vs. what is easy to assess and to use every day, real work frames of authenticity to judge output. The new plumbing leaks or it doesn't, the automobile can power itself out of the repair garage or it can't. Likewise, personal best—the LIFESKILLS in action—should be a daily, minute-by-minute expectation of students and of ourselves. Doing something over until we "get it right" is essential if we are to create a life-long skill that will assist adults in their everyday experiences and, ultimately, society as a whole.

Assessment of the emotional impact of a lesson is just as important for every learning experience as content assessment. Feelings developed while learning something new become the attitudes we hold for the rest of our lives. How often have we heard, "I wasn't good in that when I went to school, so I'm not surprised my child isn't doing well either" or "I've never liked math or science or reading, etc."

A daily journal is a way to allow students to express their emotional responses to their learning. After a vigorous lesson (such as dissecting owl pellets), it is imperative to allow the students to ponder how this experience was perceived and what the implications of this will be on their future experiences. Never discount their feelings; acknowledge that feelings are part of being alive and, more importantly, they are the toll keeper to the cognitive domain. Everyone has emotions; unguided or ignored emotions usually hinder learning rather than assist.

If an activity has generated feelings of indignation, outrage, or heightened personal interest and concern, it is time for political action, a time to write letters to the editor, school board, planning commission, Save-the-Whales Committee, a chemical company, the President of the United States, local businesses, Sierra Club, etc. Learning and internalizing information are not enough in today's society. Individuals must realize they have a right and a responsibility to get involved and that their opinions and concerns need to be heard.

Taking action politically gives content a sense of importance. It provides a real world context in which to fully explore the content, gives an audience (and a reason) for exercising a wide range of communication skills, and prepares one to deal with future experiences.

STEP 6—OUTREACH: THE CONSEQUENCES OF WORTHWHILE LEARNING ARE OBVIOUS

Outreach is the purposeful connection of classroom activity to someone or something outside the classroom—a way of applying lessons to reality. Outreach can be planned by contacting a resource person or it can be spontaneous when the students suggest a course of action or a visit. In essence, outreach asks the question, "Knowing this information leads me where or to whom?" To have knowledge and skills is to be responsible. Does it demand we take action? In a democracy, if we don't take action to correct problems or social ills, who will? Perhaps the students want to share with other classes or schools, produce a videotape, invite someone in to answer questions, start an information center, or set up a display at the local library or school district office. Educating others is a major responsibility of us all. Outreach demands application of what is studied. It may have long-range effects or short-term impact, but it is an important classroom structure, one which gently prods both the students and the teacher into looking at content in an active, meaningful way.

When looking at outreach, called "political or social action" in the ITI model, we need to use the language arts skills of reading, writing, listening and speaking. Outreach activities provide real audiences and a clear sense of purpose. What better environment in which to master these skills? In students' minds it becomes clear that these skills are a means to an important end—abilities to cope in the real world.

The best tool we know of to assist you in planning for outreach is *Kid's Guide to Social Action: How to Solve the Social Problems You Choose—And Turn Creative Thinking into Positive Action* by Barbara A. Lewis, winner of the 1991 Susan Kovalik and Associates Gold Medal Award for the best student resource book in supporting Integrated Thematic Instruction. The book is full of how tos, suggestions for getting involved, and vignettes of student political action from around the country. It will assist your students with form, content, addresses, procedures, and presentations. It is comprehensive and written as a user's guide.

When to use the discovery process? Whenever you are introducing a firsthand item—a specimen (owl pellets, worm farms, kiwi fruit), something unusual (starfish, oak galls, nests, etc.).

Enjoy the moment. The students will!

APPENDIX C

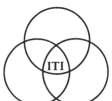

COMMUNICATING WITH PARENTS

Communication with parents is a completely understated, largely overlooked opportunity for the teacher because it is one of your most powerful sources of support. We recommend that you begin communication with the students even before school begins. Send a letter to each student welcoming him/her to school and include an invitation to the parents to attend a Back to School night held the very first week of school. The sooner you communicate with parents, the less time for assumptions or misunderstandings. Your ITI program may be new and different from what they have known in the past, so capture their attention and spread your enthusiasm in the same way you do with your students. Remember, parents are the first and foremost teachers in their children's lives. Do not wait for the traditional Back-to-School Night in October; it is entirely too late in the fall to serve as a tool for creating an anticipatory set.

PARENT PACKET

APPENDIX C: PARENT PACKET

Dear Parents,

Integrated Thematic Instruction, based on brain-compatible learning, is an innovative and proven method of integrating skills and content into a meaningful yearlong theme.

The following pages will introduce you to many of the concepts, terms, and resources which will be used in your child's classroom this year. I am looking forward to working with you to create an extraordinary year for your child.

PARENT INFORMATION PACKET

CONTENTS

1. Recommended Books
2. A Week in the Life of My Child
3. Triune Brain
4. Lifelong Guidelines/LIFESKILLS
5. Food and its Effects on Learning
6. Yearlong Theme
7. Public Library
8. Research Project
9. Mindmapping
10. Homework
11. Letter to Parents
12. Possible Family Field Trips
13. Contacting the Teacher

RECOMMENDED BOOKS

1. RECOMMENDED BOOKS FOR PARENTS TO READ

Your Child's Growing Mind: A Guide to Learning and Brain Development from Birth to Adolescence by Jane Healy

A clear translation of the most current scientific theories on brain and nervous system development into practical information for parents. Provides a detailed explanation of how children develop language and memory, and addresses academic learning—reading, writing, spelling, mathematics.

MegaSkills®: How Families Can Help Their Children Succeed in School and Beyond by Dorothy Rich

According to the author, the MegaSkills® are the values, attitudes, and behaviors that determine a child's achievement. "They are our children's inner engines of learning." The 10 MegaSkills® are: **Confidence:** feeling able to do it; **Motivation:** wanting to do it; **Effort**: being willing to work hard; **Responsibility:** doing what's right; **Initiative:** moving into action; **Perseverance:** completing what you start; **Caring:** showing concern for others; **Teamwork:** working with others; **Common Sense:** using good judgment; **Problem-Solving:** putting what you know and what you can do into action. Each is presented with multiple, practical activities to do in the home. For students aged 4-12.

Unplugging the Plug-In Drug: Help Your Children Kick the TV Habit by Marie Winn

Filled with practical advice from children, parents, and teachers, this book explains TV addiction and how to fight it. Includes tips on how to plan ahead, making a week without TV a time for more reading, more play, and a more enjoyable family life. The research into the effects of TV on children will jar you!

The Hurried Child by David Elkind

Often with the very best intentions, parents and schools expose children to overwhelming pressures by blurring the boundaries of what is age-appropriate, expecting or imposing too much too soon. The effect of such hurrying is crippling.

APPENDIX C: PARENT PACKET

In Their Own Way by Thomas Armstrong

Practical advice for parents on how to develop children's strengths by encouraging preferred learning styles. Never labeling students "gifted," or "learning disabled," the author identifies the various learning styles that make independent success possible. Examples of how to assist children to develop their latent abilities, both inside and outside the classroom, are provided.

Seven Kinds of Smarts: Identifying and Developing Your Many Intelligences by Thomas Armstrong

Provides a clear, understandable overview of the theory of multiple intelligences; a 40-item assessment inventory, and everyday examples of high capability and of the consequences of low capability in each area.

Insult to Intelligence: The Bureaucratic Invasion of Our Classrooms by Frank Smith

The author examines many of the time-honored approaches to learning and shows how these traditional techniques insult our brain's capacity. He squarely confronts the basal reading programs, worksheets, electronic workbooks, and other tools which impede the brain's progress.

Raising Self-Reliant Children in a Self-Indulgent World by H. Stephen Glenn and Jane Nelsen

The authors offer an original, convincing, and easy-to-understand explanation of why so many of our young people don't feel capable. As culprits, they point to the drastic declines in educational levels, family interaction and values, and community involvement—as well as an increase in emphasis on instant gratification. The authors focus on solutions, giving parents an invaluable, detailed, seven-step blueprint designed to help children.

Miseducation: Preschoolers at Risk by David Elkind

According to Dr. Elkind, early miseducation can cause permanent damage to a child's self-esteem, loss of the positive attitude a child needs for learning, and the blocking of natural gifts and potential talents.

Human Brain and Human Learning by Leslie Hart *(The Diamond Award Recipient from Susan Kovalik and Associates for the most important book of the century)*

This is the most significant book on brain research and its implications for the classrooms of America. The term "brain-compatible" was coined by this author. His examples of how learning goes astray inside schools will remind all readers of their own experiences as children. This is the foundation book for Integrated Thematic Instruction, which is based on brain-compatible learning.

All Grown Up and No Place to Go by David Elkind

Teens are expected to confront adult challenges at an early age without preparation. The normal adolescent rituals have disappeared, their symbols and trappings usurped by younger children, thus leaving teens with no markers for their own passage into adulthood. Worse, adults often mistake teenagers' outward sophistication as a sign of emotional maturity. This book offers helpful advice to parents to help them cope with these pressures and guide their teens through turbulent years.

2. A WEEK IN THE LIFE OF MY CHILD

The grid on the next page is for recording the activities of your child for one week. This is useful for you and your child so that you can get a picture of your child's "education" when outside of school. Remember, you are the child's first teacher. Seeing exactly where and on what your child spends his/her time is the beginning step in examining how you might play a more powerful supportive role with your child this year. Also, I would be happy to discuss your child's schedule with you and its possible impact on your child's learning.

The time chart is broken into four sections to help you capture a full 24-hour day look over seven consecutive days. Record the adult and peer influences your child experiences each day. How much support time are you able to give your child. The more detailed your information, the more valuable it will be.

	Monday	Tuesday	Wednesday	Thursday	Friday	Saturday	Sunday
BEFORE SCHOOL							
AT SCHOOL							
AFTER SCHOOL							
AFTER DINNER							

3. CURRENT BRAIN RESEARCH

The ITI model is based upon the findings of brain research from the past 25 years. Gleaned from many fields and supported by research made possible by high tech instruments such as CAT scans, PET scans, MRI, and fast MRI, we can now literally watch a brain in action. For 25 years, the research has provided very consistent findings which are summarized in the ITI model as:

- the brain has three parts, each with different functions (triune brain)
- intelligence is a function of experiences which cause physiological growth in the brain; genetics plays a lesser role than generally believed
- we have at least seven intelligences. An intelligence is defined as a problem-solving and/or product-producing capability. Each of the them functions from a different part of the brain.
- the brain, when learning, uses a pattern-seeking process; it is not logical and sequential when making meaning (however, it can be very logical and sequential when it is using information that it has learned
- most useful information is embedded in mental programs; information that does not become embedded in a program for using it in real world applications is largely forgotten

Because of these findings, the ITI classroom is dedicated to providing a learning environment with the following brain-compatible elements:

- absence of threat
- meaningful content
- choices
- adequate time
- enriched environment
- collaboration
- immediate feedback
- mastery and the ability to use concepts and skills in real life

Each of these concepts about how the brain works and the brain-compatible elements will be discussed at parent night and in home-school communications throughout the year. However, because we will be spending a great deal of time at the beginning of the year on the triune brain and how to create an environment with an absence of threat, the triune brain is described briefly here. As you read along, you will recognize the actions of the triune brain in your child's daily activities at home as well.

One of the more fascinating brain concepts developed in recent years comes from Dr. Paul MacLean's work on the triune brain. He believes that the brain can be viewed as having three parts, each of which constantly monitors our surroundings: the brain stem, the limbic system, and the cerebral cortex.

The cerebral cortex is the part of the brain which processes language and enables us to learn the academic subjects of school: to reason, to plan ahead, to deal with symbols, and to develop our culture. Because it analyzes input from all 19 senses (yes, *19!*), it is relatively slow-moving. Therefore, as Leslie Hart has noted, if the cerebral cortex senses "threat"—real or perceived—the resulting behavior is "downshifting," a physiological process that interferes with learning. Fear of failure, frustration, anxiety and grades, are all emotions which result in downshifting, reducing the capability to learn.

When we "downshift" from the cerebral cortex to the limbic system, we no longer can process language at a level necessary to learn our academic subjects. The limbic system regulates eating, drinking, sleeping, waking, body temperature, chemical balances such as blood sugar, heart rate, blood pressure, hormones, sex, and emotions. It's also the focus of pleasure, punishment, hunger, thirst, aggression, and rage. The limbic system converts information that the brain receives into appropriate modes for processing, constantly checking information relayed to the brain by the senses and comparing it to past experience. The limbic system also directs information to the appropriate memory storage areas of the brain. The limbic system is also involved in the information transfer from short-term to long-term memory.

The brain stem, responsible for survival, is fast acting but has neither language nor visual memory. This is the part of the brain we downshift to when confronted with life-threatening situations.

The following illustration is a representation of the three separate levels of the brain by Dr. Paul MacLean.

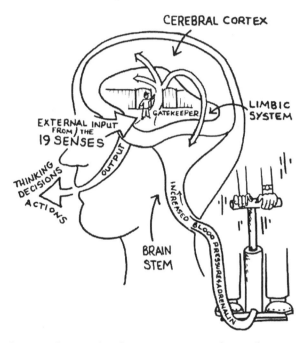

Realizing how the brain reacts when threatened and what behaviors are possible and not possible can assist parents, teachers, and students improve communication and performance.

4. LIFELONG GUIDELINES AND LIFESKILLS

Our classroom is practicing Lifelong Guidelines and LIFESKILLS. These differ from regular school rules because they apply to all age groups in all situations, thus the term LIFESKILLS. They form the basis for agreement between teacher and students, and among the students, about behavior and expectations (social and academic). I encourage you to learn about them (ask your child!) and I ask that you reinforce them at home.

APPENDIX C: PARENT PACKET

LIFELONG GUIDELINES

Trustworthiness
Truthfulness
Active Listening
No Put-Downs
Personal Best

LIFESKILLS

Integrity—to act according to a sense of what's right and wrong

Initiative—to do something because it needs to be done

Flexibility—to be willing to alter plans when necessary

Perseverance—to keep at it

Organization—to plan, arrange, and implement in an orderly readily useable way

Sense of Humor—to laugh and be playful without harming others

Effort—to do your best

Common Sense—to use good judgment

Problem-Solving—to create solutions to difficult situations and everyday problems

Responsibility—to respond when appropriate, to be accountable for your actions

Patience—to wait calmly for someone or something

Friendship—to make and keep a friend through mutual trust and caring

Curiosity—a desire to investigate and seek understanding of one's world

Cooperation—to work together toward a common goal or purpose

Caring—to feel and show concern for others

Courage—to act according to one's beliefs

Pride—Satisfaction from doing your personal best

5. FOOD AND ITS EFFECTS ON LEARNING

There are two books, both very readable, which offer some sound advice and suggestions for feeding children in a healthy manner. I recommend them as a beginning point in understanding the powerful influence food (especially junk food) has upon the chemistry of the brain and, therefore, its ability to learn.

Good For Me! by Marilyn Burns

This is a great book to read with your child. There are also many "things to do" that families will find fun and informational. A quick look at the table of contents gives you an idea of the excitement of this book: Biting In, What's the Use of Food, Anyway?; You Can Hurt Your Stomach's Feelings; The Fizz in Your Diet; The National Meal in a Bun; The Ice Cream Story; Learning to Read Labels; and, Will an Apple a Day Keep the Doctor Away?

Food For Healthy Kids by Dr. Lendon Smith

Another resource that should be on every parent's shelf is this very thorough look at food, behavior, allergies, and addictions from ages pre-birth to adulthood. Chapter headings include: Hyperactivity and Tension at All Ages; Sugar Cravings—Foods and Moods; Sleep Problems—Foods for Restless Children.

Included are over a hundred recipes for healthy and tasty meals for children.

6. YEARLONG THEME, KEY POINTS, AND INQUIRIES

The basis for Integrated Thematic Instruction is the brain research of the past twenty years. The model was designed to best fit the brain's natural way of learning. It consists of identifying a single, yearlong theme through which all content and skills are taught. This is a dramatic departure from the fragmented day during which each subject is taught separately.

The intent is to better provide our students with the capabilities that come with understanding at the level of application and the ability to problem-solve in the real world.

The enclosed mindmap illustrates the yearlong theme for our classroom. As you can see, the topics that we will be studying are varied and exciting.

To help make this year as rich an experience as possible, I would appreciate any and all support from parents, e.g., serving as a resource person in the classroom, providing materials, generating ideas for possible class field trips, assistance with field trips, etc.

Key points are statements of what is most essential for students to learn—the essential core of knowledge and skills in each of the subject areas included in our yearlong theme. Key points are identified for each day, week, month, and year. They are the content every student needs to learn and be able to apply.

Inquiries are the activities your child will do in order to "learn" the concepts and skills identified in the key points. Inquiries require the application of reading, writing, computing, and best of all, thinking!

In developing inquiries for class work and homework for this class, I have utilized the conceptual framework of Howard Gardner as presented in his book, *Frames of Mind: Theory of Multiple Intelligences*. Gardner suggests that we are all born with at least seven different problem-solving and/or product-producing capabilities, each one operating from a different location in the brain. Each of us develops a propensity for using one or more capabilities in our everyday lives. In the classroom, the more options that are available, the greater the success for students, and the greater the development of all seven intelligences, all of which are necessary to succeed in life beyond our school years.

Gardner's seven intelligences and Benjamin Bloom's Taxonomy of Cognitive Objectives were used to create the ITI Inquiry-Building

Wheel; using it as we write our curriculum ensures the broadest possible range of choices for the learner.

Here are some inquiries written for the study of owls. They illustrate the range of problem-solving and product-producing capabilities that can be tapped and nurtured.

- Design a shoe box habitat which illustrates the food chain of an owl
- Select any one of the owl poems mentioned this week and present it to the group. Make sure you add rhythm and sounds to it. You may use musical instruments
- Demonstrate the triangulation method used by owls to pinpoint by sound the exact location of their prey. Make sure you include the roles of: left ear, right ear, beak, and a squeaky mouse

These are examples of the types of activities your child will be involved in during our course of study.

7. THE PUBLIC LIBRARY

Your public library should become your child's favorite place to find information and have questions answered. According to an article published by Northwest Airlines, "There are more than 115,000 libraries serving the American public; libraries employ over 300,000 people and spend almost $3 billion per year on materials and services—less than a dollar a month for every man, woman and child in the United States. America's public libraries circulate more than one billion items per year—everything from books to computer software to children's toys, games, audio cassettes, videotapes, art prints, and films."

It is ironic that some libraries are closing for lack of support in this country. It is the last "free" source of information available to all, regardless of income or education, and deserves to be used and supported. Interestingly, even during a recession, libraries which are heavily used and strongly supported by their communities are never cut from the budget. Libraries which close are eliminated more because public use is limited, not because public funds are limited. Support your library!

The public library is your closest and easiest vehicle to adventure. And, it's free. If your child does not already have his/her own library card, apply for one immediately. We have application cards available at Parent Night. Set a goal of visiting the library twice a week. Teach your child how to browse through the library and how to use the card catalog (or computerized system!).

Check the schedule for special events for children. Most libraries provide a surprisingly wide array of cultural events for children.

Lastly, teach your child how to read public transportation schedules and how to use public transportation. When your child is old enough, teach him/her to go alone. Going to the library will become as typical an adult behavior as turning on TV to watch the news.

8. YEARLONG RESEARCH PROJECT

As part of the Integrated Thematic Instruction model, each child is requested to choose a topic of interest that relates to our theme and to begin to collect information regarding this topic. Information can be gleaned from the newspaper, magazines, encyclopedias, and museum pamphlets, at all readability levels designed for both children and adults. This is your child's chance to develop practical, everyday information-gathering skills.

Resources are as near as the yellow pages of your phone book and as far away as those listed in the *Encyclopedia of Associations*, a remarkable publication available through your public library. It contains over 30,000 addresses of public and private organizations that have been formed to "get the word out"—information on all subjects. Writing letters to request free information provides a real audience for your child's writing skills. And when the information arrives in the child's mailbox with his/her name on it . . . well, of course, it will be high interest reading material!

The research project articles should be kept in a three-ring binder; each article is read, highlighted, and at least three facts that he/she thinks are interesting or important are mindmapped. Copies of letters sent and answered belong in the binder. At the appropriate time during the year, the teacher will ask for the expertise of your child to be presented to the class. This is the beginning of a lifelong habit of collecting, analyzing, synthesizing, and using information.

The long-term research project is the best "homework" you can do with your child. It provides a point of discussion and analysis. Pride in accomplishing a significant task, deep knowledge, and lifelong learning skills are the end products.

9. MINDMAPPING

This year your child will be introduced to a concept called mindmapping. The rationale for using this methodology is that students can literally see the connections between concepts and ideas when done in a visual fashion. Pictures, as well as colors, enhance retention. Mindmapping is a skill and, like other skills, it demands practice in order to do well. Learn and practice it along with your child.

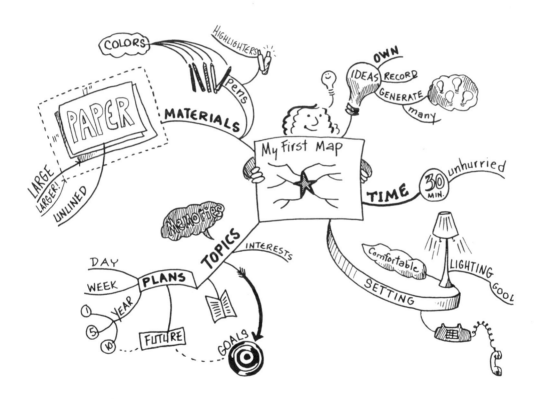

Mindmap by Nancy Margulies

Recommended book: *Mapping Inner Space: Learning and Teaching Mind Mapping* by Nancy Margulies (1992 Susan Kovalik Gold Medal Award for the best teacher resource book)

10. HOMEWORK

Homework is best assigned when it has meaning and purpose (from the learner's perspective. It should support and expand the skills, content, and concepts that were presented in the class. It should be supplemental to what has gone on in the classroom that day—something which could not be done at school, either for lack of time or of materials necessary to do the job well.

Do not expect your child to bring home "dittos" or "worksheets." perspective). Such busywork is demeaning, kills the joy of learning, and, worst of all, seldom enhances learning. The intent of homework is to contribute to the building of *mental programs* which are the fundamental key to producing intelligent behavior.

The best homework is the time you spend with your child reading, answering and posing questions, and investigating areas and concepts that will generate a sense of purpose and value.

11. LETTER TO PARENTS

Because your participation in your child's education is so critical to his/her progress this year, I will send you a letter at least twice a month to keep you up-to-date with happenings in the classroom—what we are currently studying, how you can support your child in mastering the key points for the month, what you might do to assist your child in learning how to apply what he/she is learning to real life (in your home, neighborhood, community), and, lastly, how you might assist the class as a whole—in the classroom or on a field trip.

The letter will typically take the following format:

Dear Parents,

　　We are into our third component of this year's theme, and our weekly topics for this month will include:
　　1.
　　2.

3.
4.

This week we will be working on inquiries for these key points in our content study:

1.
2.
3.

Our key points in the basic skills area (reading, writing, and mathematics) are:

1.
2.
3.

I invite you to assist your child in understanding those inquiries your child has selected to work on (or that I may have assigned), which support the key points. In particular, I invite you to help your child apply this information to real life situations.

Your continuing to work with your child on his/her yearlong research project is appreciated and makes the efforts all the more worthwhile.

Our resource person for this month (week) will be _____. If you have any additional suggestions regarding resources, especially non-print ones, please let us know.

Our next field trip:_____

Our next learning celebration event: _____

These are special days. Please mark them on your family calendar.

Sincerely,

12. POSSIBLE FAMILY FIELD TRIPS WITHIN A FIFTY MILE RADIUS

Parents are not only the first teachers of their children but also the most important. Schools are but a supplement to the educating process of the parents. Your modeling of being a lifelong learner is the most important gift you can give your child. Make a list of all the possible educational points within a fifty mile radius of your home (for small towns, increase the radius to 75 or 100 miles; rural areas, 100–300 miles). For example:

- parks
- museums
- historical sites
- cultural centers
- natural environments: lakes, rivers, mountains, oceans, etc.
- neighboring cities
- plays
- concerts
- fairs
- other

Set as your goal at least one field trip every four weeks. Remember, intelligence is a function of experience.

13. CONTACTING YOUR CHILD'S TEACHER

If you need to contact me, please feel free to call the school and leave a message with the school secretary.

I appreciate your willingness to spend quality time with your child, investing in the role of "first teacher," modeling the behaviors and values of lifelong learners and contributing members of society. Do know that I will be doing everything possible in the classroom to support those goals for your child and I am looking forward to form-ing a close working partnership with you so that together we can ensure that your child fulfills his/her capabilities.

GLOSSARY

Age-appropriate—concepts and/or facts which are understandable (versus memorizable) by students, given the current degree of development of the brain. Dr. Larry Lowery discusses the biological stages of thinking and learning in his book, *Thinking and Learning: Matching Developmental Stages with Curriculum and Instruction*

Authentic Assessment—focus of a nationwide movement in education which advocates using a variety of assessment tools by which students can demonstrate their ability to apply what they have learned to real world situations; such tools use standards of performance from the adult world

Back-to-School night—an integral part of the ITI model where teachers invite the parents of their students into school one evening during the first week of school to explain the ITI model and the yearlong theme. Teachers present them with a parent packet containing information which explains the brain research behind the ITI model and gives a preview of the upcoming school year

Basic skills—integration through yearlong theme, see Chapter 14

Being There —the most powerful input to the brain is being in a real world location; activates all 19 senses, thereby significantly increasing learning (pattern identification and program building)

Bloom's Taxonomy—a model by Benjamin Bloom, et al, originally designed for developing questioning strategies for college exams. In the ITI model, the process verbs characterizing each level are used to develop inquiries

Brain stem/reptilian brain—one of three parts of the triune brain described by Dr. Paul MacLean; responsible for survival during life-threatening situations. There is no language or visual memory associated with this level of the brain

Brain-compatible learning environment—coined by Leslie A. Hart in his book *Human Brain and Human Learning*, it is a key concept in the Kovalik Integrated Thematic Instruction (ITI) model. A brain-compatible environment is one which allows the brain to work as it naturally, and thus most powerfully, works

Brain-compatible elements—are the basis for the ITI model. They are: Absence of Threat, Meaningful Content, Choices, Adequate Time, Enriched Environment, Collaboration, Immediate Feedback, Mastery/Application

Celebration of Learning—an integral part of the ITI model where students invite their parents into school and instruct them in the concepts they have been learning

Cerebral cortex—one of the three parts of the triune brain described by Dr. Paul MacLean; the part of the brain where cognitive learning takes place, e.g., reading, writing, mathematics, geography

Collaboration—one of the eight brain-compatible elements of the ITI model which stresses the importance of allowing students not only to work in groups but to be involved in the processing of information in collaborative ways

Common core of knowledge—defined in the ITI model to mean those concepts, skills, and significant knowledge all students are expected to master and that are essential to sustain a democracy and participate in our high-tech society

Curriculum frameworks—curriculum guidelines for each subject area drawn up by state departments of education for use in local districts

Dendrites—structures found on the neurons which are responsible for transmitting messages from one neuron to the next. One dendrite has the capability of communicating with at least 600,000 other dendrites

Direct instruction—the 11 to 16 minutes of teacher presentation of a key point which provides the focus of the classroom activities; direct instruction is only *one* way of orchestrating key points

Downshifting—shifting out of the cerebral cortex where cognitive learning takes place in response to a life-threatening situation

Hands-on experiences—a term describing two levels of input: of the real thing and hands-on of something that is symbolic or representing a real thing, such as a real frog or a plastic model

Imaging—refers to the ability to create a visual image in one's mind representing what words mean, i.e., DOG—seeing a big, fluffy Collie, etc. According to brain research, the brain processes and stores images, not the sound of words (unless there is a highly emotional event). Students who cannot do this have difficulty comprehending what they read or hear

Immersion—an environment that simulates as richly as is possible the real life environment being studied, such as transforming a classroom into wetlands or a pond or a period of history to allow students the opportunity to experience or role-play as if they were actually there

Input, types of—1. *Being there*, physically being in the real world environment; 2. Immersion—full simulation of the real world environment, includes many real world things; 3. Hands-on of the real thing, e.g., (frog); 4. Hands-on of representation (e.g., plastic model of a frog); 5. Second-hand—pictorial representation, written word (e.g., pictures, videos, or stories about frogs); 6. Symbolic—mathematics, phonics, grammar (scientific definition of a frog)

Inquiries—a key curriculum development structure in the ITI model, inquiries are activities that enable students to understand and apply the concept, skill, or essential knowledge of a key point. The primary purpose of inquiries is to enable students to develop mental programs for applying, in real world situations, the key point. They make learning active and memorable. See Chapter 13

Inquiry Builder Chart—a circular graphic that organizes the process verbs of Bloom's Taxonomy of Cognitive Objectives according to five of Howard Gardner's seven intelligences

Integrated Thematic Instruction (ITI)—the name given to a brain-compatible, fully integrated instructional model developed by Susan Kovalik. The model consists of a central yearlong theme, monthly components, weekly topics, key points, inquiries, and social/political action

Key Point—essential concept, skill, or significant knowledge all students are expected to master (know and be able to use). The primary purpose of key points is to enhance students' ability to detect pattern, i.e., to readily identify the collection of attributes that is essential for understanding the concept, skill, or significant idea of the key point. They also provide a clear focus for the teacher for instructional planning and for orchestration of learning. See Chapter 12

Learning—defined by Leslie Hart as the acquisition of useful programs

Learners' Manifesto—developed by Frank Smith in *Insult to Intelligence: The Bureaucratic Invasion of Our Classrooms*, includes the following maxims: The brain is always learning; Learning does not require coercion or irrelevant reward; Learning must be meaningful; Learning is incidental; Learning is collaborative; The consequences of worthwhile learning are obvious; Learning always involves feelings; Learning must be free of risk

Lifelong Guidelines—the parameters for classroom/schoolwide interactions with other students and staff. They are TRUSTWORTHINESS, TRUTHFULNESS, ACTIVE LISTENING, NO PUT DOWNS, and PERSONAL BEST

LIFESKILLS—15 personal/social parameters that promote implementing the Lifelong Guideline of **PERSONAL BEST.** They include: Integrity, Initiative, Flexibility, Perseverance, Organization, Sense of Humor, Effort, Common Sense, Problem-Solving, Responsibility, Patience, Friendship, Curiosity, Cooperation, Caring

Limbic system—one of three parts of the triune brain described by Dr. Paul MacLean; the processor of emotions, it is the gateway to the cerebral cortex and academic learning. The brain downshifts to this area when confronted by a highly emotional situation–positive or negative. There is little or no language associated with this part of the brain. It also regulates eating, drinking, sleeping, waking, body temperature, chemical balances, and emotions

Memes—ideas with considerable power to direct other ideas; they are passed on from generation to generation

Mid-California Science Improvement Program (MCSIP)—a seven-year, $3 million effort funded by the David and Lucile Packard Foundation. Uses the ITI model with a focus on science K-6. Involves 250 teachers from 21 schools in six California counties

Mismemes—memes which are mistakes, wrong in their conceptual and/or factual content

Mindmapping—an instructional strategy where information is represented visually, usually as a web or cluster around the main idea with symbols and colors rather than in traditional outline form

Component—an integral structure of the ITI model; the framework for one month (approximately) of the yearlong theme

Neurons—The building block of intelligence. The human brain is thought to have over 100 billion neurons. They cannot repair or reproduce themselves. One neuron has the capability of communicating with at least 600,000 other neurons

Neurotransmitters—the chemicals produced by the brain which enable neurons to communicate with each other. There are at least fifty known neurotransmitters produced by the brain. The ten major ones are: endorphin, dopamine, adrenalin, noradrenalin, acetylcholine, serotonin, GABA, glycine, histamine, and glutamic acid

New memes—correct ideas about how students learn which the author believes should become the basis for public education in the future

Paradigm—a set of rules or boundaries through which we filter incoming information. Rigid, inflexible paradigms can make change almost impossible

Pattern-seeking—a key concept of brain-compatibility; describes the means by which the brain makes meaning from incoming data bits. Some of the major pattern categories include objects, actions, procedures, situations, relationships, and systems (for definition by Leslie Hart, see p. 47)

Program—a key concept of brain-compatibility describing how the brain stores and uses what it learns. It is defined as "a personal goal achieved by a sequence of steps or actions" which becomes stored in the brain for later retrieval when an action is required. Every goal we accomplish is due to implementation of a program or programs (for definition by Leslie Hart, see pp. 70-1)

Seven Intelligences—defined by Howard Gardner as "problem-solving or product-producing capabilities": logical-mathematical, linguistic, spatial, bodily-kinesthetic, musical, intrapersonal, and interpersonal. We are born with all seven but will develop each according to family and cultural preference, demands of one's environment, and the individual's inclinations and experiences

Social/political action—an integral part of the ITI model which provides students a vehicle for applying what they learn to real world problems. It assists students in becoming contributing citizens

Theme math—using the content subject areas to frame math problems. To integrate math, all you need are numbers plus events, places, or things for context

"3 Cs" of Assessment—an acronym describing the three ways information can be presented in order for the learner to readily retrieve it. The "C"s stand for: Correct—the information used is accurate. Complete—the assignment is done to the defined specifications. Comprehension—multiple resources have been used to arrive at the final product.

TRIBES—a practical book by Jeanne Gibbs for social development and cooperative learning; identifies the steps of group development, such as inclusion, influence and affection

Triune brain—refers to the three levels of the brain as described by Dr. Paul MacLean. The triune brain is a way of looking at the brain as the organ for learning and survival

Upshifting—refers to the brain being able to move from the lower levels of the triune brain (brain stem and limbic system) to the cerebral cortex where cognitive learning takes place

Weekly topics—an integral part of the ITI model; framework for dividing each monthly component into weekly topics or areas (weekly is an approximate duration)

Yearlong research projects—topics students choose during the first two weeks of school to become the "expert" on for the class. They will research and present their information toward the end of the school year

Yearlong theme—the content organizer for all skills and concepts

NOTES

Introduction

[1]Richard Bergland, *Fabric of Mind* (New York: Oxford Press, 1985), p. 7.

[2]Bergland, pp. 26-7.

[3]Bergland, p. 26.

[4]Bergland, p. 27.

[5]Bergland, p. 28.

[6]Pat Roy, "Revisiting Cooperative Learning," presentation at Outcomes-Based Education Conference, November 17, 1992, Phoenix, AZ.

[7]Pat Roy, "Revisiting Cooperative Learning."

[8]Marion Brady, *What's Worth Teaching? Selecting, Organizing, and Integrating Knowledge* (New York: New York State University Press, 1989), p. 122.

[9]Brady, p. 122.

[10]Brady, p. 123.

[11]Brady, p. 120.

[12]John Gatto, "Houses, Boats, Families, and the Business of Schooling," *The Sun: A Magazine of Ideas*, December, 1992.

[13]Brady, p. 125.

[14]Brady, p. 125.

[15]Carl Glickman, *Renewing America's Schools, A Guide for School-Based Action.* (San Francisco: Jossey-Bass, 1993), p. 8.

[16]Glickman, p. 8.

[17]Glickman, p. 9.

[18]Glickman, p. 9.

[19]Mihaly Csikszentmihalyi, *Flow: The Psychology of Optimal Experience* (New York: Harper & Row, 1990), pp. 74-5.

[20]Renate and Geoffrey Caine, *Making Connections: Teaching and the Human Brain* (Virginia: ASCD, 1991), p. 156.

[21]James Beane, pp. 4-6.

Chapter One—The Model

[1]Marion Brady, *What's Worth Teaching? Selecting, Organizing, and Integrating Knowledge* (New York: State University of New York Press, 1989), p. 3.

[2]David Elkind, *Miseducation of Preschoolers* (New York: Knopf, 1989), back cover.

Chapter 2—Absence of Threat

[1]Robert Sylwester. The Effects of Electronic Media on a Developing Brain (Theme Issue: *Education Leadership: Realizing the Promise of Technology,* April 1994).

[2]Ned Hermann, *The Creative Brain* (North Carolina: Brain Books, 1990), p. 34.

[3]Hermann, p. 33.

[4]Robert Sylwester, *Celebration of Neurons* (Virginia: ASCD, 1995), p. 44.

[5]Hermann, p. 31.

[6]Thomas Radeski, National Coalition on Television Violence (1989), p. 28.

Chapter 3—Meaningful Content

[1]*USA Today*, May 13, 1992, p. 9.

[2]Jane Healy, Ph.D., *Endangered Minds: Why Our Children Don't Think* (New York: Simon & Schuster, 1990), p. 81.

[3]Frank Smith, *Insult to Intelligence: The Bureaucratic Invasion of Our Classrooms* (New Hampshire: Heineman, 1986), pp. 29-30.

[4]Lawrence F. Lowery, *Thinking and Learning: Matching Developmental Stages With Curriculum and Instruction* (California: Midwest Publications, 1989), p. 2.

[5]Lowery, p. 20.

[6]Lowery, p. 18.

[7]Lowery, p. 31.

[8]Lowery, p. 33.

[9]Lowery, p. 34.

[10]Lowery, p. 36.

[11]Lowery, p. 41.

[12]Lowery, p. 37

[13]Lowery, p. 41.

[14] *California State Language Arts Framework* (California: State Department of Education, 1987.)

[15]Leslie A. Hart, *Human Brain and Human Learning* (Washington: Books for Educators, 1983), p. 57.

[16]Hart, p. 125.

[17]Hart, p. 65

[18] Hart, p. 56.

[19] Paul Messier, *The Brain: Research Findings Undergoing Innovative Brain-Based Learning Model,* reprinted in *1990 Summer Institute: Decade of the Brain* by Susan Kovalik and Associates (Washington, 1990), pp. 1-2.

Chapter Four—Choices

[1]Frank Smith, *to think* (New York: Teachers' College Press, 1990), p. 27.

[2]Rita Kramer, *Maria Montessori, A Biography* (New York: Addison-Wesley, 1988), pp. 373-4.

[3]Jane Healy, *Endangered Minds: Why Our Children Don't Think* (New York: Simon and Schuster, 1990) p. 277.

[4]Howard Gardner, *Frames of Mind: Theory of Multiple Intelligences* (New York: Basic Books, Inc., 1985), p. xi.

[5]Gardner, Chapter 7.

[6]Thomas Armstrong, *In Their Own Way* (New York: Tarcher Press, 1987), p. 21.

[7]Gardner, Chapter 5.

[8]Armstrong, p. 20.

[9]Gardner, Chapter 8.

[10]Susan J. Kovalik and Karen D. Olsen, *Kid's Eye View of Science: A Teacher's Handbook for Implementing an Integrated Thematic Approach to Science, K-6* (Washington: Susan Kovalik & Associates Press, 1991), p. 21.

[11]Armstrong, p. 21.

[12]Gardner, Chapter 9.

[13]Armstrong, p. 23.

[14] Gardner, Chapter 6.

[15]Armstrong, p. 22.

[16]Gardner, Chapter 10.

[17]Armstrong, p. 24.

[18]Gardner, Chapter 10.

[19]Armstrong, pp. 23-24.

Chapter Five—Adequate Time

[1]Richard Saul Wurman, *Information Anxiety* (New York: Doubleday, 1989), p. 34.

[2]Leslie A. Hart, *Human Brain and Human Learning* (Washington: Books for Educators, 1983), p. 82.

[3]Hart, p. 190.

[4]Hart, p. 88.

[5]Hart, pp. 85-6.

Chapter Six—Enriched Environment

[1]Frank Smith, *Insult to Intelligence: The Bureaucratic Invasion of Our Classrooms* (New Hampshire: Heinemann, 1986), pp. 16-7.

[2]Robert Rivlin and Karen Gravelle, *Deciphering Your Senses* (New York: Simon and Schuster, 1984), Chapter 1.

[3]Rivlin and Gravelle, p. 15.

Chapter 7—Collaboration

[1]Frank Smith, *Insult to Intelligence: The Bureaucratic Invasion of Our Classrooms* (New Hampshire: Heineman, 1986), pp. 32-4.

[2]Elizabeth Cohen, *Designing Groupwork: Strategies for the Heterogeneous Classroom* (New York: Teachers College Press), p. 25.

[3]Marion Brady, *What's Worth Teaching: Selecting, Organizing, and Integrating Knowledge* (New York: State University of New York: 1989), p. 6.

[4]Jeanne Gibbs, *Tribes: A Process for Social Development and Cooperative Learning* (California: Center Source Publications, 1987), p. 20.

Chapter 9—Mastery

[1]Howard Gardner, *The Unschooled Mind: How Children Think and How Schools Should Teach* (New York: Basic Books, 1991), p. 186.

[2]Caine, *Making Connections: Teaching and the Human Brain* (Virginia: ASCD, 1991), p. 156.

Chapter 10—Curriculum: What's Worth Learning

[1]A useful tool when developing brain-compatible curriculum for science is *Benchmarks for Science Literacy* by Project 2061. It is a rich resource of science concepts and elegantly written. The MCSIP sork committee used it in the last stages of editing to check for completeness.

Chapter 14—Integrating Skills

[1]Frank Smith, *Insult to Intelligence: The Bureaucratic Invasion of Our Classrooms* (New York: Arbor house, 1986).

[2]Sara Goodman Zimet, *What Children Read in School* (New York, 1976).

[3]Susan Torrence and Leslie Polansky (Oregon ABC Book, T.P. Publications, 1983).

[4]Smith, *Insult to Intelligence*

Chapter 15—Transitions

[1]William Bridges, *Managing Transitons: Making the Most of Change* (Addison-Wesley Publishing Company, Inc., 1991), p. 3.

[2]Bridges, p. 3.

[3]Bridges, p. 4.

[4]Bridges, p. 5.

[5]Bridges, p. 5.

SELECTED BIBLIOGRAPHY

Armstrong, Thomas. *Awakening Your Child's Natural Genius: Enhancing Curiosity, creativity, and Learning Ability.* New York: Tarcher Press, 1991.

Armstrong, Thomas. *In Their Own Way.* New York: Tarcher Press, 1987.

Bell, Nanci. *Visualizing & Verbalizing for Language Comprehension & Thinking: A Teacher's Manual.* California: Academy of Reading, 1991.

Brady, Marion. *What's Worth Teaching? Selecting, Organizing, and Integrating Knowledge.* New York: State University of New York Press, 1989.

Butzow, Carol and John Butzow. *Science Through Children's Literature: An Integrated Approach.* Colorado: Libraries Unlimited, 1989.

Caine, Geoffrey and Renate Caine. *Making Connections: Teaching and the Human Brain.* Virginia: ASCD, 1991.

Cohen, Elizabeth with Foreword by John Goodlad. *Designing Groupwork: Strategies for the Heterogeneous Classroom.* New York: Teachers College Press, 1986.

Elkind, David. *All Grown Up and No Place to Go: Teenagers in Crisis.* New York: Addison-Wesley Publishing Co., 1984.

Elkind, David. *The Hurried Child: Growing Up Too Fast Too Soon.* New York: Addison-Wesley Publishing Co., 1988.

Elkind, David. *Miseducation: Preschoolers at Risk.* New York: Alfred A. Knopf, 1987.

Ellingsen, Robert. *Classroom of the 21st Century: Integrated Thematic Instruction.* Washington: Susan Kovalik & Associates, 1989.

Ellingsen, Robert. *Classroom of the 21st Century* (videotape). Washington: Susan Kovalik & Associates, 1989.

Gardner, Howard. *Frames of Mind: Theory of Multiple Intelligences.* New York: Basic Books, Inc., 1983.

Gibbs, Jeanne. *TRIBES: A Process for Social Development and Cooperative Learning.* California: Center Source Publications, 1987.

Hart, Leslie A. *"Anchor" Math: The Brain-Compatible Approach to Learning.* Washington: Books for Educators, 1992.

Hart, Leslie A. *Human Brain and Human Learning.* Washington: Books for Educators, 1983.

Healy, Jane Ph.D. *Endangered Minds: Why Our Children Don't Think.* New York: Simon & Schuster, 1990.

Healy, Jane Ph.D. *Your Child's Growing Mind: A Guide to Learning and Brain Development from Birth to Adolescence.* New York: Doubleday, 1987.

Hermann, Ned. *The Creative Brain*. North Carolina: Brain Books, 1990.

Kaufeldt, Martha. *I Can Divide and Conquer: A Concept in a Day* (videotape). Washington: Susan Kovalik & Associates, 1987.

Kindrick, Karen and Cynthia Black. *Adventures Down the Mississippi: A Year's Integrated Thematic Curriculum for Grades K-8*. Washington: Susan Kovalik & Associates, 1990.

Kovalik, Susan and Karen D. Olsen. *Kid's Eye View of Science: A Teacher's Handbook for Implementing an Integrated Thematic Approach to Science, K-6*. Washington: Center for the Future of Public Education, 1991.

Lazear, David. *Seven Ways of Knowing*, with Foreword by Howard Gardner. Illinois: Skylight Publishers, 1991.
Lazear, David. *Seven Ways of Teaching*. Illinois: Skylight Publishers, 1991.

Lewis, Barbara A. *The Kid's Guide to Social Action: How to Solve the Social Problems YOU CHOOSE—and Turn Creative Thinking into Positive Action*. Minneapolis: Free Spirit Publishing, 1981.

Lowrey, Lawrence. *Thinking and Learning: Matching Developmental Stages With Curriculum and Instruction*. California: Midwest Publications, 1989.

Magid, Ken and Carole McKelvey. *High Risk Students: Children Without a Conscience*. New York: Bantam Books, 1987.

Margulies, Nancy. *Mapping Inner Space.: Learning and Teaching Mindmapping*. Arizona: Zephyr Press, 1991.

Montessori, Maria. *The Absorbent Mind*. New York: Delta Press, 1967.

Olsen, Karen D. *The Mentor Teacher Role: Owners' Manual*. Washington: Books for Educators, 1989.

Rich, Dorothy. *Megaskills: How Families Can Help Children to Succeed in School and Beyond.*, revised and updated edition. Boston: Houghton-Mifflin, 1992.

Smith, Frank. *Insult to Intelligence*. New Hampshire: Heineman, 1986.
Smith, Frank. *to think*. New York: Teachers College Press, 1990.

Society for Neuroscience. *Brain Facts: A Primer on the Brain and Nervous System*. Maryland: Work Press, 1990.

Winn, Marie. *Unplugging the Plug-in Drug: Help Your Children Kick the TV Habit*. New York: Penguin Books, 1987.

INDEX

Age-appropriate, 6, 7, 13, 14, 36, 41, 45, 46, 144, 160, 175, 178, 196, 199
Assessments, 108-117, 130, 132, 178, 184, 234, 243

Back-to-school night, 249
Basic skills, 10, 37, 113, 142, 201
Being there, 6, 7, 37, 38, 39, 40, 80, 83, 84, 100, 126, 127, 129, 141, 142, 144, 147, 149, 151, 158, 160, 172, 177, 178, 190, 191, 197
Bloom's Taxonomy, ii, 191, 193, 194, 195, 198, 205, 216, 260
Brain stem, 18, 256-7
Brain-compatible learning environment, iv, 13, 16, 78, 87, 143, 238
Brain-compatible curriculum, 122, 124, 128, 129, 130-2, 173
Brain-compatible elements, xxiii, 3, 10, 13, 122, 255-6

Celebrations of learning, 235, 238
Cerebral cortex, 18, 19, 20, 37, 256
Collaboration, xxiii, 10, 27, 86-9, 90-1, 94-5, 218, 235, 232, 244-5

Dendrites, 78, 84
Direct instruction, 12, 22, 23, 24, 102, 178, 183, 184, 196, 199, 210, 223
Downshifting, 18, 19, 20, 54, 69, 256

Hands-on experience, 36, 172, 197, 215

Imaging, 19, 20, 60, 61, 79, 90, 145, 146
Immersion, 78, 80, 83, 172, 177, 212
Inquiries, 9, 24, 54, 89, 91, 92, 102, 114-6, 129, 130, 139, 182, 189, 190, 191, 193, 195-9, 200, 217, 260-1, 304-317
Inquiry Builder Chart, 191
Integrated Thematic Instruction (ITI), 1, 3, 121, 190, 201, 203
ITI Components 4, 8, 9, 25, 113, 139, 140, 142, 147-9, 151, 153, 155, 158-168, 171, 175, 183, 185, 193, 194, 203, 206, 207, 209, 213, 215, 217

Key points, 124, 129, 130, 139, 142, 149, 158, 171, 173-185, 189, 190, 195, 197-9, 200, 217, 260, 299-303

Learner's Manifesto, 69
Learning, 20, 25, 31, 32, 36, 37, 39, 40-3, 46-51, 53-6, 62, 68-70, 73-5, 78, 80-1, 83-4, 86-92, 95, 98-102, 107-115, 117, 121-3, 127, 131, 146-8, 151, 157, 167, 171,

172-3, 176-8, 184, 189-191, 198-9, 200, 202-3, 205-8, 214, 218-220, 222, 225, 228
Lifelong Guidelines, 10, 23, 25, 31, 90, 108, 109, 240, 258
LIFESKILLS, 23, 28, 29, 31, 90, 92, 95, 108-9, 168, 239, 257
Limbic system, 18-9, 256

Mismemes, viii-xiv
Memes, viii, xvi, xviii-xx
Mental Programs, 9, 13-5, 20, 27, 37, 38-9, 41, 47, 54, 68, 70-4, 76, 78, 90, 98-9, 101-3, 107-8, 110-2, 115, 117, 122-5, 127-132, 139, 184, 189, 191, 198-9, 200, 204, 206-7, 209, 211, 213, 219, 220, 225, 232-3, 235, 255, 265
Mid-California Science Improvement Program, 41, 124, 125
Mindmapping, 240, 260, 264

Neurons, 78
Neurotransmitters, 51, 99

Paradigm, ix, 53
Pattern-seeking, 122, 123, 127, 128, 139, 145, 150, 151, 179
Political action, 113, 166, 246

Seven Intelligences, 57, 58, 64, 191, 193, 195, 198, 255
Social Action, 113, 246

Theme Math, 213, 214, 217
TRIBES, 27, 88, 90, 91
Triune brain, 17, 20, 54, 69, 256

Weekly topics, 139, 140, 142, 147-9, 152-3, 155, 158, 160-1, 171, 183

Yearlong theme, 4, 5, 8, 9, 10, 22, 115, 139, 140-2, 146, 151-2, 159, 161-2, 169, 171, 175, 232, 260
Yearlong research project, 263, 270